This remarkable book is the memoir of Kathleen Dayus, who was born in Hockley, Birmingham, in 1903. She grew up in a city of grand architecture and civic splendour, but her own story is a very different one. Her childhood was spent in the slums of the city, in a district of small engineering works and metal-working foundries called 'The Jewellery Quarter'. Her early life was one of appalling poverty, inadequate food and clothing and cramped and overcrowded living conditions in one of the densely populated courts built to house Birmingham's working poor. Yet this memoir is full of humour and rich in incident. Written out of a concern that 'her people' shall not be forgotten, Kathleen Dayus vividly evokes her family and neighbourhood life, dominated by her much-feared mother. *Her People* speaks with an authentic working-class voice. It is both a unique historical document and a rare piece of autobiography, in the splendid tradition of *Lark Rise to Candleford*.

Kathleen Dayus left school at the age of fourteen. She worked at various jobs, including enamelling, before getting married in 1921. Left a widow with four young children when she was only twenty-eight, she has twelve grandchildren and five great grandchildren. Now in her late seventies, she regularly plays bowls for Warwickshire and is writing another book in which she describes her life in the 1920s and 1930s.

If you would like to know more about Virago books, write to us at Ely House, 37 Dover Street, London W1X 4HS for a full catalogue.

Please send a stamped addressed envelope

Book Tokens

Give them
the pleasure of choosing

Book Tokens can be bought
and exchanged at most
bookshops.

Kathleen Dayus

HER
PEOPLE

With an Introduction by
John Rudd

Virago

To Christina Rainey,
my granddaughter

Published by VIRAGO PRESS Limited 1982
Ely House, 37 Dover Street, London W1X 4HS

Reprinted 1982

Copyright © Kathleen Dayus 1982

Introduction Copyright © John Rudd 1982

Printed in Great Britain by litho at
The Anchor Press, Tiptree, Essex

British Library Cataloguing in Publication Data

Dayus, Kathleen
  Her people.
  1. Labor and laboring classes—England—
  Birmingham (West Midlands)
  2. Birmingham (West Midlands)—Social
  life and customs
  I. Title
  942.4'96082'0924   DA6 90.B6

ISBN 0-86068-275-7

Contents

Introduction by John Rudd   vii

1 Our Yard   1

2 The Pig's Pudding   10

3 Saturday Night in Our Yard   20

4 My Brother Jack's 'Ghost'   32

5 Christmas 1911   43

6 The Free Samples   54

7 Frankie's Illness   60

8 Granny Moves In   75

9 Mum Decides to Take Us Hop-picking   92

10 Our First Day in the Country   108

11 Settling In   119

12 The Hop-pickers   130

13 Our Last Day on the Farm   139

14 Our Homecoming   153

15 Our Jack's Trial   171

16 How Things Turned Out   188

List of Illustrations

Between Pages 66 and 67

Kathleen Dayus' mother and sister Mary with Mary's daughter and granddaughter, 1932

Kathleen's brother Jack, 1914

Kathleen's father, 1921

Kathleen's brother Charles with her first born son, Camden Street, 1923

Kathleen Dayus in 1933

The Bull Ring, c. 1895

Colemore Row, c. 1895

Number 1 Court, Camden Grove, c. 1905

Number 4 Court, Back of 21 Holland Street, 1905

Interior, c. 1905

'Children of the poor', 1898

Hop pickers from the Black Country, Witley, 1896

Flower Market, Bull Ring, 1900

Great Hampton Street, 1901

Brass bed-stead makers, 1905

St Paul's churchyard, c. 1895

Family photographs reproduced by kind permission of Kathleen Dayus. 'Hop Pickers' reproduced by permission of the Reference Library History & Geography Department (Stone Collection), Birmingham Public Libraries. All other photographs reproduced by permission of the Reference Library Local Studies Department, Birmingham Public Libraries.

Introduction

Autobiographies are usually written by people who have witnessed or been involved in great events, or who have themselves performed notable feats or known famous people. They tend to present the public with their memoirs in order to set the record straight or to forestall historical judgement. They give their own, necessarily biased, personal viewpoint of the events of their lives. In the canon of autobiographical literature those who have risen to eminence from poverty and obscurity have a particular place. If they have been political figures, fierce resentment of social inequality has usually provoked a reforming zeal. And they are often more than usually complacent in their certainty of social progress and their own part in its achievement. But in the entire literature of autobiography there have been few men or women whose account of their lives has been interesting and compelling but who have lived in total obscurity until the publication of their reminiscences has propelled them into the limelight: Kathleen Dayus is one of these, and her book stands as an important addition to the literature of democratic, feminist autobiography.

When I first leafed through the pages of closely written children's sketchbooks in which for several years Kathleen Dayus had been recording her life's story in the delicate, yet strongly stylised hand of her Edwardian schooldays, I had the strong presentiment that hers was a tale which deserved to be read by a wider audience. My initial reaction to discovering that the grandmother of a friend's pupil was writing about her early days was to expect a short, possibly not very literate, but probably vivid account, that could be lodged in the local history section of the public library where it would serve to provide a footnote for some earnest student's thesis. How far from the truth one's preconceptions can lead one I was soon to find out. For I found a narrative of power and sensitivity. I was struck by Kathleen Dayus's command of detail and memory for the minutest aspects of her home, her family and her neighbourhood, but above all for her own childish thoughts and emotions. This was a story of pathos, ironic humour and literary ability which gave a vivid evocation of a lost culture which is usually only dimly perceived in the condescending statements of middle-class observers, but rarely in the authentic voice of articulate participants.

When I had completed that first, excited reading I felt convinced this could become a classic story of slum childhood which would touch many hearts. It does not set out to recreate that lost world in order to correct or bolster some contemporary academic interpretation. Even less is it a response to the questions of a modern investigator. It stands as the voice of childhood recollected in old age, expressing the fears, hopes and joys of growing up poor in the industrial slums of Edwardian Birmingham. For this reason much of the world which is revealed here is vaguely perceived and seems to shimmer tantalisingly beyond our grasp. It seemed useful, therefore, to set the specific historical and social context more clearly in order to illuminate what the slums of Hockley and the Jewellery Quarter of Birmingham were like.

In 1911, Birmingham was a city of 525,000 people, of whom nearly half[1] were crammed into the central industrial area within a mile radius of the city centre. Although the extension of the local rail network had enabled some of Birmingham's citizens to move out to the green suburbs of King's Norton, Acock's Green and Handsworth, the central areas, the historical focus of the city's industry, remained densely populated. One hundred and fifty people to the acre was not uncommon, but actual overcrowding was made worse because of the concentration of workshops and factories in this same area. Birmingham was still the compact city it had been during the nineteenth century: the majority of its working population lived within walking distance of their place of employment and did not use the trains, trams and trolley-buses which carried artisans and clerks to work from their suburban terraced villas.

The city centre had been transformed by late-Victorian improvements (in scale not unlike the recent comprehensive, redevelopment programmes). Areas of small workshops and densely packed housing were swept away and replaced by the modern boulevards which some thought could bear comparison with those of Paris. New Street, Corporation Street and Colemore Row and the streets between were lined with tall blocks of offices and shops. Their elaborate facades of Baroque, Gothic or Flemish splendour were the visible signs of Birmingham's commercial and industrial prosperity. The focus of this civic pride was Thomason's gaudy Council House, from which Joseph Chamberlain's Liberal Party had engineered the whole process. However the gold-lettered and etched-glass shopfronts, in front of which the carriages of the wealthy inhabitants of Edgbaston parked, created a false impression of progress and prosperity. Despite advances in such basic amenities as running water, flush lavatories and gas lighting which Chamberlain's municipal socialism had wrought in the newer suburbs, Birmingham with its 43,000 back-to-back houses remained dirty, overcrowded, insanitary and unhealthy. Many thousands of its Edwardian citizens would have laughed at Chamberlain's boast that local government was a more fruitful field of endeavour than national government. Certainly his claim that an extension of the functions and authority of local government was the means of equalising the condition of men must have seemed empty posturing as it applied to Birmingham.

By 1900 Birmingham had amassed a municipal debt of £10 million – the bill for its extensive improvements. Yet virtually nothing had been done to improve the condition of those who lived in the densely populated wards of St Paul's, All Saints, St Mary's or St George's which formed a garland of poverty around the crowning achievements of the central shopping and business district. On the contrary, it is more likely that these 'improvements' increased overcrowding; many thousands being made homeless in the clearances which preceded. The net result was that poverty was banished from the sight of Birmingham's complacent bourgeoisie into the districts immediately to the north and east.

Although a campaign of the 1870s against poor housing conditions probably did lead to improvements – certainly the death rate decreased in that decade – by 1900 Birmingham's position relative to other cities had deteriorated. Cross's Artisans' Dwelling Act, which had provided powers for compulsory purchase and the building of model housing, was not used for its original purpose by the city council. Large numbers of courts and workshops were compulsorily purchased to enable the city's prestigious rebuilding to proceed but they were not replaced with new dwellings for the thousands thus displaced. They were forced into the already overcrowded districts like St Paul's, which is the area where Kate Dayus was born and grew up.[2]

Birmingham did not develop an enlightened policy on the basis of the council's improvement scheme, and later when powers to build better housing were increased by the 1890 Housing of the Working Classes Act they remained a dead letter in Birmingham.

Kate Dayus was born in one of the courts of back-to-back houses which were characteristic of Birmingham's working-class districts at the turn of the century. Despite the clearances already described and earlier ones to build the city's main-line railway stations, the back-to-back court house remained typical. There were 43,000 in 1913 and, because of a chronic shortage of cheap accommodation, little progress was made in slum clearance between the wars; and even in 1960, after a decade of improvements, Birmingham still had 25,000. In the areas discussed here 65 per cent of all houses were of this kind before 1914.[3]

The court where Kate lived throughout her childhood was typical. It contained five houses in a row, with five at their back sharing a common party wall. Each row faced a dividing wall between adjacent courts. Some courts ran directly off a street, but most were approached through alleys beside 'front houses' which were themselves often built in back-to-back rows. Alternatively, the approach was through the 'tunnel' under a front terrace of two- or three-storey individual or back-to-back houses.

Camden Street still exists, but its houses were amongst the 12,000 swept away by Hitler's own slum clearance programme in 1941. The claustrophobic overcrowding is not difficult to visualise. Camden Drive is ten feet wide – too narrow for two vehicles to pass each other. The ten courts which abutted on to this street were perhaps ten feet wide and the houses had a ground area of about 100 square feet. In Kate's court lived fifty individuals; a level of overcrowding which was common throughout the industrial parishes. These houses had no rear access of course, and light and air circulation was wholly inadequate. There was little space inside the house and most social life took place in the yard in full view of the neighbours. This lack of privacy especially annoyed Kate's father. He discouraged contact with neighbours and disliked the frequent rows which his wife provoked and mostly won. For him the public house provided the comfort and dignity which his overcrowded home and its public court could not. In general the noise and stench of humanity must have been very great. Any domestic disagreement would be witnessed by all and events like Billy Bumpham's shell-shocked, drunken cavorting must have provided regular distractions from people's own problems.[4]

Such houses consisted of three habitable rooms. In Birmingham it was usual for each dwelling to be occupied by a single family. Cellars were common but used for fuel storage rather than habitation. Using cellars to keep animals in was probably more common than Kate's story indicates.

In these three rooms up to a dozen people experienced all their family life together; from birth to death, and each mundane or traumatic event between. In Kate's case the eldest boys shared their parents' bedroom. There can have been little opportunity for love-making, even if Kate's mother had been less reluctant than it appears she was. In practice, older boys like Charlie and Jack left home at the earliest opportunity. Although unmarried, Charlie seems to have left home by the time Kate's story starts and, like most Edwardian children, she seems to know little of the lives of her elder brothers and sisters. Jack still lived at home but he appears to have spent as little time as possible there. Kate, Liza and Frankie, who were still children, slept together in the other bedroom in which their older sister, Mary, had a separate bed. Yet despite the apparent lack of privacy possible in these circumstances, or perhaps because of it, it was normal for Edwardians like Kate to grow up with only the vaguest ideas of sex and childbirth. Many girls expected their child to appear miraculously from their navel up to the very moment of birth. Knowledge of contraceptive methods was rudimentary in the extreme (apart from abstention), and Kate herself gave birth to five children without knowing that precautions against pregnancy were possible.

These slum houses had no mains water supply and few even had a sink before 1914. Water was obtained from a standpipe in the yard. There were two wash-houses with coal-fired boilers for household laundry and five dry privies were shared by ten households. The stench that these created can be imagined. It was particularly acute in hot weather when the chances of diseases, caused by the multiplication and transmission of germs, increased and typhoid often resulted. The hazard these privies presented was both invisible and, in view of the lack of knowledge of hygiene, very severe. The inadequate sanitary arrangements and the ashpits in which household refuse was tipped was perhaps the worst aspect of Birmingham's working-class housing. Pan closets and, later, water closets were introduced but the disgusting condition of these communal buildings remained and was not eradicated until the 1930s or later.

In the newer suburbs the introduction of building by-laws

led to improved terraced 'tunnel-back' housing which is found throughout industrial England; but older houses continued in use until the 1960s.

Perhaps the root cause of poor building design standards was the profit motive which drove small speculators to skimp on materials to strive for maximum densities. Even so rents were comparatively high, averaging three shillings and sixpence to five shillings per week (or a quarter to a third of the weekly income) for inner-city court houses, compared with only five shillings per week on the competently managed, garden city development, the Harborne Tenants' Estate, built on the outskirts of Birmingham in 1908 with fewer than ten houses per acre.[5]

In these central industrial areas in the midst of this tightly packed hive of humanity was situated most of the city's traditional industry. Birmingham had for long been a centre of metal-working and, at the turn of the century, was emerging from a period of industrial decline and transition. Long-established trades like gun-making were being replaced by newer electrical, chemical and component manufacture and mass production assembly lines were replacing hand manufacture as the dominant mode of production. However, despite these recent trends, the central area remained, and still is to some degree, an area of small workshops and foundries producing a multitude of metal products, particularly brass, from pans to buttons and from diamond rings to steel pens.

Contemporary observers were struck by the large number of chimneys emitting smoke and contributing to the generally polluted environment. The enormous numbers of poor people to be seen hanging around the streets had to put up with the dull and gloomy conditions resulting from the sooty, smoke-filled atmosphere and the absence of trees and open spaces.[6] In the whole district of Hockley in which Kate Dayus grew up, St Paul's churchyard – 'Titty-bottle Park' – was the only green grass to play on. Even today, the uncleaned smoke-blackened exterior of this fine Georgian church, built when this was an upper-middle-class residential square, bears testimony to the area's industrial past.

The area was the centre of the electro-plate trade, bedstead and other brassware manufacture, sewing-machine production and nut- and bolt-making. Some trades, like pen-making, were in decline because of the invention of alternative products, others like brass-bedstead-making were the victim of changes in fashion as wooden beds became more popular. However, whether in decline or not, the typical workshop was small, employing at most a few dozen workers, whilst many trades, particularly in jewellery, remained one-man operations. Typically a small master, himself once a journeyman, would employ a number of skilled workmen and a larger number of semi-skilled or unskilled labourers, many of whom might be women or teenagers. Unions were mainly craft-based and often their interests were closer to the masters', whose ranks it was still possible to join in some trades. All that was needed was sufficient capital to rent a small workshop and contacts to obtain orders for work. Traditional unions of this sort were the Brassworkers' Union, the Flint Glass Makers', and the Tinplate Workers'. There had been some progress by general labourers' unions by 1900, the National Union of Gas Workers and General Labourers for example, but it was in the years after 1914 that the general labourers made progress, particularly in the growth of the Amalgamated Engineering Union and the Transport and General Workers' Union.[7]

The main aims of the trade unions were to obtain better wages and protection for their members during unemployment; brassworkers were eligible for superannuation through the Brassworkers' Union for example. Attempts were made to exclude girls and women and the introduction of new machinery was opposed, in order to prevent the de-skilling and decreases in wages which usually resulted. None of these campaigns was successful and craftsmen found themselves increasingly ousted by unskilled women and children straight from school, who were able to operate the new lathes, drills and presses, in pearl-button manufacture for example. Only unions which covered small unmechanised trades like flint-glass manufacture made any progress in limiting entry to the trade and maintaining high wage levels in the Edwardian period. However even the Flint Glass Makers' Friendly Society had to give grants to some members to enable them to emigrate.

The skilled man who stayed in Birmingham during the first decade of this century saw further building of three- and four-bedroomed terraced and semi-detached housing with individual gardens and modern facilities for men like himself. These developments were in areas such as Balsall Heath, Small Heath and Sparkhill; but the central slums remained untouched. Here the intermittently employed, unskilled labourer and his family lived, or, more accurately, subsisted, on the doorstep of the works.

Observers found large numbers 'of persons in very poor circumstances'.[8] Here it was discovered that poverty of the most intractable kind was the norm. The basic deprivation was extreme, and the weakest, the very young, literally died like flies. The diet was, at its best, only barely adequate for physical efficiency and most survived in a state of semi-starvation. It was found that 45 per cent of households in the central districts had total household incomes from all sources of under twenty shillings per week and 20 per cent had less than ten shillings per week.[9] This was during a period of trade recession in 1908 to 1909 but in normal times the situation was little better. When a survey of working mothers was undertaken in order to investigate infant mortality, 15 per cent of husbands were found to be totally unemployed.[10] The extent to which family survival was dependent upon the efforts of all its able-bodied members is graphically illustrated by Kate's story. She and her young brothers and sisters were forced to spend all their spare time begging for scraps, or earning halfpence to buy food to supplement their meagre meals at home. Their father was given the choicest food because he needed all his strength to perform his strenuous labour as a brass caster. The older brothers and sisters who were at work contributed to the household economy and Kate's mother 'charred' to earn a few extra shillings. This picture was typical and, despite the meagre standard of living which resulted, Kate's family was more fortunate than some in having several working members. Those with young families, the elderly and the single-parent family were much worse off.

In most families it was vitally important for the wife to work. In Birmingham as a whole 19 per cent of married women did so, as compared with 17 per cent in London and 24 per cent in Nottingham. In the central districts of Birmingham over 50 per cent of married women worked.[11] It was conditions such as these which were described as 'most inimical to infant life'. Fifty per cent of mothers had to work during pregnancy, frequently up to the last possible moment before the onset of labour. In these conditions of poor diet, physical hardship and strenuous toil it is hardly surprising that 14 per cent of pregnancies ended in miscarriage or stillbirth, and premature birth and congenital deformity was the second greatest cause of death of infants under one year of age. Before 1914 female employment in engineering was confined almost totally to the Birmingham area,[12] and there was little information available on occupational disease in women, but during the First World War it was found that working mothers were more than normally susceptible to prolapse of the womb as a result of long hours standing and heavy lifting; varicose veins were regarded as inevitable.[13]

Women in Kate's neighbourhood worked after marriage as a matter of course but employers were reluctant to employ them, and the slightest unpunctuality caused by the need to feed infants, or any absence from work, resulted in dismissal. The type of work they undertook was either related to the job they had done prior to marriage (70 per cent of all working wives were employed in factories in 1910); or, like Kate's mother, they undertook 'charring' or took in washing as an extension of their household duties (20 per cent).[14] The kind of work women undertook was unskilled or semi-skilled. Light presswork was the most common although heavy presswork, brass polishing and operating general machinery were usual types of employment pursued by mothers. It was noted at the time that few were employed in the skilled trades. The average wage of working mothers was eight shillings and fivepence per week but this figure disguises considerable variation between those who earned under five shillings per week for homework like hook-and-eye- or button-carding and those who earned ten shillings per week for factory work.[15]

Few women worked unless it was essential to the household economy. Indeed, it was the proud boast of the respectable, high-wage-earning, skilled man that his wife stayed at home managing the household. The gulf that existed between the skilled minority and the unskilled majority is well illustrated by the fact that even where women did work the household income was still less than where the family depended solely on the husband's income. The necessity of working added greatly to the burden of wives, and working mothers were less capable of attending to household tasks, important to maintaining a foothold on the ladder of 'respectability' and, more importantly, they had less time to devote to their infants' welfare. It is staggering today to discover that 20–25 per cent of their babies died in the first year of life.[16] They could not breast-feed their infants if they were at work, and bottle-fed children were found to succumb to diarrhoea and enteric illness thirty times more frequently than naturally suckled children. The women Kate observed giving suck in the streets and on doorsteps were consciously or unconsciously preventing their baby ingesting the germs which generally went with unsterilised bottles, milk and generally poor hygiene, but none could avoid the foul sanitation, the dirty clothing and polluted atmosphere. Middle-class observers like Birmingham's medical officer of health, John Robertson, whose prejudice was that working itself led to greater risk to the children of the poor and who argued that working mothers had no time to 'make themselves practically familiar with . . . apparently unimportant details . . . [of] a well-ordered home', were forced to conclude that it made little difference whether a mother worked or not, bottle-fed or breast-fed, because infant death was related to poverty itself. Most women must have suffered to a greater or lesser degree from malnutrition. They had a diet which was insufficient to ensure proper foetal development before birth or a healthy sustenance after it.[17] Dr Jessie Dawson, a pioneer worker in women's health problems upon whom Robertson relied for his information, was drawn to the conclusion that working mothers sacrificed themselves for their husbands and children whilst they themselves lived in 'semi-starvation'.[18] 'The life of a mother among the poorer classes is always a strenuous one if a family is large, but when hunger is added . . . the condition is a particularly distressing one.'[19]

Dr Dawson proved her point. At this time there was no original research data on the relationship between diet, nutritional value of human milk and infant health, although, as Dr Dawson pointed out, male doctors had carried out exhaustive research on cows! So she instituted an experiment of giving a group of nursing mothers one good meal each day. Though there were wide variations in results, this was largely because many of the group stopped eating any meals at home except tea, bread and lard, but Dr Dawson nevertheless showed there was a considerable increase in the quantity and food value of mother's milk as a result of a more adequate diet.[20]

It is hardly surprising that mealtimes and food are one of the main themes of Kate's story. The eugenically inclined Robertson might have seen the social problem of poverty as owing its origin primarily to the 'good deal of inefficiency one finds so prevalent among adult men and women' in Birmingham's slums. But for thousands of families like Kate's it was a question of survival on the margins of industrial society. Kate was usually hungry; she probably suffered to some degree from malnutrition and writes of being 'fattened up' when she neared school-leaving age in order to be physically capable of factory work.

Kate's father was intermittently employed in a casting shop and would have brought home about £1 per week when working. However, he had three dependent children. His wife and older children were contributing to the household so he was amongst the more fortunate of the poor. Kate's house had a certain amount of dilapidated furniture although many had only orange-boxes to sit on. They had best clothes which could be pawned each Monday after washing, to be reclaimed the following Saturday for their weekly airing when Kate's parents visited the local pub to celebrate what little they had to be happy about. Although seven of Kate's mother's children died in infancy, six did survive and Kate was resented as a late and unlooked-for addition to her mother's domestic burden and seems to have been picked on by her mother as a result. The family would certainly have had to struggle against greater poverty until the older children began work. The moderate, relative prosperity of Kate's childhood would have been matched by an earlier period of sufficiency before marriage or the birth of her parents' children and was itself the prelude to an inevitable decline into dependent old age as physical strength was exhausted and Kate's father became incapable of his strenuous job. The only prospect for most middle-aged slum parents was eventual destitution, and perhaps for the wife a few twilight years in the workhouse whence she would be consigned (with her husband if he were still alive – although to separate 'wards') when she became incapable of supporting herself and was forced to apply to the Guardians for relief. It is true that this situation was modified slightly by the introduction of the ten-shilling weekly pension in 1909 but infirmity would eventually lead to the workhouse if death did not intervene.

In a much more fundamental sense Kate was fortunate. She actually survived infancy: seven of her siblings had not. The high levels of infant mortality in the Birmingham slums have been mentioned but just how immense was this loss of young life it is difficult to imagine. Premature birth and deformity were common. If the child survived the ministrations of the 'midwife', then it stood a one in five chance of dying before its first birthday. Health care in the modern sense was unknown. Doctors were called only if the person was an adult or older child, was obviously in great pain or near death. Although

Birmingham had had health visitors since 1899 there were only twenty-one in 1913 for a city with a population of 500,000.[21] Children of school age benefited from the introduction of regular medical inspections, and when Kate's brother Frankie contracted scarlet fever he was immediately hospitalised.

Attempts were being made to improve the medical treatment of mothers and babies and Dr Dawson had pioneered the opening of twice-weekly clinics in rented rooms in the slum districts in about 1908, but by 1913 Kate's district still did not have one. In any case, working mothers could not leave work to visit them and large numbers of the destitute had no decent clothes and were too ashamed to visit.

The weak were carried off and the strong survived; Social Darwinism could have had no better proof than Kate Dayus's Birmingham. However the death rate fell rapidly with age. In 1913, whilst 129 infants in 1000 aged 0–1 year died, in the 0–3 year age group this figure had fallen to 75, and a mere 2 in 1000 of the 8–15 age group succumbed to fatal illness. Thus it seems that poverty itself killed the young.[22] There is no evidence that the poor themselves wilfully allowed their children to die. If they had been able to afford better clothing, food and heating, and if mothers did not have to go out to work, then fewer children would have perished. Had the conditions of insanitary housing been improved the efforts of mothers to keep their dwellings and children clean might have borne better results. This conclusion is clear from the fact that infant mortality was 50 per cent higher in households where the father was unemployed or earned less than £1 per week, as compared with households where the father was earning £1 per week or more. Seventy-two per cent of children of fathers in this latter category were in good health after a year of life as compared with only 50 per cent of children of fathers in the former category.[23]

If children survived this terrible culling of the weakest, they had a good chance of surviving to adulthood. But they would still experience continual hunger and be expected to perform a large number of household chores. 'Little drudges' like Kate might have to clean the communal privies, fetch and carry water for all household purposes, run errands to the shops, help prepare meals, wash dishes and clothes and look after younger brothers and sisters. Boys would probably be let off more lightly, but they would be expected to contribute their small earnings from running errands and doing odd jobs from an early age. Children were expected to contribute to their own and their family's survival: there was no money for material luxuries like toys or even fresh fruit and, in some households, little time for the emotional luxury of warm understanding relationships between parents and children. When fathers returned home they were habitually worn out after ten to twelve hours' heavy toil and mothers were equally drained of energy and vitality by the even more exhausting demands made upon them by work, child-rearing and domestic duties. In this position a sensitive and neglected child like Kate might lavish a great deal of unreleased emotion on a tatty rag doll or dote on sympathetic older brothers. Although some Edwardian girls were ignored by their brothers because other boys regarded playing with sisters as 'cissy', Kate's brother Frankie and her rather bullying sister, Liza, formed a close group who provided each other with mutual support and aid in the continual search for additional food and in presenting a united front against the harsh discipline demanded by the adult world as represented by their hot-tempered mother.

Many boys worked long hours before they left school as errand boys, either riding heavy trade bicycles delivering goods or helping van drivers. Girls were less likely to take paid employment outside the home before they reached the minimum school-leaving age of fourteen although they might assist in the sweated labour of button-carding and the like. It was reported in 1913 that many school boys found employment in factories after school hours, and that perhaps 1000 or more worked as van boys for shops or at the main-line stations. They worked up to sixty hours per week, although twenty-five was more normal, for which they earned between nine shillings and sixteen shillings per week for delivering up to 200 parcels per night. It was illegal for children to work later than 9 p.m. or earlier than 6 p.m., but even under these conditions it was thought that their health must suffer and the boy's ability to benefit from his hours at school be reduced.[24] 'He arrives at school physically tired, he is in school all day and when he comes out of school, completes the process of undermining his health by working till late at night.'[25] Other lads with initiative travelled to suburban golf courses to caddy for middle-class patrons for two shillings to three shillings per day.

Kate had innumerable chores to perform but perhaps the most strenuous for both her and her mother was doing the weekly wash. This involved firing the boiler, fetching buckets of water, violently scrubbing the wash with the paraphernalia of scrubbing boards, brushes and washing-dollies and finally mangling the wet clothes before hanging them out to be spotted with soot and dust from the effluent of factory chimneys. Co-operation between neighbours was essential to economise on soap and hot water, and in Kate's yard this required the authority and organising ability of a natural leader like her mother. It is not difficult to imagine the infirm or exhausted mother being less than willing to perform these arduous tasks with the vitality and enthusiasm of Kate's mother. The reward of a tot in the local when the clothes, freshly laundered, had been pawned was well earned.

In the face of such a continuously grinding struggle to clean, wash and feed a family, many women became short-tempered, disinclined to lavish affection and answer childish questions. Many may have sought solace in drink as their husbands often did, but Kate's story bears ample proof of the pivotal role of the mother in keeping the family together through good times and bad.

Children lived most of their waking hours that were not spent at school on the street, and street-wise boys and girls like Kate and her brothers and sisters quickly learnt where to pick up broken cakes or bread or over-ripe fruit, how to earn a copper or two and how to avoid the eye of the local policeman.

In many poor families the father was emotionally closer to his children than their mother. He was out of the house a great deal, at work or looking for it, and in the evening if he could afford to he would visit the local pub. He did not have the problem of looking after a large family and could enjoy the luxury of talking and listening to his children without being required to contribute in the way of disciplinary supervision. He could indulge them in drunken generosity and provide occasional treats such as visits to the cinema. Kate's father himself suffered from his wife's fierce temper and tried to moderate her treatment of the children. His was an erratic protection because he saw few of the blows dealt out, but Kate was assured that she had less to fear in the evening when he returned home.

The evening meal was a ritual in his honour as it was in many Edwardian homes. Kate fetched his bowl for his wash. He sat in his favourite armchair whilst the meal was prepared and placed before him. Quiet and unobtrusiveness was his only demand from his family, but more often than not he had his exhausted and querulous wife's nagging to contend with. Her turbulent conduct involved her in numerous rows with the neighbours whom she dominated much to her husband's embarrassment. If he could not find peace and quiet in his cramped home, he, like many Edwardian men, retreated to the bar of the local, but on occasion he found that he was not safe here from his indomitable wife.

If discipline could be harsh at home, Kate, like many Edwardian children, found that at school it could be draconian. Kate's teacher was sympathetic to her sensitive, thoughtful pupil, but many teachers could only control classes of forty or fifty, especially if they were all boys, by imposing the most sadistic regime upon them. Teaching large classes was difficult, resources were meagre and learning by rote the norm. Most pupils would in any case be tired from work and hungry, and concentration must have been difficult. Many children played truant habitually but at Kate's school the daily provision of breakfast seems to have ensured a more regular attendance. Throughout the poorest areas parents relied on the annual dole of boots and clothing to maintain their children in decent dress.[26]

In addition many families like Kate's were dependent during the worst times on parish doles. The rigours of the Victorian Poor Law had been softened to the extent that outdoor relief was given in the form of food and clothing vouchers, often on a weekly basis. Those who were periodically employed usually did odd jobs or earned money in any way they could find to supplement their relief, despite the fact that this amounted to fraud punishable by imprisonment.

After children left school, the prospects of employment were good, contrary to what might be expected: indeed we have seen that many found paid employment before leaving. This was the result of changes in the structure of industry in Birmingham which had been underway for decades and were accelerated by demands on output created by the First World War. Many traditional, skilled crafts, as we have seen, had declined in the face of foreign competition or changes in fashion and the small workshop economy was withering in the face of improvements in production brought about by the introduction of machinery, standardisation and production-line methods. Outworking and skilled hand labour were giving way to the modern factory. When she left school in 1917, Kate went to work in a succession of these new engineering works which had appeared in the Hockley area before 1914. She readily found semi-skilled factory work and was able to change jobs frequently in search for better pay or conditions. The quality of finished product depended less on the individual craftsman's skill than on well-integrated machine production and a well-disciplined, unskilled, largely female workforce who assembled components made by machinery or operated the presses, lathes and drills themselves. What was required was a 'series of operations of a light, repetitive character' and girls passed from one trade to another as 'lathe' or 'press' hands.[27]

In 1917, when Kate started work, there was a chronic shortage of such hands and this goes some way to explain why she found herself earning fifteen shillings per week – treble what she would have earned in 1913 when young women like herself were reported to be earning five to six shillings per week for similar work in the brass trade: then the trade had been subject to irregularity of employment, the summer months were slack and seasonal unemployment averaged 25 per cent.[28] Fluctuations in trade resulting from declining bedstead-making or lack of demand for ecclesiastical brassware had given way by 1917 to a continuous demand for army buttons, buckles and such like and cartridges for the Front. Employment was constant.

Nationally, the numbers of women employed in engineering increased from 170,000 to 440,000, a large proportion of whom were employed in the Birmingham area.[29] Girls were working sixty hours per week in Birmingham's engineering trades in 1916 and wages were increasing through the introduction of piecework.[30] Despite these long hours and the physical strain of standing for such long periods and lifting heavy loads, some observers concluded that 'some of the girls under discussion were now adequately nourished for the first time in their lives'.[31] However, there was some evidence of occupational illness resulting from these long hours of strenuous labour, particularly gastric problems, anaemia and menstrual disturbance, and the girls themselves are described as 'languid and lacking in vitality', 'pale and nervous' and being 'incapable of taking an interest in anything'. Working conditions were not attuned to a female workforce and middle-class visitors to Birmingham's small workshops found that sanitary conditions 'were not always ideal' and that changing facilities 'often fall short of a reasonable standard of decency'. Had these same observers known what standards of decency were possible in the average court dwelling in the area they might have been even more shocked.[32]

Despite Kate's apparent good fortune in obtaining work, wartime conditions had merely reinforced factors which already existing in the economy of juvenile exploitation. This marked central Birmingham's main industries, and would leave her and her contemporaries unemployable when wartime demand gave way to peacetime slack, and when marriage made them less attractive to employers. Before the war it was noted the major factor affecting youth employment and consequently the whole life chances of young slum-dwellers was the predominantly young and female nature of the workforce locally. In the brass trade which, with jewellery, was the most important employer in Kate's district, more than a quarter of the workforce was female, although some branches of the trade, like casting in which her father was employed, remained male preserves. But even where men and boys prevailed, de-skilling was underway. Boys were given no formal training and were expected to learn to operate machinery by 'using their eyes'. Employers had less need of skilled craftsmen except in trades like gun-making, spinning hollow-ware for the electro-plate trade and certain branches of jewellery, and even in skilled jobs like pattern-making, apprenticeship was unknown. Employers acquired nimble-fingered, healthy, unskilled workers who could be quickly trained and as easily replaced. By 1913 apprenticeship was the exception even in jewellery where small manufacturers were wary of teaching a trade to young workers who might set up in opposition to them.[33]

As a result the practice had grown of employing children straight from school who could be quickly trained and paid at juvenile wage rates until adulthood and then, when they needed higher wages to get married and support a family, they would be sacked or leave to find more highly paid heavy labouring jobs in foundries and press shops. Many young men joined the army, as Kate's father had, in order to escape the labour market altogether, at least for a few years. There was little incentive to seek the initial low pay of apprenticeship, even if these had been more readily available. Thus, when a young man had reached the maximum wage of fifteen shillings per week that he could earn in machine-operating, his only prospect was a life of heavy labouring between periods of unemployment. Such jobs were subject to the worst conditions, and industrial illnesses such as bronchitis and intestinal weakness were common amongst brass casters like Kate's father. This long-term underemployment is one characteristic of early twentieth-century Birmingham. The myth of Birmingham's prosperity, if it applies at all, belongs to the post-Second World War period.[34]

Kate herself found that she was locked into this cycle of relatively highly paid youth, marriage and the inevitable poverty which it brought, to be followed by a grim struggle to improve her standard of living as the family grew up. After a succession of pregnancies and the birth of five children, one of whom died in an accident, Kate's husband died, having been unemployed for most of their married life. She was then faced with a terrible struggle. The single-parent family was virtually unknown before the coming of the Welfare State and she had to allow her children to be taken away from her. The fact that she overcame these difficulties and has written a story which provides a moving example of female strength and courage was the result of her efforts to break the cycle of poverty described in these pages. It was also the result of the possibilities which existed, and still exist, of finding an economic niche in the jewellery trade which assured her own children's future. She had mastered various aspects of enamelling by changing employers and picking it up a bit at a time until she knew enough to grind and mix the powdered glass, prepare the paste, lay this on to the design, and then fire the article.[35] Thus she was able to work as a skilled enameller until the coming of the Second World War brought another boom to central Birmingham's Jewellery Quarter and enabled her to set up a small workshop to take advantage of the established firms' inability to cope with the increased demand. She has long since retired, of course, and is able now to contemplate from the tranquillity of her modest home, which she shares with one of her daughters and her husband, a life which has seen such enormous social and economic changes in the area which she has lived all her years.

John Rudd

NOTES

[1] Forty-three per cent: *Victorian County History, Vol. VII: The City of Birmingham* (1964), p. 53.

[2] For details of these changes see A. Briggs, *Victorian Cities* (1968), Penguin, pp. 225–40. Also numerous references in *Victorian County History, Vol. VII: The City of Birmingham* (1964), pp. 342–5, 332–3.

[3] ibid, p. 54.

[4] See pp. 27–31 in Kathleen Dayus's account.

[5] ibid, p. 53.

[6] City of Birmingham Health Department, *Report on Industrial Employment of Married Women and Infantile Mortality* (1910), pp. 3–4.

[7] *Victorian County History*, pp. 178–84.

[8] *Employment of Women*, p. 4.

[9] ibid, p. 5.

[10] ibid.

[11] ibid.

[12] D.J. Collier and B.L. Hutchins, *The Girl in Industry* (1918), pp. 17–18.

[13] Barbara Drake, *Women in the Engineering Trades*, Fabian

Research Department (1917), p. 7.

[14] *Employment of Women*, p. 12.

[15] ibid, p. 11.

[16] ibid, p. 10. For rates for different parishes for 1904-9, see p. 3.

[17] ibid, p. 17.

[18] ibid, p. 18.

[19] ibid, p. 19.

[20] City of Birmingham, Public Health and Housing Department, *Report on Infant Mortality* (1912), p. 17.

[21] City of Birmingham, *Report of the Medical Officer of Health on Child Welfare 1913* (1914), p. 5.

[22] ibid, pp. 3-4.

[23] *Infant Mortality*, pp. 11–13.

[24] L.A.M. Riley, *Report on Vanboy Labour in Birmingham* (1913), pp. 5, 12.

[25] ibid, pp. 5-6.

[26] The Birmingham Schools Dinner Society had been instituted in 1886 and its function was continued by the education committee after the passage of the Education (Provision of Meals) Act 1906. The meal actually supplied was, as Kate testifies, breakfast, and up to £3052 was spent annually before 1914, but in that year the sum rose to £8025 as a result of fathers departing for the war. *Victorian County History*, pp. 496-7.

[27] *Women in the Engineering Trades*, p. 8.

[28] R.S. Smirke, *Report on Birmingham Trades . . . for the Juvenile*

Employment Exchange: The Brass Trade (1914), pp. 6–8.

29 *Women in the Engineering Trades*, p. 41.

30 *The Girl in Industry*, p. 7.

31 ibid.

32 ibid, p. 25.

33 R.S. Smirke, *Report on Birmingham Trades prepared for . . . the Juvenile Labour Exchange: Jewellery* (1913), pp. 3–8; *The Electro-Plate Trade* (1913), p. 3; *Pattern Making* (1913), pp. 10–12.

34 R.S. Smirke, *The Brass Trade*, pp. 4–7.

35 For the jewellery trade, see R.S. Smirke, *Jewellery*.

1
Our Yard

One day, a few years ago, I found myself walking through a part of Birmingham I hadn't seen for a long time. Hockley is an area of warehouses and factories today and I shouldn't think anybody lives there except the landlords of the pubs that are dotted about here and there on corners. It was a different story seventy years ago, though. Then this whole district was so crammed with humanity it was more like a rabbits' warren. There were still factories and lots of small workshops and foundries and the same pubs were crowded all day long, not just at lunch-time when the workmen were having a break like today. Then, this was what people today would call a 'slum' I suppose, and the people who lived there would be pitied as the 'have-nots', but then there was no pity and we were left to sink or swim, rise or fall, as best we could. Yes, this was where I was born in 1903 and the poor people who struggled to live until that struggle killed them were my people.

So as I was walking by the George and Dragon where I had shivered on Christmas Eve singing carols for a few pence to buy a small treat that my mother and father couldn't afford, I thought, these people may have had nothing, but they don't deserve to be forgotten. My people; my parents and their friends and my brothers and sisters and the rest of us who fought for a crust here ought to be remembered now that the National Health Service, council houses and colour television have clouded our memory of where we came from and who we are.

People then were superstitious. They had no education and some couldn't even read and write: they never had the chance to learn like everyone has today. What we didn't have we had to do without, and what we didn't know we had to find out the

1

hard way, although more often than not it was the wrong way! The menfolk were mostly out of work and the women had to earn a living by taking in washing, or carding linen buttons, or sewing on hooks and eyes by the light of a piece of candle. There was never much of a fire in the grate but plenty of ashes from old boots or anything else that could be found to burn to warm ourselves. When we were fortunate enough to have coal, every lump was counted! Us kids would run a mile for a farthing or a piece of bread and dripping which we'd have to share with the rest.

The grown-ups always tried to help each other the best way they could, but they found it very hard, for some had large families to feed and clothe; ten, twelve and even sixteen in one family was not uncommon. Sometimes their language was terrible but they had harsh conditions to put with. Consumption was well known in our district and there were plenty of burials. The only people who did a good trade were the undertaker and the midwife. However, if you couldn't afford a midwife one of the neighbours would oblige, which resulted in many a baby dying before it had even opened its eyes and many a young mother as well. They were worn out and old women at forty, with children dragging at their dry breasts, a practice which was prolonged because they believed that if they kept a child to the breast until it was three years old they wouldn't become pregnant again. However, this rarely stopped them producing a large family despite the warnings they were given. I can recall many young children pulling at their mothers' skirts, crying to be picked up for a feed. You would hear the child cry out, 'I'm 'ungry, I want some titty.' Then the mother would lift her child up and pull out a breast while she walked along or sat on a step. There was often no milk there nor the bosom there used to be, only an empty flat piece of flesh, but this comforted the child and the mother, who hoped that the child would get something out of it even if it was only wind. Still most of these women wanted a large family, 'the more the better', they used to say. I imagined the reason for this was because they were jealous of the others having more than themselves, but this was not always so; and as I grew older I learned that the true reason for having a large family quickly was to replace the children that died, which many did, sometimes at a very early age. Diseases that were common at that time were rickets, 'wasting disease', fever, consumption and the rest. Those who did survive had to begin work at a very early age to help feed themselves and their parents, otherwise it was starvation or the workhouse.

Our street was called Camden Street. Along one side of this street facing the high school wall ran ten terraces called 'groves'. Ours was called Camden Drive. There were five houses or hovels with five more back-to-backs to each terrace. They were all built the same; one large living-room, one bed-room, and an attic. There were also cellars that ran under each house, damp, dark and cold. Here was where they kept their coal, 'slack', or wood when they had any, which was never very often. For this reason there was usually some rubbish tipped in the cellar ready to be put on the fire for warmth or for cooking. I don't suppose this habit would be regarded as altogether healthy today but then it was essential.

Sometimes the shopkeeper down the next street would leave an orange-box with a few specked oranges left in it outside the shop, or a soap-box or perhaps a wet-fish-box. Then there would be a mad rush of us kids and many a fight would ensue as we dragged the box home for our parents to put on the fire. We'd skin away the mould on the oranges and share them out with those not lucky enough to grab a box.

My mum and dad slept in the main bedroom over the living-room and my brothers, Jonathan and Charlie, slept in another bed in the same room. My other brother, Francis or Frankie, and my sister, Liza, and I slept in the attic over the bedroom and my eldest sister, Mary, had her bed in the other corner of the attic facing ours. Mary was twenty and was going to be married soon, when she was twenty-one. She had to wait because Mum and Dad would not give their consent until she was of age. In 1911 my brother Jonathan (Jack) was nineteen and Charlie was eighteen, Liza was eleven, Frankie was ten and I was eight years old. Us younger ones slept three in a bed; Liza and I at the top and Frankie at the bottom.

One night I asked Mary if I could sleep with her in the big bed but she told me, 'No! It's for me bottom drawers.' Now this puzzled me somewhat because I couldn't see how she could get a big bed like that in her bottom drawers.

We all lived in the first house in the fifth 'grove' which we all called 'our yard'. Next door lived Mr and Mrs Buckley and their six boys and one girl. In the third house lived Mr and Mrs Huggett with ten children: five boys and five girls. Next door to the Huggetts lived Maggie and Billy Bumpham. They had no children, or none that I knew of anyway. The neighbours used to say they weren't married and I could never understand this because I used to watch them undress and get into bed together – they never drew their blinds because they had none. What they did have that I loved was a little bull-terrier called Rags. Mrs Taylor lived in the last house in our yard. She had seven children and as many cats of both sexes who were continually producing offspring of their own: Mrs Taylor gave them to neighbours who needed them, to eat or clear away the mice. Everybody in our district had plenty of these. What she couldn't give away she drowned in the maiding-tub. No one knew what had became of Mr Taylor. Some people said she was so expert in drowning cats that she must have drowned him too.

At the end of the yard stood three ashcans and five lavatories, or closets as we called them. These each consisted of a square box with large round hole in the middle. Us children had to hold the sides of the seat otherwise we could have fallen in. These were dry closets. You can imagine the stench in summer! Next to the closets were two wash-houses where every washday everybody did their weekly wash. Like all the outhouses they were shared between the five houses in our yard and the five that backed on to us. There were always rows over whose turn it was to clean the closets so to save further quarrels Dad put a big padlock on one and gave Mrs Buckley next door a key to share. We kept our key on a cotton-reel tied with string behind our living-room door. The other closets were left open for anyone to use and they were filthy. We had to hold our

4

noses as we passed by, but Mum and Mrs Buckley always saw to it that ours was kept clean: her girls and Liza and I had to do it in turns while the women looked on. Finally, there was a gas-lamp in the centre of the yard and also a tap where everybody got their water for all household uses.

No one had a garden, not a blade of grass. There were cobblestones everywhere. If we wanted to see any flowers we went to the churchyard to play. We were often sent there, out of the way of our parents. We would take a bottle of tea and some milk for the younger ones who were transported in our go-cart. We nicknamed the churchyard 'Titty-bottle Park', a name that stuck with us for years. We'd tie the go-cart to a tree or a tombstone and play at hide-and-seek or perhaps some of us would change the stale water in the jam jars and rearrange the flowers. We'd be happy for a while playing at our games until the vicar appeared with his stick to chase us away. But try as he might he could never get rid of us; we always returned the next day.

All our homes were in old buildings that were tumbling down. The rent was usually three shillings a week; that was when the landlord was lucky enough to be paid. I've seen him wait until his tenants came out of the pubs at eleven at night. Often he wasted his time and if they couldn't pay their arrears he'd send along the bailiffs, but as often as not they'd already done a 'moonlight flit'. Down the street some one would borrow a hand cart, on the chattels would go and into another house they would move, for empty houses were common at that time. They were still the same old sort of hovel, though. The landlord rarely did any repairs, as the reader can imagine. So people did their own after their own fashion. When Christmas was drawing close they scraped together a few pence to buy some fresh wallpaper to brighten up the walls. I remember Dad used to paste ours with a mixture of flour and water and when Mum wasn't watching he'd mix in a bit of condensed milk. He swore it stuck the paper better but Jack said it only gave the bugs a good meal. Dad never stripped the old paper off. 'I daren't. It's only the bugs and the paper that's holding the walls up.'

They were dirty old houses; everyone had vermin or insects of some description. There were fleas, bugs, rats, mice and cockroaches – you name it, we had it. But I'll still say this for our mum; although we were as poor as the rest, she always kept us clean. Many times we had to stay in bed while she took the clothes from us to wash and dry in front of the fire so that we could go to school the next day looking clean.

Our mum was also very cruel and spiteful towards us, especially to me, and I could never make out why until I was old enough to be told. I can picture her now as I write. She was a large, handsome woman, except in her ugly moods. She weighed about sixteen stone and always wore a black alpaca frock, green with age, which reached down to her ankles, and a black apron on top. On her feet she wore button-up boots, size eight, which it was my job to clean and fasten with a steel button hook that hung by the fireplace. Mum always pretended she couldn't bend when she wanted her boots buttoned. She had long, black hair which she was always brushing and combing. She twisted it round her hand and swung it into a bun on top of her head. Then she'd look in the mirror and plunge a long hatpin through the bun. She called this hatpin her 'weapon'. Sometimes when she went out she'd put Dad's cap on top which made her look taller. She was always on the go, one way or another. I felt sorry for her at times and I tried my best to love her but we all lived in fear when she started to shout. When she did start you knew it. You had to move quickly, for it was no sooner the word than the blow!

Many a time we felt the flat of her hand, Liza, Frankie and me. We never knew what for at times, but down would come the cane from its place on the wall. If we tried to run away then we really had it. Neither our parents nor the neighbours had any time to give us any love or affection and they didn't listen to our troubles. We were little drudges and always in the way. You may ask who was to blame for us growing up like this in squalor, poverty and ignorance. We were too young to understand why then, and I don't think I understand yet, but there it was, we had to make the best of it. My dad would listen to us sometimes but only when Mum wasn't about, or if he'd had an extra drop of beer. It was at these times that I liked him best because sometimes, not always, he was jolly. This wasn't very often because he was out of work, and had only Mum or his pals to rely on to buy him a drink. He had to do an odd job or two before Mum gave him his beer money. Sometimes he did odd jobs for other people on the sly, before the relief officer made his visit.

Our dad never hit us. He would tell us off and show us the strap but he left the correcting to Mum, and she did enough for both. So we young ones tried very hard to behave ourselves when Dad was out and he was more times out than in. He always said he couldn't stand her 'tantrums' but my brother Jack took over when Dad was out, pushing us this way then that and giving us the occasional back-hander if we didn't do what he told us.

We saw very little of my brother Charlie; he only came home to sleep. Mother's tantrums got on his nerves also.

Frankie and I were the best of pals. He always tried to get me out of trouble, but he often got me into some. But I still loved him.

My sister Liza was very spiteful to me as well as being artful and although I tried to love her she pushed me away and pinched me on the sly when she had the chance. I couldn't do much about this because she was bigger than I was and very fat besides. When she did give me a sly dig I just had to grin and bear it and keep out of her and Mum's way. I still had to sleep with Liza and if she didn't pinch me she'd kick me out of bed. It was no good complaining, because Liza was always telling lies and Mum would believe her: she couldn't do wrong in Mum's eyes.

I remember one night very clearly. It was about one o'clock in the morning. I woke very thirsty so I crept quietly out of bed so as not to wake Liza or Frankie and went downstairs to get a drink of water. There wasn't any in the house, only a drop of warm water in the kettle. After satisfying my thirst I tiptoed back upstairs but when I got halfway up I heard Mum say, 'No! You can put it away! I've already had a baker's dozen. I'm 'avin' no mower so yow can get to sleep!'

I was always a very inquisitive child so I sat on the stairs to listen for more but I only heard the bed creak, so off up to the attic I went. I was feeling cold in my torn and threadbare chemise, one of Mary's cutdowns. I lay awake that night trying to puzzle out what my mum meant. I thought maybe she had eaten too much and wasn't feeling well so next morning when I came downstairs I said, 'Don't you feel well, Mum . . . have you eaten too much?'

At once she glared down at me and shouted, 'What do yer mean . . . 'ave I eaten too much?'

'Well, I heard you say to Dad you'd already had a baker's dozen,' I answered, trembling a little.

Mum went red in the face and cried out, 'And where did yer 'ear that?'

Then timidly I explained how I came down the stairs for a drink of water but before I could finish she slapped me across the face and shouted, 'That'll teach yer ter sit listenin' on the stairs!'

I moved back quickly as she lifted her hand once again so I was quite surprised when she seemed to have second thoughts.

'I'll get yer dad ter settle with yow.'

Whether she told him or not I never found out but I was determined to find out one way or another what was meant by a baker's dozen. So that same night I waited for Mary to come up to bed and after Liza and Frankie fell asleep I crept over to her bed.

'Are you awake, Mary?' I whispered in the dark.

'Yes. What do yer want?' she snapped. She didn't usually snap at me, but I could see why she didn't want to be bothered at that time of night. I began to tiptoe back to bed when she lit the candle and called me.

'Come on, Katie. What is it you want?' she asked more pleasantly.

Just then Mum shouted up the attic stairs. 'Let's 'ave less noise up theea!'

Mary smiled as she put her finger to her lips. 'Hush,' she whispered. 'Come and get into bed beside me and get warm then you can tell me all about it.'

I snuggled up close and felt very comforted. I could have gone straight off to sleep, but Mary wanted to know what was troubling me.

'Can you tell me what a baker's dozen is, Mary?' I managed to ask between yawns.

'Why? Where did you hear that?' She sat up in bed looking at me quizzically, and as I told her a broad smile spread across her face.

'You were lucky to get away with only your face slapped.' I was wide awake by now.

'Well, what does it mean?'

'It means Mum didn't want Dad to love her and to have any more babies. She's already had thirteen which is what's called a ''baker's dozen'' and you being the thirteenth, Mum calls you the ''scraping of the pot''.'

I could still see her smiling in the candlelight as she whispered to herself, 'I must tell Albert about this when we meet.'

'But if I'm the last, what became of the others in between?'

'They all died before you were ever thought of,' she answered sadly. 'Now lie down and go to sleep.'

We both snuggled up to keep warm after she blew out the candle. Although I was warm and comfortable I couldn't help but think about those other seven who had died. Maybe they were happier in the other world, I thought. There wouldn't have been room for them here, and Mum and Dad wouldn't have been able to feed us all. And with all these thoughts in my mind I eventually dropped off to sleep.

2
The Pig's Pudding

Everyone in our district was more or less poor. They never knew from where or when the next meal was coming. Most of them had to have parish relief[1] but what they received was insufficient to feed us growing children, let alone our parents as well. Each Friday morning or afternoon, according to their surname, they queued up for their rations. Each person had a card for coal, bread, margarine, a tin of condensed milk, tea and sugar. They received more and some less according to their circumstances and the size of their family. No one was given any money. The officers in charge decided this would be spent on beer, tobacco, snuff and other unsuitable commodities. Therefore those that didn't indulge in those habits had to suffer for those that did, but everyone did little odd jobs on the quiet to get some extra coppers. Some didn't care, as long they could manage to borrow or beg a cup of sugar, a piece of soap or half a loaf until they could collect their next ration card. They were artful: they never returned the same quantity. It was a smaller cupful or less than half a loaf and no soap. They said the kids had left it in the water and it had melted away or they had thrown it down the 'snuff'[2] with the water. Thus they wore out their welcome. It only happened once to Mum – 'once bitten twice shy', she used to say. No one ever came to borrow at our house a second time.

She was independent-minded and, although we too had to have parish relief sometimes, she wouldn't ask a neighbour for anything. She used to say, 'What we ain't got we'll goo without.' Nor would she have any neighbours in our house unless it was essential. She said they only came to see if you'd got more than them. If anybody did call and ask Mum to help them out, her reply would be blunt.

'I don't arsk yow fer anything so don't arsk me! I don't borra and I don't lend!'

With that they'd get the door slammed in their face for their pains. Mum was very hard, but then the neighbours said she

10

could afford to be because they thought she had more coming in than they did. Perhaps they were right: Jack was at work as was Mary, but Jack didn't give Mum much and nor did Mary, who you'll remember was saving to get married. At this time Charlie had already left home and Dad was unemployed like the other men. So we can't have had it much better than other families in our yard.

We were forbidden to play with the kids who had dirty heads but how we were to know they had dirty heads I never understood. We saw more scratch their heads and others were sent home from school, but they were our friends, so we still played with them despite what our mum said. I came indoors one day with one of my girlfriends and Mum pounced.

'Come over 'ere, yow! What yer doin' with yer fingers in yer 'air?'

I walked slowly towards her. I was afraid. She knew and I knew that I had disobeyed her. Suddenly she slapped me across the face and grabbed me by the hair.

'Kneel down 'ere and put yer 'ead between me legs!' she shouted.

I did as I was told and she combed my hair so hard with the steel comb that I began to scream.

'That'll teach yer ter defy me . . . And if I do find anything 'ere I'll cut the lot off!'

I hoped she wouldn't because a previous occasion was fresh in my memory. I had come home with a note and Dad had held my head down over a piece of newspaper and after pouring paraffin over my hair he had cut the lot off. I wasn't allowed to grow my hair long after that. I had to have it in two plaits but on this day they survived. Mum found nothing to tell Dad about. I would still rather lose my hair than my little friends so I continued to play with them. However, I kept my distance just in case.

Later that evening I waited for my sister to go to bed first, then I lit my candle and crept up the stairs so as not to wake her. I checked to see that she was asleep then I blew out the candle and slipped into bed beside her, but as usual she was only catnapping and all of a sudden she kicked me out of bed.

11

I fell with a bang on the floor.

'You ain't sleepin' with me! You've got ticks in yer hair!'

'No I ain't! You ask Mum!' I shouted back at her with tears in my eyes.

At that moment the attic door flew open and in came my brother Jack.

'What's all this bloody racket about?' He bawled. 'I carn't get any sleep!'

'Liza's kicked me out of bed,' I cried, hoping to get a few words of comfort from him, but all he said was, 'Shut yer cryin', yer big babby.'

He struck a match and gazed down at Liza who was pretending to be asleep again.

'She's not asleep. She's only pretending,' I cried.

'Don't you dare to answer me back!' he said sharply, and he pushed me into the corner between the bed and wall and left me there and returned downstairs.

During all this commotion Frankie had lain quietly at the bottom of the bed but, when Jack had gone, he jumped out of bed and pulled all the clothes off Liza.

'If you don't keep yer hands off Katie and give her more room in bed I'll pay you out when I get you on yer own.'

Liza was afraid of Frankie when he was in one of these moods so she moved over without saying a word and I climbed back into bed. She still gave me a couple of sly digs but I didn't care while Frankie was there to protect me. So it just my luck and his when the very next morning he should feel ill and so wasn't able to go to school. Dad told Mum, 'Polly, I'll light a fire in the attic grate so Frankie can stay in bed.'

'You'll do nothing of the sort! I carn't spare the coal,' she shouted.

'Oh well,' replied Dad, 'he can sleep down on the sofa in front of the fire. Anything for a bit of peace.'

Mum went mumbling out of the room. She always sulked when she couldn't have her own way. So Liza and I had to leave for school without Frankie. Liza never spoke to me all day. She pushed past me in the playground and ignored me. When I returned from school Frankie was huddled by the fire on the sofa. I asked him how he was but he could hardly speak, he had such an awful cold. Dad asked me to get the blue paper sugar bags which we always saved for slack or tea leaves to bank up fire. Mum was out, so Dad gave us our tea. Then we did our jobs. I didn't want to finish because I was afraid to go to bed. Frankie wouldn't be there to protect me from Liza and when she went to bed first I stayed up to give her plenty of time to get to sleep. To kill time I looked for things to do. I washed all the crocks twice over, very slowly, then I went up the yard to fill the kettle for the next morning. I even went down the cellar again to fetch up another bucket of slack. I searched around the room for more to do but I hadn't escaped Mum's notice. She turned round in her chair.

'Why are yow still up?'

'I was wondering if you want anything else done, Mum,' I said nervously, with my back to her.

'No, there ain't. So yer can get up ter bed!'

'Can I stay up a bit longer, Mum? I'm not tired.'

But I was tired, very tired; I was only making excuses and I guessed Mum wouldn't let me stay up any longer.

'What ain't done tonight yer can do tomorra night! Now be off with yer,' she shouted.

She always frightened me when she shouted. I wished her and Frankie good-night, but only Frankie answered. I prayed God that Liza would be asleep. I prayed also that the stairs wouldn't creak, but they were like everything else in the house, very old, so I wasn't surprised when they did. When I reached the top of the stairs I knew my prayers hadn't been answered. There was Liza wide awake, sitting up in bed, waiting for me.

I crept into bed beside her, afraid to speak and scared of what she would do now Frankie was not there to defend me. Suddenly she sprang on me.

'You ain't got yer pal tonight, have yer?' she hissed in my ear. I didn't answer, thinking it was best not to, but she continued louder, 'Did you hear what I said?'

I still didn't answer, I was too afraid. Then she grabbed hold of my two plaits and shouted in my ear again, 'Get out of this

13

bed. There's no room for two of us.'

Then I finally lost my temper and cried out, 'If you wasn't so fat there'd be room enough for the three of us!'

But I knew I'd get the worst of it for calling her 'fat' so I crept down into Frankie's place. Then she pushed her feet out and I fell with a thump on to the floor and there I stayed. I sobbed quietly to myself, afraid Mum would come up to see what all the noise was about and I knew I'd be blamed. After a while, I pulled one of the coats off the bed and crawled into a corner to cry myself to sleep. I don't know how long I had been asleep when I awoke with a terrible fright. Something warm and soft brushed against my face. My first thought was that it was a mouse; we had plenty and they always came out at night, but when I put my hand up to face I could feel that it was our cat, Pete. I pulled him to me and hugged him tightly and like that we slept right through the night.

Next morning Liza went down first and we washed for school. I looked for Dad but he wasn't around, only Frankie who was sitting up on the sofa.

'Are you better, Frankie?' I asked.

'Yes,' he replied.

Before I could say another word Mum beckoned me over.

'Come 'ere, yow!'

I went slowly towards her, thinking to myself what have I done wrong now.

'What was all that bangin' I 'eard larst night?'

'It wasn't me, Mum, it was Liza. She kicked me out of bed again.'

'What do yer mean, "again"?' She shook my shoulders roughly.

'I never did, Mum.' Liza lied. 'Katie's telling lies.'

I was surprised when Mum turned to Liza and said, 'You speak when yer spoken to . . . I know who's telling lies.'

Then turning to me again she spoke angrily, 'I'll put the cane across yer backs if I 'ear any mower from either of yer! Now get yerselves off to school.'

I was always glad when she stopped shouting. When she started you never knew when she was going to stop and her

14

language was usually terrible. I remember Mary telling her to be quiet.

'Oh, shut yer face! You like to hear the sound of yer own voice.'

Mary and Jack were the only two who could speak to Mum this way and attempt to put her in her place. What they said usually quietened her because they threatened to leave home if she kept on with her tantrums, but we all recognised that Mum changed her tone and moods when it suited her.

Frankie got off the sofa and got himself ready for school. His job every day was to take the tin bowl to the tap in the yard and fetch our washing water. But on this morning the tap was frozen when he went out. The Jones and Buckley kids were already there waiting for the water to thaw. I took a burning piece of paper which I pushed up the spout. It started to trickle and eventually Frankie managed to half fill the bowl. We took it inside and stood it on the stool.

'Can I have a drop of hot water in here, Mum?' he asked. We were both shivering with the cold.

'No yer carn't! I ain't got none till the fire's lit, so hurry yerselves or yer'll be late agen fer school and miss yer breakfast.'

On and on she went, jumping off the chair and she was sitting on and pulling Frankie by the ear and holding his head over the bowl and rubbing his neck with carbolic soap so hard that he began to cry. Frankie was a tough lad and it took a lot to make him cry; even when Mum caned him he would grin. But on this occasion he wasn't well and if Dad had been there he wouldn't have allowed him to go to school. Mum was only stopped by the sound of the school bell. We dashed out of the house and arrived just in time to receive our 'parish breakfast'.

All the poor children in our school were provided with a breakfast, so when the bell rang out at five minutes to nine we had to be ready and waiting. The kids from our yard would rush up the street like a lot of ants because if you were not in line when the bell stopped you would be lucky to get any at all. The breakfast consisted of an enamel mug of cocoa and two thick slices of bread and jam. The bread was usually stale or soggy. Dad would get up very early some mornings and earn himself a few extra pennies fetching the big urn which contained the cocoa, and the bread and jam. He had to wheel it along to the school in a basket carriage and when he passed our yard Mum would be waiting with a quart jug hidden underneath her apron. When she could see no one about, Dad used to fill it with cocoa. She would have helped herself to the bread and jam too but Dad stopped her because they were all counted. Mum and Dad would have been in trouble with the authorities if they'd ever been found out; but they never were. Our parents were both too cute to be caught, and although I knew what they were up to I never told anyone. I was too afraid in case they were sent to prison.

One morning we were dashing up the lane to get there in time for breakfast but the bell stopped ringing. Frankie grabbed my hand and dragged me along.

'Come on! We can still make it, Katie!' But I started to cry.

'We're too late now and I'm hungry!'

We hadn't had anything to eat since tea-time the day before, and then only a piece of bread and dripping.

'Shut yer blarting!' Liza hissed as she pushed us inside the door. Our teacher was calling the last name from the register when she saw us come in.

'I see you three are late again. I'm afraid you are too late for your breakfasts.'

'But we're hungry, miss!' pleaded Frankie.

'Well you can stand at the back of the line. You may be lucky,' she answered sharply.

We reached down a mug each from the ledge but when it came to our turn all we had was some warm cocoa, watered down, but no bread and jam. There was none left, and by the time our lessons were over at twelve o'clock we were very, very hungry.

On our way home from school we had to pass a homemade cook shop where we always paused to look through the window at all the nice things on show. This particular morning we stayed longer than usual, pressing our noses to the pane of glass, saliva dripping down our chins. There was pig's

16

pudding, hot meat pies, hocks, tripe and cakes of every sort staring back at us. Worse than the sight of this potential feast was the smell. It was too much for Frankie who burst out: 'I'm so hungry I could smash the glass in and help myself.'

'And me!' I said.

'Don't you dare,' said Liza, who was afraid he would.

'Well, why should they be on show when we're so hungry?' asked Frankie.

Liza had no answer; she too was dribbling down her chin and she didn't stop Frankie who glanced quickly up and down the street to see who was about and hissed: 'If you two look out for me and as soon as ''Skinny Legs'' goes around the back of the shop I'll nip in quick and help myself to a few.'

Every one called the shopkeeper this because he gave short measure and he never gave you a stale cake or a loaf like other shops did. Anyway, it seemed ages before Frankie did anything but at last he saw 'Skinny Legs' go through to the back of the shop and he dived in whilst Liza and I watched the street to warn him if anyone came along. I saw his hand in the window as he grabbed hold of a roll of pig's pudding and several hot meat pies. He came out, stuffing them under his gansey,[1] and the three of us ran off down the street as fast as we could but before we had gone many yards Frankie stopped.

'Catch hold of these pies, Liza, they're burning my belly!'

'No,' she replied, 'I don't want any part of them!'

'No? But you'll take your share to eat 'em, won't you!' he snapped.

I was sure someone would come along and overhear us so I put my hands up his gansey and pulled down the pies. He wasn't kidding, they were hot, but my hands were so cold I was glad of the warmth.

'Did anyone see me?' he asked anxiously.

'Yes. He did.' Liza was pointing at Jonesy, one of the lads from our yard.

'Hello, how long have you been there?' said Frankie.

'Long enough, and I seen what yer bin dooin' an' all, an' if yer don't give me some, I'll snitch on yer.'

17

We all knew he meant it, so reluctantly Frankie pulled down the roll of pudding from his gansey and handed it over to Jonesy who dashed off home after saying he wouldn't tell anyone. But I knew he'd snitch all right. His mum went out cleaning on a Tuesday, so thinking she wouldn't be at home and he'd enjoy himself with his pudding he ran indoors. However he was unlucky: she was there.

'Where ever 'ave yer 'ad that from?' we heard her shout.

We heard his cringing explanation and Frankie shouted in the door, 'Yer traitor.'

Then the three of us ran down the yard to the wash-house to eat our pies. I don't think I ever tasted anything like that meat pie. It was delicious. Afterwards as we came from the wash-house we saw Mrs Jones walking towards our house. We knew we were in trouble but we didn't care now that our appetites were satisfied. Mrs Jones didn't like our mum, in fact I don't know who did, so I wasn't surprised by what happened next. Mrs Jones knocked loudly on our door and Mum lifted the corner of the curtain to see who was there. Seeing Mrs Jones she opened wide the door and shouted for all to hear, 'What do yow want?'

Mrs Jones stood on the step with her hands on her hips, grinning like a Cheshire cat. She always liked to get a dig at Mum, so she shouted louder so the neighbours could hear. 'I've got news for you, Polly. Your kids 'ave pinched some of ''Skinny Legs'' ' pies.'

She didn't mention the pig's pudding though.

'I don't believe yer and get away from my dower, the lot on yer! Goo an' look after yer own kids.' And Mum slammed the door shut.

I thought, one day the door is going to fall off.

When Mrs Jones had gone away she came out again to call us in. Mrs Jones was still gossiping with the others.

'Come in, yow three. I want some explainin'.'

We went in timidly, but before we could utter a word she began angrily, 'An' what's this I 'ear about some pies?'

Liza quickly unburdened herself about how Frankie had

18

stolen the pies and the pig's pudding.

'Pig's pudding. She never said anything about any pig's pudding.' She was furious.

'Frankie gave it to Jonesy,' said Liza.

'Well, we'll see about that!' said Mum.

She was fuming. She couldn't get out of the house quick enough. On went Dad's cap, off came the apron, and round the backyard she marched. When she got to Mrs Jones's door she banged twice, as hard as she could. All the neighbours lifted their windows and popped their heads out while some of them crowded round to watch developments more closely. They knew Mum was big enough to eat Mrs Jones. There was no answer so she knocked again, louder and shouted, 'Yow can come out. I've seen yer be'ind the curtin.'

Slowly, Mrs Jones opened the door a little way to face Mum standing there, hands on hips, chest puffed out.

'Yer crafty old sod! Yow never told me that my Frankie giv' your lad a roll of pig's pudding. Now what about it? An' I ain't gooin' from 'ere till I get it.'

Mrs Jones was scared now, thinking what Mum might do, so she shut the door quickly and we all heard the bolt rammed home. But Mum wasn't finished. She banged again, louder than ever.

'Yer better 'and over that puddin' or else!' demanded Mum, her fist in the air.

Then suddenly the window shot up and the pig's pudding came flying out. It caught Mum on the head and everyone began laughing, but Mum ignored them and grabbed hold of us and the pudding and marched us indoors. She never bothered about what the neighbours thought or said as long as she didn't hear them. Woe betide them if she did.

'Get yer clo's off and get up them stairs. I'll get yer dad ter deal with you two when 'e comes 'ome.'

She pushed us towards the stairs and Frankie and I ran quickly up to the attic. We didn't go back to school that afternoon because Mum kept us up there until Dad returned in the evening and all we had to eat that day was the meat pie each.

It was late when we heard Dad come up the stairs so we

pretended to be asleep. We knew he wouldn't wake us. Sure enough we soon heard his receding footsteps on the stairs. In the early hours of the morning Frankie crept downstairs and brought a cup of water and a thick slice of bread and lard. We shared this between us while Liza slept on. Then we climbed back into bed and finally fell asleep.

NOTES

[1] For parish relief see pp.xx and p.197.

[2] The cesspit.

[3] A corruption of 'guernsey', originally a fisherman's woollen jumper, but meaning here any thick, woollen sweater with a round or slit neck.

3
Saturday Night in Our Yard

The next afternoon Dad came home pleased and excited. This was pleasing for us as well because he wasn't often happy.

'Where's yer mum, Katie?' he asked.

'Down in the wash-house, filling the boiler,' I answered.

'Well, go down and tell her I've got a lovely surprise for her.'

I hadn't seen Dad so cheerful for a long time so I ran down the yard and, seeing Mum through the steam in the wash-house, I called out to her, 'Come quickly, Dad's got a surprise for you!'.

'What's 'e want now? Mower money for beer I suppose,' she snapped.

'No, Mum. I don't think so. He's too excited.'

'Hm . . . we'll see,' she mumbled.

She stopped to put some more slack under the boiler, then, with me trailing behind, marched down the yard. She never walked like other women, she always seemed to stride along, taking big steps with her back straight and her head held high. When we were indoors she took Dad's flat cap and her hessian apron off, then staring at Dad she said, 'Now, what do yer want this time?'

'Give us a kiss first, then I'll tell yer,' he replied, putting his face forward close to hers.

'Don't be daft!' was her reply to this show of affection. 'I ain't got time any mower fer that sort of thing.' She turned her back on him.

I felt so sorry for Dad; he looked so dejected as he stood looking at her. I can never remember Mum and Dad kissing each other: they were always snapping or not on speaking terms. I stood by Dad, watching and waiting. I, too, was eager to know what the surprise was, but Dad didn't say a word. He just flopped down in his chair and lit his pipe. Then Mum raised her voice and shouted at him. 'Well, come on, Sam! Let's know what it's all about.' She was getting impatient.

Dad turned around in his chair and told her he'd got a job. 'It's hard work, and it's only twenty-five bob a week. I don't mind the hard work, Polly, but it's long hours, six in the morning until six o'clock in the evening.'

'That ain't much money for all them hours,' was all she said.

Then she turned and went out again to the wash-house with her apron over her arm. I stood there waiting for Dad to say something more, but he just got up from his chair and walked out.

'Can I come with you, Dad?' I asked.

He just nodded, so along I went, walking behind him. I knew he was going to the Golden Cup to have a drink. He met Mr Taylor inside, and thanked him for getting him the job. Mr Taylor bought Dad a pint and a pop for me. I sat just inside the door, filling a Woodbine packet with sawdust from the floor, when I noticed four navvies stroll in. I could see they were already well oiled. They called for a pint each and then began a song. Some of the songs they sang I knew so I joined in.

'Come and give us a song, littl' 'un,' said one. But I was too shy, so Dad came over to me, picked me up and sat me on the counter.

'You want to hear my Katie sing?' Dad asked proudly.

'Yes, mate,' they replied.

Dad knew when I sang someone always gave me a halfpenny and sometimes a penny, so with this in mind I burst forth with my favourite, 'Mid Pleasures and Palaces'. Everyone in the pub joined in after I had sung a few lines, including the publican and his wife. When I had finished my song I heard one of the navvies say to Dad, 'That kid's got a sweet voice, yow ought to get her trained, mate.'

They each gave me a penny. I felt like a queen when they applauded me and asked me to sing some more, but Dad lifted me down from the counter.

'You better be off now before yer mum sees yer.'

He took threepence from me and left me with a penny and the excuse that I could have the rest when he came home. I never did, but I went home happy knowing that Dad had the threepence instead of Mum.

Monday morning came and Dad rose early to start his first day at the casting works. He had to get himself up because Mum said it was too early and too cold for her to get up first. When Dad returned home that evening I thought he looked miserable, tired, dirty and wet through: it hadn't stopped raining all day.

'It's hard and dirty work in that casting shop, Polly,' he sighed as he flopped into his chair. Mum was preparing supper, but she appeared not to hear him.

'Shall I pull your boots off, Dad?' I asked.

He neither said yes or no, nor did Mum, so I bent down on the floor and untied the laces, pulled off his boots, stood them on the fender to dry and passed him a torn piece of towel to dry off his hair.

'I don't mind the hard work, Polly,' he continued at last. 'But last night I couldn't sleep.'

'Why? I dain't keep yer awake,' was her sharp answer.

'Oh no,' replied Dad. 'I was afraid to get to sleep in case I overslept on my first day. Anyhow, where's the alarm clock gone from off the mantel-shelf?'

'Why ask? You know it's in pawn with the rest of the things. I'll get them out at the end of the week.'

'I carn't wait until then,' he pleaded.

Mum went on preparing supper which was bread and cheese, a pint of ale and a bit of Spanish onion.

'I know what I'll do,' he said, jumping up from his chair and reaching for his cap.

'Now where yer gooin'?' Mum shouted across the table.

'I'm going to ask Fred the lamplighter to tap his pole on the bedroom window when he comes in the mornings. Keep my supper till I get back.'

He swallowed three parts of his pint and, as he dashed out to see the lamplighter, Mum finished the rest. Fred happened to be coming down the yard to light the gaslamps when Dad bumped into him.

'Hello, Fred,' Dad said. 'You're just the chap I'm looking for. I've got a job for you. Will you tap my bedroom window every morning?'

'Why, Sam, you've got a job then?'

'Yes,' said Dad.

'It'll cost you a tanner a week and a pint,' said Fred, scratching his head.

'Very well, you old fraud,' smiled Dad. He knew very well what the charge was.

'That's what all the others pay me,' said Fred, a bit indignant. 'But don't tell anyone, Sam. If the Gas Department find out I'll lose my job.'

'You can trust me,' Dad told him, and they shook hands and wished each other good-night.

So each morning at break of dawn Fred did his job as promised. Then on the following Saturday night Dad met him in the pub. Fred was about to take his sixpence when Dad pulled him to one side and whispered in his ear, 'Fred, I want a few words with you.'

'Make it quick, Sam, I've got me rounds to do.'

'You'll have to tap our window a bit harder. Some

23

mornings I carn't hear yer.'

'I'm sorry, Sam, but yer know how it is. If the others hear me knock your window loud they won't want to have theirs tapped and I'll lose their tanners. You know what I mean?' he said slyly, and winked at Dad.

'Yes, I know what yer mean. You're a crafty old sod,' smiled Dad, returning the wink. 'But you'll do till the missus gets the alarm clock out of the pop-shop.'

I was an inquisitive child and always followed Dad or any-one else I knew to find out what was happening, but on this occasion they turned and noticed me drawing in the sawdust behind the door.

'You'd better be off before yer mum comes after yer,' the lamplighter said, pressing a halfpenny into my hand as I followed them out. Reluctantly I walked home with the coin safely hidden down my stocking.

When I arrived at our house I noticed Mum was standing on the step with her arms folded across her chest and looking like thunder. Now what have I done, I thought to myself. She was glaring all the while as I approached her, then she bellowed, 'Where 'ave them two gone?'

I acted as though I didn't know, hoping I would not be forced to tell her.

'Who do you mean?' I asked.

'Yer know who I mean! That Fred an' yer Dad.'

'They went in the Cup, Mum, but they've left now and gone down the street,' I answered truthfully.

'I think I know where they are. If there's any treatin' to be done they can treat me.'

She mumbled to herself as she went inside, snatched down a flat cap from the back of the door and slapping it on top of her bun, she marched down the street. I trailed behind her as usual to watch developments. She arrived at the King's Head, flung wide the door and shouted, 'Anybody seen my Sam?'

Everybody looked round, but no one answered; they only shook their heads.

'I'll find 'im if it's the larst thing I do!' she fumed, as the door banged after her.

24

I looked up the street and saw Dad walking towards the Cup. He didn't see Mum, but she saw him just as he was going inside. Her strides grew bigger and when she reached the pub door she pushed it wide and entered. Kicking the sawdust out of her path she went up to the counter.

'Mine's a pint!' she called out to Dad.

Everyone stopped talking, and a hushed quiet descended. They all knew what Mum was like when she was in one of her moods. I watched her bosom heave up and down as she breathed heavily. Then she flopped down on one of the benches, all sixteen stone of her. Little me climbed up beside her, hoping she wouldn't have another of her tantrums.

Dad came over to her and gave her a pint. Poor Dad, I thought. She tipped her head back and drank it down. Dad was always giving into her when she was in a bad mood. He tried not to answer her because we all knew she would have the last word. It was the only time we got any peace when Dad took no notice of her. I often looked at the picture of Mum and Dad that hung on one of our walls. Mum had been quite a good-looker and Dad was handsome when he was young. Dad was still handsome, despite his years of worry and toil, but Mum looked older than her years. Today I realise why she was like she was. It must have been a terrible ordeal for her and the rest of the women who had to live in one room and two bedrooms and bring up thirteen and even more children. They had no bathrooms, no hot or cold water in the house and had to live on relief when they could get it. These women were tired and worn out when they reached the age of forty. Some never lived to that age; many were claimed by consumption, childbirth or plain hard work.

Now that Dad had started work we all had more to eat. He would bring in a joint of meat for Sunday, whereas before I used to fetch fourpenn'orth of pieces. Our clothes and knick-knacks started coming out of pawn, and life in general at our house seemed more pleasant for a time. However, Dad still collected the relief without telling them he was working. Then one day I remember Mum warning him, 'I think yer better sign off, Sam, before they find out.'

25

'I'll stay on a bit longer, Polly. I don't know how long me job's going to last.'

'Oh, well! Please yourself. If yer goo ter prison, don't say I didn't warn yer,' was her only answer.

No matter how bad our neighbours seemed, they always tried to help one another in their own kind of way. They would never 'snitch' on each other, because they were all doing odd jobs on the side without reporting them to the relief officers. They had to do this; it was the only way to make ends meet. But they had to be extra careful to hide things away when the visitor came to call because they were always poking around to find out what was happening. With that in mind, Dad signed off after having two free weeks.

Saturday dinner-time, Dad had his first wage packet and, after giving Mum hers, he went off down the pub to get his quota. Later, when he came back, he lined us up. There was Frankie, Liza, several of our school friends and me and he took us to the Saturday afternoon matinée. We used to make an awful clatter in our clogs and Dad in his heavy boots, and even the horses turned their heads to see where the noise was coming from. Along the cobbled street we marched in a line like little soldiers, so proud were we to be treated to the pictures. Up the stone steps to the top of the gallery we climbed, then rushed madly to get a good seat on one of the low forms. It was wonderful to watch the silent films and hear the pianist banging away at the piano. We were sad when it was all over because we never knew when we'd get another treat like this. As we went out the 'chucker-out' who stood on the door gave each of us a bag of sweets.

'You've been behaving yourselves, haven't you?' he said.

We couldn't do anything but behave with Dad with us. When we got home it was growing dark and Mum was waiting for Dad to take her out for the usual Saturday-night drink. I can see her now, standing on the doorsteps in her white starched pinafore which she kept especially for these Saturday nights, with her arms folded across her huge bosom and Dad's flat cap stuck on top of her head.

'And about time too! I've bin waitin' for yer this larst 'arf 'our, and I want these kids in bed!'

Dad didn't answer, so she turned to me. 'There's tea in the pot an' bread an' drippin' on the table and when you've 'ad it get up to bed. An', yow two . . .!' she called out to Frankie and Liza.

Dad had walked off while she was giving us our instructions but she didn't let him get far before she caught him up. Frankie and Liza didn't drink their tea. They said it tasted like old boots, and no wonder, the enamel teapot was chipped and cracked through being stewed on the fire so often. I was too thirsty to care what it tasted like; I even drank Frankie's and Liza's share. After feasting on the bread and dripping, we lit our piece of candle and went up to bed. However, we didn't get undressed that night: this was the Saturday night and we were going to be entertained.

We all looked forward to these Saturday nights when we saw Battling Billy, as he was universally known, who became a little peculiar when he'd had to much to drink. He would then offer to fight anyone in sight. Our parents never took any notice of him. They understood why he was like he was: Dad said he was more to be pitied than blamed. He'd fought alongside Dad in the Boer War and was shell-shocked.

None of the pubs would serve Battling Billy because of his antics, so his wife Maggie used to fetch drink in bottles from the outdoor for him and he always seemed to have plenty on a Saturday night. Downstairs we hurried and when we emerged into the yard we saw some of our neighbours already there. The children were sitting on old mats and coats on the wall, waiting for Battling Billy to appear. Our friend Jonesy and his mum kept our places. We hadn't waited long when Billy dashed out of his house, just like a bull at a gate. He was only a small man, but he had a lot of strength, the more so when he'd had too much to drink. He was swearing and performing worse than ever, and soon everyone was laughing at him. He looked very comical, running back and forth in bare feet and red flannelette combs.[1] He reminded me of one of the warriors out of our school history books. The cats flew in all directions to get out of his way. He stared to the right and left and with the yard broom in one hand and a dustbin lid in the other he yelled at the top of his voice, 'Charge!'

Using the lid for a shield, and thrusting the broom handle forward, he yelled again, 'Charge! . . . Let 'em all come!'

Suddenly, he shot a glance up at the wall and saw us sitting there. He put the shield up to his face and peeping round its edge he shouted at us, 'Come on down, all you bloody Boers!'

Then we all began to scream. We'd never seen Billy in such a fierce mood before. But Maggie and his bull-terrier were used to him and they both stood on the step waiting for him to tire himself out so that he could be put to bed. To us he seemed worse than ever and we clung to our places on the wall for all we were worth. He was going strong. He ran down the yard, yelling, 'Charge!' again and this time thrust the broom handle through Mrs Taylor's only unbroken window. As the glass shattered, someone shouted down the yard that the cops were on their way. But Billy was too wrapped up in what he was doing. In fact he was enjoying himself so much that he was oblivious to our warnings. We all managed to scramble off the wall and run indoors, from which place of refuge we watched the finale from our bedroom window. Billy was still peering over his shield, waving his broom about and shouting as four burly policemen came marching towards him. Two stood at the entrance to the yard and the other two tried to catch poor Billy, but he was like an eel slipping between their legs. After a lot of struggling, Billy tired, and the policemen managed to hold him down so that they could talk to him quietly.

'Now come along peaceably, Billy,' and in the morning when you've sobered up you can be bailed out.'

All the police in the local lock-up knew Billy, and they never took him to the cells unless he became too dangerous.

'If you don't behave yourself we'll have to drag you there.'

We'd all heard this but he continued to kick and struggle so that the other two policemen had to help take him away. By this time Billy's dog Rags had seen what was happening and he too joined in. He grabbed hold of Billy's combs and tried to prevent him being carried off. During all this performance Maggie still stood on her doorstep watching. However, when she saw that things were threatening to get out of hand she walked over to Billy and spoke to him.

'Go along quietly, Billy, and I'll bring the rent book in the morning to bail you out,' she said, soothingly.

Then she gave him a kiss, picked up the dog and walked away, but before she could get to her door one of the policemen called out, 'I'd like a word with you before you go.'

'I ain't done nothin',' she answered, scared.

'Maybe not, but he's worse than ever tonight. Why's that?'

'Well, it was his birthday and I bought him a drop of the best.'

'You should be ashamed and have more sense. But I'm warning you now, next time he may go to prison for a long time and you with him!'

She didn't answer. She probably thought it better not to, and her eyes were cast down to the floor, but she did have a last word with Billy.

'Good-night, Billy, love, and behave yourself now. I'll be round in the morning, early, and I'll bail you out.' She didn't seem to care whether he went or not.

Then he was taken away, with crowds of people following behind to see the poor chap taken to the station house.

As Maggie walked towards her door with the dog still under her arm, Mrs Taylor shouted from her attic, 'You ought to be ashamed of yourself, Maggie, letting the cops take your Billy away. And remember, I want me window mended.'

'Push your head back in and look after yer own! I'll look after mine,' she yelled back. 'Anyway, if you want ter know it's the only time I get a wink of sleep when the cops tek 'im in.'

Then she went off and we heard the door slam behind her. I often wondered why some of the doors did not fall off, the way everyone slammed them shut? Tempers were always getting frayed because things never seemed to go right for these people. They skimped and saved to make ends meet, but they knew it was hopeless, so they gave up trying, or, worse, caring. Many's the time I've heard and seen them quarrelling with each other and coming to blows over the least little thing, but they didn't mean to say or do these things. They would be friends again the next day, and meet in the pub to discuss their troubles again.

The following morning, after putting Mrs Taylor in her place as she put it, Maggie knocked on her neighbour's door to ask her if she could take her rent book along to the station to bail poor Billy. In the end she had to ask Mrs Taylor for her book because she was the only one with a clean sheet. So they forget their argument of the previous night and hurried along to the lock-up. They were not alone. Nearly the whole street had risen early to meet Billy. We had hoped to see him appear in his combs but after confessing to the officer in charge that she'd forgotten to bring Billy's clothes, one of her friends volunteered to lend some of her own husband's. After a brief delay while the garments were found and handed over, Billy emerged from the station. We couldn't see his hands or feet, the borrowed clothes were so large; we could only make out the top of his tousled head and part of his dirty face. Maggie grabbed him to her, hugged and kissed him, then we all trooped off to the Cup to celebrate his release. Everyone crowded in round him and pushed through the door so Billy could be smuggled in, but unfortunately the publican spotted him and rounded angrily on the crowd.

'I ain't servin' 'im! I'll lose my licence!'

'Well, if you don't serve 'im yer don't serve us!' was the reply, and there was a general movement towards the door.

The landlord couldn't afford to offend so many customers so he called them back.

'All right, he can have one pint but no more.'

They sat Billy down and warned him to be quiet while drinks were called for and Billy given his. There was quite a crowd round him waiting to hear what he had to tell them about who else had been in with him. Billy was reluctant to divulge his exploits. 'If you buy me a drop of the best, I'll tell yer what happened.'

But the landlord heard this and adamantly refused, and Maggie backed him up. 'No!' she shouted. 'He ain't 'avin' any mower! I want 'im back 'ome, not back in the lock-up!'

Somebody had already slipped him a couple of whiskies which he drained quickly before the barman could jump over the counter to prevent him.

'Right! That's it! Clear out! Clear out, the lot on yer, before I call the cops.'

The pub emptied in no time but it was too late for Billy. When he emerged he started to rave again and wave his arms in the air. Maggie pleaded for help and between several of them they managed to carry him home where Maggie put him to bed and locked him in the bedroom before returning to the pub to continue the days gossiping.

NOTE

[1] 'Combs': all-in-one sets of underwear of vest and long pants. Abbreviation of 'combinations'.

4
My Brother Jack's 'Ghost'

It was the middle of winter and our boots were letting in water. It was no wonder we had snotty noses, coughs and colds. Each winter all our parents put in applications for boots and clothing. Our teachers would inspect us then, after giving us each a form for our parents to fill in, she would warn us that everything must be written down correctly. If not, our parents would be in trouble.

I always read our leaflet to Mum and Dad and explained what it was all about because Mum couldn't read or write, and although Dad could write, he could only manage to read the newspaper (when he could afford to buy or maybe borrow one). Some people tried to claim what they were not entitled to, but the teachers could tell who was in need just by looking at us all. In our street alone there were at least sixty or seventy poorly clad children and most of them were at our school.

The annual distribution used to be an exciting day. We

went along to the supply office to be fitted out with clothes, boots or clogs, as well as being given a mug of hot soup which the Salvation Army supplied. The girls were fitted for woollen combs or vests and bloomers, navy blue woollen slips or jerseys, and thick black woollen stocking. The boys had vests or combs, navy-blue woollen ganseys and trousers that hung over their knees, because most of these clothes were ill-fitting. We had to wear them or go without. I told my teacher once that I didn't like any of the clothes because they were so coarse and rough to wear and she shouted at me, 'You should be very grateful. Beggars can't be choosers.'

When we emerged from behind the screen in our clobber, Frankie and I had clogs, and Liza had boots. Mum asked us why we didn't get boots. Frankie lied and said there were no boots left to fit us, but really we preferred clogs. We loved dancing a clog dance on the cobbles down our street. These articles all had to have holes punched in them or be marked with an arrow so that our parents couldn't pledge them. If they had done, they could have been fined or sent to prison. Everything else of any value went into pawn, sometimes for food, but mostly for beer. There were pots, pans, clocks, kettles and umbrellas, if you were lucky enough to own one. Everything went to the pop-shop, or 'uncle's', as we called it. I used to hate the pawnshop as much as I did washdays, because there were always rows on these occasions.

Mum always did the washing on Monday morning, wet or fine, and when she was finished in the wash-house she left the hot suds in the boiler for the next woman. This went on day after day, each one leaving the soapy water for the next in order to save buying extra soda or Hudson's Powder, Lively Polly or Rickett's Blue. There was always plenty of blue in the water because it was thought things looked better blue than grey: they never managed to get clothes really clean or white. Some women would scrub their wash until nearly dark, sometimes by the light of a piece of candle or the glow of the boiler fire. On a rainy day this washing would be taken indoors to dry, ready for the pawnshop. I remember two lengths of rope nailed across our kitchen as a permanent fixture. We had many a back-hander off Mum if we didn't duck our heads low enough under the washing. The washing had the distinctive smell of carbolic soap. It took up every available space – hung over the fireplace, draped on the fire guard, on the pictures, in fact anywhere where there was space to be found.

When it was fine Mum and Mrs Buckley from next door would be up very early before anyone was awake to get their washing done and hung out on the clothes line in the yard. Nobody got any extra sleep when it was Mum's washing-day Bang! Bump! Bang! Bump! The maiding-tubs[1] made a dreadful noise as they rolled them round to the wash-house. Then they would start agitating the washing with their dollies,[2] singing at the tops of their voices in time to the rhythm. Mum had a powerful voice and she knew it. She always let rip for anyone to hear and Mrs Buckley tried to keep up with her. It was always the same song and Mrs Buckley always sang it off-key, but Mum's rendering of 'My Old Man Said Follow the Van' drowned Mrs Buckley out. Then when they'd eventually finished and the clothes were pegged out on the line, the next two neighbours would begin theirs. Mum used to fold and squeeze the washing through the mangle to remove the water and to press it if the iron was being used by one of the other women. The old mangle squeaked and groaned each time the handle turned. The cogs wanted oiling but we had no oil, so Dad poured paraffin over it.

'It helps,' he maintained. He also sewed rags round the rollers to stop the rotten wood getting into the clothes, the mangle look as if it had come out of hospital. Then when everything was folded up and ready for the pawnshop, Mum would called out down the yard, 'Maggie! Nell! Liz! Are yer ready?'

'Yes, we're ready.'

Then down the street they'd go with their bundles under their arms to the three brass balls.[3] I followed, as usual. They knew I was following behind but they never took any notice of me. They never did, unless it was to run their errands for them. When they arrived at 'uncle's' Mum was the first, as usual.

'Can yer loan me fower and six? I've put in extra today.'

He gave the washing a good going over before he replied, 'I'm sorry, these are getting a bit worn but you can have three and sixpence.'

Mum gave him one of her dirty looks, but he wasn't afraid of her and just glared back.

'Take it or leave it! Next one.'

So Mum quickly grabbed what was offered, less a penny for the ticket, and went down he entry to wait for the others. They came, all moaning and saying what a skinny, bloody Jew he was. Then off to the local they went to wet their whistles. This routine was repeated week after week. In, out, in, out, more often in than out, it was never any different.

It was on a washday like this when Mum gave me sixpence wrapped up in paper.

'Katie!' she called down the yard. 'I want yer to goo down ter Longman's and tell 'im I want a fresh rabbit. Tell 'im it must be fresh or else! And 'urry, I want to get it in the pot.'

I did as I was told, but when I got there he just glared down at me.

'Does she want it skinned?'

'I don't know,' I answered timidly.

He left the skin on, wrapped it up and I ran back with it clutched under my arm. It didn't smell very fresh to me, and when Mum took it from me she sniffed it, then threw it across the table and began raving.

'Now yer can tek it back right now! It stinks!'

I picked it up. On dear! It smelled awful but I wrapped the newspaper round it as best I could and took it back to the butcher's. When I arrived Mr Longman was still standing outside in his blue and white striped apron with his straw boater on the back of his head. I peered up into his huge, round face trying to appear confident as I timidly spoke to him.

'Mum says you've got to change this rabbit.'

'What's the matter with it?' he bawled at me.

'It stinks!' I bawled back, and pushed it under his nose.

'I'm not changing it. What's yer mum want for a tanner?'

But I was feeling courageous now, and I attacked him.

'I don't know. I know this though, Mum'll give you what for if you don't change it.'

'Be off with yer, yer cheeky little sod!'

Next then I knew he hit me across the head with the rabbit and it fell to the floor. After this I was afraid to go home but I knew I had to face Mum with an explanation, so I picked the rabbit up off the floor and wrapped it up in the newspaper and off home I went.

'He won't change it,' I wailed, hardly before I had entered the door.

' 'E won't, won't 'e. Well I'll see about that!'

The neighbours heard Mum shouting, and came out to their doorsteps to see what it was all about. Mum went in and on went Dad's cap, off came the apron and, holding the rabbit at arm's length, she marched down the street. Some of the neighbours with their children followed. So did our cat, Pete, and some of his friends. Mum knew they were all behind her to see the fun but she didn't mind, She enjoyed having an audience and encouraged her followers.

'I'll show 'im.'

When she saw Mr Longman she flung the rabbit across the counter and shouted for all to hear, 'What yer mean by sayin' you ain't changin' this? I asked for a fresh one and I want a fresh one!'

'But I ain't go another one,' he replied nervously.

Mr Longman saw the size of Mum and how angry she was, and hurried back into his shop. Mum glanced up and saw a large rabbit hanging from his wall on a hook. She didn't need prompting, and stretched up on her toes and reached it down and call into the shop, 'Then I'll tek this one.'

This brought him running after Mum, but she was striding back up the street with her prize.

'Come back here!' he shouted. 'I'll call a copper.'

Mum looked back over her shoulder and, to the immense amusement of the crowd that had gathered, yelled back at him, 'Yow do! An' I'll 'ave yer pinched for sellin' rotten meat!'

With her head held high she marched back home with the

parcel under her arm, smiling all over her face.

'It's a woppa,' she kept saying to herself.

I watched the crowd dwindle by the time we were home. We entered and Mum kicked the door shut. Dad was there to greet us.

'What's all the commotion about? You've had the bloody street in uproar again.'

Then she told him the story.

'But 'e dain't get the better of me. An' 'e 'ad the cheek to say 'e'd call a cop.'

She tossed the parced on to the table for Dad to see and when he saw what it contained he was first surprised, then angry.

'It would've served you right if he had called a cop. This ain't a rabbit, it's a bloody hare!' He glared at her.

' 'Are or no 'are, it's goin' into the pot,' she replied, and began to skin it. Dad knew it was no use arguing, so he stamped out of the house leaving Mum to prepare our dinner.

I helped scrape the carrots and peel the onions and when everything was ready Mum put all the ingredients into the pot which was like a witch's cauldron hanging over the fire from a hook that swung out from the grate. This completed, she went out mumbling about the day's washing and how it would never be done.

'Come an' tell me when it starts to boil an' I'll be back to mek the dumplin's,' she called back to me.

Just then Frankie came in and I told him about the commotion. We both laughed uncontrollably about Mum's behaviour. I didn't want to fetch Mum so I asked Frankie if he thought she'd be pleased if I made the dumplings. I'd often watched them made so I foresaw no problem. Frankie agreed and stood up on Dad's chair, reached up for the mixing bowl for me and fetched the flour from the cupboard over the sink. I rolled the flour up into balls after pouring the water on. They were big and looked good enough to eat before they saw the pot but I'd forgotten to mix in the suet. Anyway, it was too late and Frankie thought they would not taste too rubbery. I felt proud of my handiwork and could hardly wait to call

Mum. After moving Mum's bloomers and Dad's pants further along the fireguard we leaned over and dropped the dumplings into the pot. The pot was boiling merrily away over a fierce fire and Frankie and I stood back to admire our workmanship. The flames licked round the pot and before our eyes the dumplings seemed to rise. We looked at each other: we couldn't believe our eyes: the dumplings grew too big for the pot and continued to swell! It was then that we realised what we'd done. We'd made them from self-raising flour and we hadn't allowed room for them to rise.

We were frightened. How big were they going to become? Then, all at once, they rolled out of the pot into the fire. The chopped hare and carrots followed. Steam and ashes filled the room as the stew boiled over into the fire, putting it out. Frankie turned and dashed out of the house. He'd heard Mum coming up the path.

'I'm off! he shouted.

'Wait for me!' I cried, grabbing hold of the back of his gansey.

We were scared but we didn't get far: as we ran round the corner we collided with Dad. Now we're really for it, I thought.

'Well, well, well, and what's this all about?' he asked, looking down at us both.

'I told him breathlessly how we'd tried to help Mum with the dinner. Frankie didn't say a word, he just looked at the floor and kicked the stones. Then I began to cry. But Dad only smiled down at me.

'Come along now, and you, Frankie.'

I felt a bit safer now my dad was there. The three of us went inside the house where Mum was standing by the wall with the cane at the ready.

'Not this time, Polly,' Dad said, taking the cane away from her. 'They only wanted to help you and give you a surprise.'

'Surprise? Surprise!' she blustered. 'Yer call this a surprise? Look at all the mess they've med.'

She was waving her arms about indicating the state of the room. She didn't stop yelling.

37

'No dinner fer anybody today. I've got no mower money to buy any.'

'I have,' said Dad gently, in an attempt to calm her down. 'I've had a sub off the gaffer.'

This seemed to please Mum, at least she altered her tone and set to to clean up the mess while Dad lit the fire again. Then Mum took the pot and the remains of the hare and swilled it under the tap to save what she could: she didn't believe in wasting anything.

'Wasn't we lucky we run into Dad?' Frankie whispered to me.

I nodded in reply and we began to see the funny side of the affair but we didn't laugh for long. Mum and Dad had fish and chips while Frankie, Liza and I had to eat the hare that had been rescued from the floor.

When Mum's birthday came round Dad told her to put on her best bib and tucker and took her out. She was dressed in her stiff white pinafore that was kept for such occasions. I'd cleaned and polished her button-up boots and fastened them for her. Dad had his white muffler on. Off they went, leaving us with the warning to behave ourselves while they were out. We watched them go out of sight, then called some of our friends in to play at shop. We had nothing to sell, but it was fun just to wrap nothing up in newspaper and pretend to buy. Little Maudie Taylor made us laugh when she mimicked Mum.

'I'll 'ave a rabbit, an' see it's fresh or else!'

All too soon it was time for our parents to return, so they all scattered. It was very late when Mum and Dad arrived home and Liza and Frankie had already gone up to bed, leaving me to let them in. We always put the bolt on the door when we were alone. I jumped off Dad's chair when I heard their footsteps.

'Why ain't yow in bed?' Mum managed to say.

I didn't answer: I could see it was no use.

'Don't stand and stare at us. Mek yerself useful an' pour me out a drink.'

Dad took four bottles from his jacket pockets and banged them down on the table. I looked from one to the other and thought how stupid they both looked. They were really well oiled.

'Come on. Do as yer told, yer know it's yer mum's birth-day.'

I knew, and I was thankful it was only once a year. After helping them to their 'lunatic soup' (this was Charlie's phrase), I sat down on the stool listening to their patter but I couldn't make out what they were whispering about. They'd forgotten that I was still there when just a few minutes later Jack came in. He glanced at Mum then at Dad, and tutted. He didn't see me at first but then I coughed. He put his finger to his lips for me to keep quiet and then he beckoned me over.

'Katie, I want you to do me an errand,' he whispered.

'Where to?' I was alarmed. 'It's late.'

'Shush,' he hissed. 'I'll give yer a penny if you'll go.'

But he needn't have whispered because Mum and Dad were asleep.

'I want yer to take a note round to Lil's house.'

'But it's late, Jack, and I'm tired and sleepy.'

'I'll come part of the way with you. How's that?'

I didn't mind when I knew he was coming with me. He handed me the letter and a penny which I slipped down my stocking, then I put on my coat and off we went. It was nearly midnight as we hurried down the narrow streets. I wasn't very brave, even with my big brother, because the moon was casting weird shadows everywhere as the clouds scudded over it. I pulled at his coat.

'Jack,' I pleaded. 'Can't the letter wait until tomorrow?'

'No!' he snapped. 'She must get it tonight. I don't want to see her tomorrow.'

'But it's late, and I'm cold.' I clung to his coat tail and shivered.

'Oh, let go and give me yer 'and. We'll go through the churchyard for the quickest,' he said impatiently and pull me along.

When we reached the other gate at the opposite end of the

churchyard, Jack pointed across the road.

'That's the house. Number seventeen. Just push the note under the door and I'll wait for you here.'

When I'd delivered the message I ran back to my brother as fast as I could.

'Are you sure you pushed it right under the door?'

'Yes, Jack, I'm sure.' I was trembling.

'Come on then. We can get back home before Mum and Dad miss you if we go back the same way.'

I felt braver now because Jack held my hand as we hurried along. The church clock struck twelve. The moon was so bright it lit up the whole cemetery. You could read the words on the tombstones. Everything was still and quiet as we scurried across the grass. Jack started to whistle a tune and then suddenly a body popped up out of a hole in the ground and spoke in a deep voice.

'Hello, mate.'

At that Jack took to his heels and ran for dear life, leaving me to escape as best as I could. I ran screaming. Then I tripped over a jar of flowers on one of the graves but Jack turned and dragged me along. We couldn't get home quick enough. We fell inside the door, waking up Mum and Dad as we flopped on to the sofa.

'What's all the bloody noise about?' Dad shouted.

'And why ain't yow in bed?' Mum cried out to me, as I edged towards the stairs and began to cry.

'I went an errand for Jack,' I managed to blurt out. But Jack wouldn't let me finish.

'I've seen a ghost tonight, Dad,' he said, still shaking and pale.

'What yer mean? You've seen a ghost. Where?' Then Jack told all.

'You had no right to take Katie through the churchyard at this time of night. Do your own dirty work!' Dad spluttered angrily. 'And another thing I want to say. I'm sick and tired of these girls you love and leave coming up to ask me if I've seen yer. If you have seen a ghost it's yer sins finding you out!'

By now Mum was fully aroused.

' 'E must 'ave seen a ghost. Look at his face.'

Jack was pale with fright and so was I, but no one seemed to notice me on the stairs, until suddenly I let out a loud scream as I felt a hand on my back. I needn't have worried though, it was only Frankie who'd crept downstairs, dressed only in his nightshirt.

'What's the matter, Katie?' he asked.

But I was hysterical and couldn't speak. Anyway, you couldn't have heard your own voice with Mum, Dad and Jack arguing.

'Be quiet, all of you!' Dad shouted. 'Now, Jack, I want the truth. Did you really see a ghost?'

'Yes. It came up out of a grave and spoke to me, didn't it, Katie?' I nodded my agreement.

'Are you sure you ain't had too much drink?'

'No. I've bin playing cards with my workmates.'

'I believe 'im,' Mum said. 'Just look at 'is face. 'Ere, tek a drop of this.' She handed him a mug of beer which he drank down in one gulp.

'If you don't believe me,' he said, 'you come with me now and I'll show you the grave he popped out of.'

'All right. I could do with a breath of fresh air,' Dad replied.

Frankie got his trousers on quicker than I'd ever seen him, and followed Dad out of the house. Determined not to be left out, I followed behind.

'I'll come as quick as I can,' said Mum.

She wasn't afraid of anyone or anything and neither was I now that Dad was with us. It was nearly one o'clock in the morning but the moon was bright enough for us to see all we wanted as we walked through the churchyard.

'Which hole is it? Is it this one?' asked Dad, pointing to an open grave.

'No,' whispered Jack. 'That's the one, next to it.'

'You must be mad!' Dad replied. 'There's no one down there.'

Dad turned to go back when suddenly a body clad in a white coat popped out of the grave behind Dad and spoke in a rough voice.

41

'What do you lot want at this time in the morning?'

Jack nearly fell into the open grave with the shock. Frankie and I stood petrified, but Mum and Dad didn't turn a hair. Dad burst out laughing.

'It's all right, Jack. I know 'im.'

We all collapsed on one of the tombstones to recover our breath, and Mum turned to go home without a word. I think she was disappointed.

'You're working late, ain't yer, Arthur?' said Dad.

'I've got to. I've got a busy day tomorrer. Another four to dig yet,' replied the ghost.

'Would yer like me to fetch yer a jug of 'ot cocoa?' Dad asked.

'Thanks, Sam,' he replied. 'It's getting a bit chilly in 'ere.'

Dad said he hadn't got anything warmer to give so we returned home where Mum had already gone to bed. Frankie and I crept quietly upstairs after wishing Jack good-night. We heard him and Dad tittering as we climbed into bed. News always travelled fast round our district and everybody pulled Jack's leg about his ghost. But Jack had a sense of humour, so each time he told the story he stretched it a bit longer.

NOTES

[1] Large wooden tubs, once a vital piece of domestic equipment but now only used to grow flowers in.

[2] Washing-dollies were used to agitate the wash in the days before washing machines. They were made of wood and looked rather like a joint stool with a three-foot-long wooden pole through the centre. At the other end was a horizontal handle, used to rotate the gadget in the washing.

[3] Traditionally three balls hanging from a horizontal beam above a shop door indicated a pawnbroker's.

5
Christmas 1911

When Christmas came, Frankie, Liza and I went into the 'better' district which was not far from our school where there was a pub called the George and Dragon. This was a large public house with a long mixed bar, a gentleman's smoke-room, a bottle and jug department, and a 'snug' for ladies only.

We all knew when Dad went there to have a drink with his mates because I always had the job of pressing his best suit and his white muffler. When Mum went there with any of the neighbours she always wore her Sunday best, a stiffly starched pinafore which she took great pride in ironing, especially the lace edges. Her hair would be plaited round over each ear, instead of the usual bun on top. She always tried to make an impression. I can remember her saying, 'We're as good as this lot 'ere, even if we ain't got much.' The kind of people Mum was talking about were mostly shopkeepers and independent, but the folk who lived in our district were happier in their own little local, the Golden Cup. They used to say, 'We feel at home here; the gaffer and the missus are like us.' How true that was: they both drank like fish too! Their moods were unpredictable, though. They would sometimes join in with their customers and sing, or alternatively throw them out if they'd had enough. This usually happened on Saturday night when a burly, punch-drunk barman was employed for the purpose. Then there'd be a free-for-all – spittoons and saw-dust flying everywhere. You never saw a pub empty so quickly as when someone peeped round the door and warned them that the cops were on their way.

The night before this particular Christmas Eve it was snowing and freezing hard when Frankie, Liza and I hurried along the street to sing carols. The shopkeepers were busy in their windows putting up their decorations ready for the Christmas spree. While this was going on, Frankie nipped smartly up the baker's entry and helped himself to a large, empty flour sack. This was to keep us warm while we waited for the shops to close and the pub across the street to fill with customers. The three of us sat on an empty shop step, huddled up close together wih the sack over our heads to keep us warm. Although we were covered in flour we didn't mind as long as we didn't feel the cold. I was lucky; being the smallest, I sat between Frankie and Liza. Even so, my feet were cold and wet because my clogs were split at the sides and my clothes were threadbare.

At last we saw the lights go out in the shop windows. The street was deserted and dark now except for the lights that shone from the leaded windows of the George and Dragon, the knight in his brightly coloured armour making red, blue, green and yellow lights that glistened on the snow. We were just about to cross the street when we saw two shadows coming towards us. Quickly we dashed back to our hiding-place, but it was too late. Before we could hide our heads underneath the sack again, a man's hand dragged it from us. He struck a match and peered down at us.

'Well, well, well and what have we here? Three little orphans of the storm?' he chuckled.

We were too scared to move. We just sat there looking up at him wide-eyed. He called back over his shoulder, 'Aggie, is there any port left in the bottle?'

Aggie brought the bottle and said, 'It's time they were in bed and dreaming about Father Christmas.'

'Here, drink this.' He offered the port. 'It'll warm yer up.'

Frankie quickly took the bottle. I thought he was going to drink the lot but he gave Liza and me the bottle, and between us we finished the rest. There was only a drop for each of us which was a good thing because otherwise we'd have been tiddly. Anyway I felt warmer. Frankie gave him back the empty bottle after draining the dregs and saluted him gratefully.

'Thank you, sir. And a merry Christmas.'

The man put his hand into his waistcoat pocket and pulled out three pennies which he dropped in my lap.

'Do you want us to sing some carols?' I asked, hoping to return his kindness.

'Don't be silly; of course he don't!' said Frankie, giving me a nudge which nearly pushed me off the step.

His lady companion walked away as the man warned us to get off home before a bobby came along. But we had no intention of doing that.

'We ain't sat on this wet step just to go back home,' muttered Frankie.

So we pulled ourselves up off the step and walked a little way to hide in a doorway until they were out of sight. Then we dashed back to sing outside the George and Dragon. We were happy to have threepence and grateful for the port wine. It gave us Dutch courage. We could've faced anybody or anything that night, we felt so happy and warm inside. The other kids at our school never sang carols here, they weren't allowed to go near this pub. Their parents used to frighten them by saying the owners were wicked people who, just like George and the dragon and the Mormons who came along our street, carried little children off. I asked Frankie if it was true about the Mormons.

'You don't want to believe everything people say. Anyway, our parents don't want us, yet they don't want the Mormons to have us either. It don't make any sense to me.'

'Shut up!' spat Liza. 'Let's get on with the carols. It's getting late.'

We stood just inside the doorway out of the snow, wiped the snow and flour off our faces, and began to sing. But we couldn't hear ourselves above the noise of merriment going on inside, so Frankie pushed open the door a little and kept his foot there. We waited until the sound had died down, then we burst with 'Hark, the Herald Angels Sing'. We sang at the top of our voices to drown Liza who was off-key as usual. Then someone shouted from inside, 'Some bloody angels!'

'Close the door,' somebody else cried.

This dampened our spirits. Frankie retrieved his foot and we walked away. However, before we'd got out into the street a kindly little lady came up behind us and gave us a silver sixpence. She told us to return on Christmas Eve, then she popped back inside, leaving us dumbfounded.

'Who was she?' asked Frankie.

'She's George's dragon we've heard so much about,' said Liza.

I was a bit disappointed. I'd imagined her to be a large woman something like our mum. We were happy, though. We ran to the fish shop to buy a pennyworth of fish and chips which we thought was plenty to share between the three of us. We ate it as we walked slowly back home. When we arrived, Frankie ran straight upstairs and put the rest of the money in a tin box which served as our savings bank. He had a good hiding-place, no one knew where, not even Mum.

The table was strewn with coloured papers which Mum had left for us to make our paper trimmings that night. We cut them all into loops and Liza made the paste with flour and water. If this failed, Frankie said he would get a tin of condensed milk to mix it with. Frankie took a little, not enough for Mum to notice, and this did the trick, and it was nice to lick our fingers each time we stuck one loop inside another and so we made the decorations for the walls and pictures. We didn't have a real Christmas tree. We had to beg two wooden hoops off a cheese tub from the grocer's. We fitted these one inside the other and covered them with different coloured tissue and crepe paper.

When Dad came home he said we'd done a good job and helped us hang the streamers across the room, high up above the clothes line: and to let people see we had some sort of tree, the paper Christmas tree was hung in the window from a nail. Every time we had a farthing or a halfpenny given us for running errands we bought white sugar mice and little chocolate Father Christmases and shiny, coloured balls and tinsel or any little thing we could afford. After we'd trimmed up the room, Dad gave us a penny each to buy extra gifts for the tree. Then, after drinking our cocoa, we went off to bed, happy and contented, knowing we had some money to spend and that we were going carol-singing again the next night to earn some more. We got up early in the morning to do our errands and daily chores around the house, then when it got dark we got ready to go out to continue our carolling. Mum watched us with keen eyes as we donned our coats and scarves.

'And where do yer think you three are gooin' this time o' night?' she asked, sternly.

'We're going carol-singing,' Frankie replied, defiantly.

'That's all right,' Dad said, 'but be back in bed before we get home.'

'Yes, Dad,' we replied in unison.

We ran out and turned up the street towards the George and Dragon. I was glad Mum and Dad hadn't asked what part we were going to because this street was forbidden territory. When we arrived we started 'Hark, the Herald Angels Sing' again, but we only got as far as 'Hark' when I felt a hard thump on my back.

'Don't sing that one,' Frankie said. 'You know what happened last time. Let's sing 'Noël'.'

Halfpennies and pennies came flying through the door and when I picked them up I counted tenpence ha'penny in all. We showed our gratitude by singing it again, only louder. But when Liza reached the high notes she gave out an off-key shriek which brought George out with the warning to 'clear off'. Frankie turned on Liza as we walked away.

'You spoil everything with yer cracked voice. I wish I'd brought one of Mum's gob-stoppers along for you.!'

She walked on, but never answered. We turned into our street where we thought we'd try our luck again. When we got to the Golden Cup, Frankie warned Liza to keep her mouth shut and pick up the money instead. We were unlucky this time, though. While we'd been up the street the other kids had been here, so we sang in vain. Next we tried the Mermaid, then the King's Head, but they told us the Salvation Army band had already called. We were reduced to singing for the passers-by, a few of whom gave us a penny. By now it was getting late and we remembered we had to be in bed before our parents returned, but we decided to satisfy our hunger first. We went to the cow heel and tripe shop and bought three pig's trotters. Frankie hid the rest of our earnings while we sat munching away. Then suddenly I remembered that Mum had

47

told me that morning to mend a hole in my stocking.

'Don't forget to sew that 'ole or Father Christmas will leave yer nothin',' she'd said.

But I was too tired now. Anyway, I thought, perhaps she'll forget about it.

'Ain't yer going to hang up yer stocking?' asked Frankie as we were undressing.

'In a minute,' I yawned.

'Never mind. I'll hang it up,' he said, as I climbed into bed. Liza and I watched him hang three stockings over the bed-stead. Then he jumped into bed and after blowing out the candle we fell to sleep.

Next morning we woke early and wished each other 'Merry Christmas' before looking to see what we'd been given. Liza jumped off the bed and grabbed her stocking while Frankie looked to see what was inside ours. Liza had an apple, an orange, some mixed nuts and a bright new penny. Frankie had the same, but when I looked in mine there was nothing, only the hole. In the dark Frankie had hung up the wrong stocking.

'Never mind.' Frankie was trying to be sympathetic and wiped my tears away. 'You can share mine.'

'But that's not the same. Mum's never loved me. I don't know why, Frankie, I always do as she tells me and I always try to please her,' I cried.

'Come and dry your eyes. It's Christmas Day. Anyway we've got our money-box hidden away for the holidays,' Frankie said cheerfully.

Liza didn't say a word. She was busy sucking her orange, sitting up in bed. So I sat up beside Frankie at the foot of the bed and he shared what he had with me. He nudged, winked and smiled at me with his big blue eyes. Then I returned his smile because his mirth was infectious.

This was the one morning in the year we had to stay in bed until Mum called us downstairs. So after eating our Christmas fare we got back under the bedclothes to keep warm, planning what we were going to do with our savings. All of a sudden we were startled by Mum's voice.

'Yer can get up now!'

We dressed quickly and went downstairs. Mary, Jack, Dad and Charlie were sitting at the table ready for us to join them. Mum was standing over a big fire frying eggs, sausages and bacon in a big pan.

'Merry Christmas,' we called out to them all. They each returned the greeting except Mum. She turned round to face us and waved the fork at the bowl of water for us to get washed.

' 'Urry yersèlves. We're waitin' to 'ave our breakfast.'

After falling over each other to get to the bowl first, we sat down in our usual places on the sofa which was drawn up to the table. Dad, Jack, Mary and Charlie each had an egg, two sausages and a rasher of bacon. On our enamel plates was half a sausage, half an egg and a piece of fried bread. By the side of my plate was a small packet wrapped in tissue paper. I smiled across at Mum. I thought, she's not forgotten me after all.

'Thank you, Mum,' I said as I opened it.

She didn't turn an eye, only said, 'Yer can look at it when you've 'ad yer breakfast.'

I didn't want any breakfast, I was too anxious to see what was in the small packet. So while Mum wasn't looking I slipped my fried bread and sausage under the table to Frankie. Then I finished my half egg but I daren't leave the table until everyone else had finished. I looked at Mum and smiled.

'Can I please open it now, Mum?'

She didn't answer, so I presumed she meant me to and I eagerly unwrapped it and dropped the paper on the floor. It was a matchbox but when I opened it and saw what was in it I burst into tears. Inside was a little ball of black wool and a darning needle. I stared hard at it. My sister Mary came round the table and picked it up.

'How could you do such a thing to her?' she said. 'What's the reason?'

All eyes were on Mum now as I blubbered.

'That's 'er punishment fer not doin' as she was told!' Mum answered sharply.

Then Mary and Mum started to quarrel, and between my sobs I heard Mary accuse Mum.

'You've never loved her. But she'll know why some day!'

Mum walked over to the fireplace and Dad joined in.

49

'Now, Mary, let's have no more of this. It's Christmas Day, remember?'

Jack went out and Charlie followed behind him, banging the front door behind him. Dad patted me on the head and said softly, 'I'll be back when you've settled your arguments.' Then he too walked out.

Frankie and Liza just looked at Mum. I didn't know what they were thinking but I knew why she'd given me the needle and wool. I went upstairs and took off my stocking and began to darn it when Mary came in to see me. She unfastened her trunk and took out a box of lace handkerchiefs. 'Here you are, Katie,' she said. 'Here's my present for you.'

I thanked her with a sob and a smile.

'Don't take Mum to heart too much, Katie. She didn't mean anything.'

I knew she was making excuses for Mum. I knew Mum didn't love me from piecing together bits of conversations I'd over-heard, and now this morning I'd heard Mary say so to Mum.

'Mary,' I asked as I put on my stocking, 'do you know why Mum doesn't love me?'

'She does, in her funny way,' she said gently.

'She can't do or she wouldn't do and say the things to me that she does. Won't you tell me why?' I sobbed.

'When you're older,' she said. Then she went downstairs.

'That's all I get off you grown-ups; ''when yer get older'',' I answered angrily, following her down.

Mary whispered something to Mum and then got her work-box out. She called me over to show me what was inside. I soon forgot my troubles as she showed me the presents the friends she worked with had given her. I couldn't believe my eyes: there were two rows of pearls, a row of blue glass beads, some more hankies and lots of other trinkets. There were also pretty Christmas cards with real lace round the edges. Before Mary closed the box she put the pearls round my neck. I saw Mum look, so I unfastened them quickly and gave them back.

'Now you just put them back on. They're yours, from me to you,' Mary said to my immense surprise and joy.

'Thank you, Mary.' I threw my arms round her neck and hugged her.

During all this time Mum never said a word until Mary went back upstairs with the box.

'Come on. 'Urry yerselves up, the three of yer. Yer gran'll be waitin' for yer.'

I was eager to go, so was Frankie, but Liza couldn't care less one way or the other. Anyway, Mum made her come along with us whether she wanted to or not. Frankie and Liza had Christmas cards in their hands to give their school friends, but I had mine in a surprise parcel for Granny. Our granny lived about twenty minutes' walk from our house – that was if we ran all the way, which we had to do that day because the snow was freezing underfoot and we wanted to keep warm. Her house was built on the same pattern as ours which meant there were no repairs done and she couldn't afford to improve it herself. Anyway, she used to say, 'I ain't spendin' any of my money to clean this place: it's the landlord's job.' She was a stubborn old woman, but I loved her. I believe if the house had fallen down she wouldn't have cared. She was very defiant and independent. When we arrived, Frankie knocked on the door with his foot and we heard the heavy bolts being pulled back. Then she peeped round the door.

'We've come to wish you a Merry Christmas, Granny.'

She glared at us. She didn't look very pleased when we handed our Christmas cards to her.

'What's there for me to be merry about?' she shook her head and dislodged some paper curlers which whirled to the floor. 'Anyway, come inside an' warm yer feet, yer must be a-freezin',' she said hobbling over to the fire.

I looked round the room. There wasn't much fire in the grate to warm us and there was nowhere to sit. Frankie rushed to sit on the only, backless, chair. Granny sat in her rocking-chair, and Liza dashed for the stool.

'Yoo ain't sittin' theea!' she screamed out at Liza. 'That's Katie's seat.'

'You don't like me, do yer?' Liza put out her tongue at Granny.

'No, I don't! Yer a little tell-tale,' she said, looking away.

'An' I don't like you!' said Liza, shrugging her shoulders.

But I don't think Granny gave Liza another thought because she turned to me. 'You sit in me rockin'-chair, Katie.'

It was a big old chair. It had to be big for Granny because she was a large woman like Mum, and when I sat down in her chair I felt lost. Whenever Granny sat in it the chair creaked, squeaked, rocked and rolled as she hummed to herself. I always expected her to tip over backwards, but she never did: she must have timed those rusty old springs to a fine point. All in all she was a very funny old granny. Sometimes she would be very kind to us, and other times her entire manner would change. She had her moods, just like Mum.

I sat trying to rock myself, but the chair was too heavy for me to get even a squeak. She stood by the table trying to untwist the paper curlers from her black hair. Then I remembered her present.

'Here you are, Granny, I've bought you some real hair curlers for Christmas.'

'Thank yer, I'm glad someone thinks about yer old granny.'

She took the box from me. Then she looked up at the alarm clock, which had only one hand and half a finger.

'Ain't it about time yer went now? It's getting late.'

We'd only been there about five minutes, but she could see we were already fidgety to be going. As we made for the door she said to Frankie and Liza, ' 'Ere y'are. 'ere's a new penny for yer.'

I felt dejected again when she said she'd not got one for me, but then, as if from nowhere, she produced a cardboard box tied with real pink ribbon.

'And that's for you,' she said with a smile.

A lump came to my throat and tears started to flow, and I threw my arms round her waist.

'Be orf with yer at once. I'm 'ungry now and me cat wants 'is breakfast too. An' don't untie that ribbon now. Wait until yer get 'ome. 'An yer can tell yer mum yer old gran don't forget yer, even if she does.'

I wondered then if she knew about the hole in my stocking, for Mum had always said she was an old witch. I felt sorry for

Granny living in that old hovel all alone with her mangy old cat.

We ran all the way home, eager to see what was in the cardboard box. When we got indoors I untied the ribbon carefully because I wanted it for my hair. Then Frankie and I tore the wrapper to see what the present was. When I removed the lid there inside lay the biggest golliwog I'd ever seen, a lovely Christmas card and a note which read, 'This is for Katie which have made all myself.' I hugged it and kissed it and tears of delight ran down my face and dropped on to the golly's.

'She might have put a few marbles in the box for me,' said Frankie, beginning to sulk. But when Liza saw my present she just said, 'Phew,' and walked away with her head in the air.

'She's only jealous,' said Frankie, smiling.

The golliwog was made out of a black woollen stocking and filled tight with straw. She, for I had decided that it was a lady, had red wool for her lips and two linen buttons for her eyes and on the top of her head was real, curly black fur. I was proud to think that Granny had made this with her own two hands. I carried her nearly everywhere and I treasured her for years.

That was one Christmas I never forget. Frankie even said I could have his new penny, but although I was grateful for his offer I only wanted my golliwog because this was the first one I had ever had of my own. I hadn't even had a doll to play with when I was younger. Liza told Mum later that afternoon what Granny had made for me but she didn't ask to see it, and I could tell she wasn't interested. All Dad said was 'That's very kind of her.'

Christmas afternoon, Frankie, Liza and me went to a tea-party at the Salvation Army Hall where there were other little girls like me with real dolls, but theirs weren't as big as mine, so there and then I decided to name her Topsey.

6
The Free Samples

After our Christmas holiday we started back to school. Each day when lessons were over and it was time to go home I would look out for the welcome sign of smoke coming from our chimney. Then I'd know Mum had lit the fire to warm us. One particular day I remember glancing up and being surprised to see that the expected trail of smoke was absent. In fact none of the chimneys was smoking. I pointed this out to Frankie.

'Did you fetch the coal up from the cellar this morning?'

'You know I did,' he answered. 'Why?'

'Well, look, there's no smoke coming from our chimney, nor any of the others.'

He agreed that this was funny and so did our friends when we showed them. It was very quiet and there seemed to be no adults about either. Then somebody noticed that some little packets had been left on each of our steps. We all made a mad dash to pick them up. Each little packet consisted of a little silver paper parcel labelled 'Ex-Lax'. We didn't know what this meant so we opened them and found five small tablets of chocolate which we pocketed, promising to say nothing to our parents. It was not long before Mum and Dad and the rest of our neighbours came walking down the yard with blankets under their arms. Then I realised where they'd been. Once a year the poor went to the church to be issued with bedclothes.

As soon as Frankie spotted Mum he cried out, 'We're hungry, Mum, and we'll be late back to school.'

'Well you'll 'ave to wait! I've bin to the church to get me issue. I couldn't miss them, could I?' she answered with a glare.

So while we waited for something to eat we slipped the chocolate into our mouths while Mum wasn't looking. She gave us each a slice of bread and lard and told us to clear off back to school.

'I'm already be'ind with me washin'.'

I thought how wicked and crafty our people were: they only

54

went to church when something was being given away free. Then of course they would smile and say, 'Oh, well, we'll 'ave to go.' The only other time they went was for weddings, christenings and funerals.

At five to two we all hurried up the street to get back before the bell stopped ringing. When we arrived we all took our places, the boys in their classroom and the girls in theirs, separated only by a glass partition so that we could see the boys and they us, if we stood on tiptoe. We had to be careful that the master or mistress didn't catch us, otherwise we had the cane or the ruler across our knuckles.

Lessons began, and after a while my tummy began to rumble as the Ex-Lax began to do its work. I started to wriggle about in my seat and when I looked around the other girls were wriggling too. Then, while the teacher was writing on the board, I stood on my toes to look for Frankie. He was also moving uncomfortably, as were the rest of the boys. I whispered to Liza, 'Liza, I got an awful pain in my tummy. I think I want to go to the lavee. It must have been that chocolate I ate.'

'And me!' she hissed back.

'Me too,' Sarah Taylor said, looking pale.

Then all the girls who'd eaten the Ex-Lax joined in.

'Oh-er, and me.'

Miss Frost, our teacher, couldn't understand why we were whispering and wriggling in our seats.

'What's wrong there?' she called out sharply, the cane at the ready.

Up shot our hands in unison as we chorused, 'Please, miss, may we leave the room?'

She looked at us over the top of her spectacles and spoke firmly. 'No you may not!'

Then the cane came down hard across the desk with a loud swish. We flinched, and practically jumped out of our skins. Matters were getting no better and we remained with our hands in the air, afraid to move in case of an accident.

'What is this?' she repeated harshly. 'Some new joke you're

55

playing? Put your hands down at once and sit down!'

Slowly our hands dropped halfway at least. But we didn't sit still. We couldn't.

'Very well,' she said deliberately. 'I haven't the time to cane you all, but you will stay in and write two hundred lines on how to behave in class.'

Then she wobbled out, locking the classroom door behind her. Liza and I managed to look over the partition to see how the lads were behaving. Although we couldn't hear them, we saw they too had their hands raised high while the master's face was getting redder and redder. I turned to Liza.

'What are we going to do? I'd do it in my bloomers if I don't go soon.'

'I've already done something in mine,' she answered, beginning to cry.

Some of the other girls were weeping too, and others were trying the door but it wanted a battering-ram to make that door yield: it was made of oak. We were all more or less in an awful mess and lessons hadn't even begun. Just then we heard the heavy tread of our teacher in the corridor. She unlocked the door and stood still. I saw her nose twitching like a rabbit's.

'What an awful smell!' she managed to say, before turning back down the corridor, leaving the door open.

This was our chance. We knocked each other over as we made a mad dash for the exit. We ran headlong down the passage, pushing past the master and mistress who were standing at the end and tearing out into the street. Once outside, we scattered in all directions towards our homes. When we got inside the door Mum was about to ask why we were home so soon when her nostrils also twitched and she sniffed at us.

'Blimey! What a pong!'

Frankie and I tried to explain, but we were sobbing by now and she wouldn't listen anyway. She pushed us away and asked Liza to explain. Usually when she had to explain anything it was a twisted version to lay the blame on us two. This time, however, she had to tell the truth. Mum went out and dragged back the big tin bath that always hung on the wall outside the door and filled it full of water.

'You sit on the stairs while I strip these two, and close the dower,' she told Frankie, pushing him in the direction of the stairs.

After our clothes were stripped off we stood up naked, waiting for some hot water to be added to the cold, but Mum was too impatient to clean us for niceties like that. She pushed us roughly towards the bath. We had to get in even though the water felt freezing. Then Mum poured in disinfectant and began to scrub us with carbolic soap. She dipped us up and down like a couple of yo-yos, swearing at us all the time. When we were dried she threw one of Mary's chemises at me and one of her own at Liza. We looked like Marley's ghost! Then we were sent straight to bed without a drink or anything to eat.

Frankie's turn was next but he had to help Mum lift the bath of dirty water into the yard and wait for it to be filled before he was performed upon. In the meantime, instead of going up the stairs as we'd been told, we sat on them and peeped through a crack in the door. We watched Frankie stripped and bundled into the bath.

'Come on! Jump in!' Mum shouted at him in exasperation.

He jumped out a lot quicker than he jumped in, and stood beside it naked and shivering, complaining that it was too cold.'

'It'll be colder still if yer don't get back in!' She was growing angrier by the second.

However, Frankie was made of different stuff from us. He had that extra bit of nerve. He refused to do what Mum told him. Liza and I looked at each other, then back at Frankie, and began to titter. We put our hands across our mouths to stifle any noise but it was too late. Suddenly the door was flung open and Mum chased up the stairs bringing the cane across our bottoms as we fled. When we tripped over our long nighties she was able to give some more. Luckily, however, she after the first flight and descended again, puf ing. We crawled into bed, sore and sorry. I stil my prayers through the tears, though. Just a

'Amen,' Frankie came into the room dressed in one of Dad's shirts. He stood there like a third Marley's ghost, all shirt and no legs. Liza burst out laughing when she saw him, but I was crying. I was too sore even to smile.

'I'm hungry,' I cried to Frankie, as he climbed in the bottom with me.

He said he was too. Then we heard Mum's footsteps on the stairs.

'Yow can stop yer cryin' or I'll come up an' give yer some mower . . . an' 'urry up an' blow out that candle!'

We heard her close the stair door but Frankie didn't intend going to sleep. He sat up and turned to me.

'Don't cry, Katie. I've got some bread and jam hidden away in the tuck-box.'

I looked at him, somewhat surprised. 'Where've you had that from?'

'Bertha Marpley gave it to me for some marbles, but you can win them back for me tomorrow.' He winked and smiled.

He knew I could and so did I because I was the champion marbles player in our neighbourhood. So the three of us sat quietly in bed while Frankie shared his swap. I didn't know how long it had been in that tin box but the jam had soaked through the bread and the whole thing had set rock hard. However, we were so hungry it seemed to taste wonderful. We finished our feast and happily settled down to sleep. I was still tired and sore but I had Topsey to cuddle. Just then Mum called out, 'Liza, are yer awake?'

'Yes, Mum,' she replied.

'Come down 'ere. I want yer.'

'I'm coming.' Liza sounded fed up.

I wondered what Mum could want, but Frankie was already asleep and I soon joined him in the land of nod. So I didn't hear Liza return, which was unusual because when she got in it always tipped up, catapulting us out.

Next morning we couldn't go to school nor could the others who had eaten the free samples. None of us had any clothes to wear until the wet ones dried, so we had to stay in bed until they were. We weren't bothered because our attic was bedroom, prison and playroom as well as anything else that was necessary. We started to play 'I spy with my little eye' but that proved too easy so we moved on to a spelling game. This also bored us quickly so we took to gazing listlessly out of the window. We saw in the yard below our bloomers and the boys' trousers billowing in the breeze on the clothes lines. Then we spotted Dad coming down the yard so we pulled our heads back inside. We'd forgotten Dad came home early when he was working the nightshift. We crept to the top of the stairs to hear what Mum had to say about us.

'An' thay ain't getting nothin' to eat till their clothes are dry.'

'But, Polly, you can't leave them kids up there without anything to eat. Don't you think they've been punished enough? I'm having my way, just for once.'

We dashed into bed as we heard him coming upstairs. He entered the room and looked at us sitting up in bed with the bedclothes wrapped round us, then he turned without a word and returned downstairs. He was soon back, this time with a large jug of hot cocoa, some bread and dripping and our three enamel mugs on a tin tray.

'Get this down yer while it's hot,' he said jovially.

He left us again without a word of sympathy, but before he could get downstairs I called out to him, 'Thank you, Dad. We're sorry we caused Mum so much trouble but we thought the Ex-Lax were chocolates.'

'Well, perhaps this'll teach you a lesson not to touch free samples that are left on doorsteps until your mum comes home.'

If only he'd forgiven us we'd have felt happier, but he never said another word. But we heard Mum carry on at him when he got downstairs.

'Yer too easy with 'em!'

'Yes, and you're too 'ard on 'em and don't you dare hit them kids again today, otherwise you'll answer to me!'

Then we heard Dad go out, banging the door to behind him. As soon as he'd gone Mum came bounding up into the room.

'You don't drink that until you drink this!'

Then she held our noses in turn and poured a large spoonful of castor oil down our throats 'to bind you up'. I swallowed mine. So did Liza. We had no option, but when she left us Frankie spat his into the chamberpot. He warned Liza with an unnamed threat.

'If you dare tell Mum . . .'

While we were drinking our cocoa I thought over what Dad had said about Mum hitting us.

'Frankie. I think our dad does love us in his funny kind of way. Don't you think so?'

'Perhaps,' he grunted.

7
Frankie's Illness

I used to like to helping people, running their little errands for them or doing small jobs, but the farthing or halfpenny or piece of bread and jam that I usually received as a reward was an added incentive. Better than these, though, was a little love, a kind word or small affection, that was all I needed really. I remember one day Dad sent me to the homemade-sweet shop to fetch a pennyworth of pear-drops. Eager to please and hopeful of reward I ran all the way there and back. I even left Topsey behind. When I returned, breathless, he gave one to Frankie, one to Liza and one he placed in my pinafore pocket, or so I thought. Then we dashed off to school. During break I put my hand in my pocket for the sweet but I was surprised to find that there were two. I ate one and although I was tempted to eat the other I didn't. I wanted to impress Dad with how honest I was. When I returned, Dad was dozing by the fire. So I tiptoed up to him and pushed the pear-drop under his nose, waking him up. He sniffed and opened his eyes.

'Dad, you gave me two pear-drops by mistake, so I've brought you the other one back.'

He yawned lazily and pushed my hand away.

'Go out and play.' He seemed unconcerned at my exemplary behaviour.

I felt dejected. If only he'd thanked me or given me a pat on the head or just a kind word I would have been proud and happy. I didn't realise that Dad didn't want to be woken up when he'd just returned from a hard day's work. It was really no wonder he was irritable, but it took me some time to forget that incident and my childish hurt. I still ran his errands when he asked me, though. I was too young to understand my own feelings and the strange ways of adults so I bestowed my love on Topsey.

I wandered out, hugging my golliwog, to look for Frankie. I found him sitting on the pavement with the other boys and girls. I soon won him the marbles he'd swopped and a few more besides. I even won some 'glarnies', larger and brighter than ordinary marbles, much to the delight of my brother who squatted nearby, watching me beat the boys and hugging my Topsey. When I'd cleaned out the opposition and we were about to leave, Jonesy and Freddie who lived in our yard began to jostle Frankie.

'Look at 'im. The silly little Topsey,' they taunted.

This angered Frankie who flung Topsey at me and jumped up so violently that one of his braces snapped. The other boys backed away apprehensively. They were alarmed because they knew what Frankie might do. He was a tough lad, not easily frightened, and on this occasion his tormentors thought better of their challenge and ran off, which was just as well because no matter what the result of the fight, their mothers would have got us into further trouble. Frankie never looked for it, he didn't have to, trouble found him. Frankie's annoyance subsided and then I noticed that he was shivering. His trousers were wet through from sitting on the moist pavement and he began to sneeze. I told him I thought he'd caught a cold and that, worse than that, Mum wouldn't like the look of his trousers. But he wasn't worried about that.

'Well, she ain't going to see them, is she?'

Nor did she. Each time Mum was about he contrived to face

her and edge about backwards which aroused no suspicion because there was precious little room to do anything else in our tiny room. The following morning he was slow to get up, but when Mum called him the second time and warned him that she was coming to get him with the cane he responded. He looked very pale when he came down, but he assured me he was all right when I inquired how he felt. So off to school we went and after eating our school breakfast we parted to go to our separate classes.

Out of all the girls in my class I was the one picked to do odd jobs. I suppose I was thought to be trustworthy and reliable. Anyway, each Friday afternoon I had to wash out all the ink-wells ready to be filled on Monday morning. I did other jobs as well, and the one I preferred was emptying the flower vases ready for the fresh ones our teacher brought each Monday morning from her garden. Secretly I thought it was a wicked waste to put them in the dustbin when some were still fresh and I sorted out the best ones and hid them behind the school door until it was time for me to go home. Mum was usually pleased with the flowers when I gave them to her for her to put in a jam-jar and stand them on the windowsill for the neighbours to see.

On this Friday afternoon I was taking the ink-wells to wash when I happened to look over the partition to see what Frankie was doing. As soon as I saw him I could tell something was wrong. He was sitting at his desk with his head on his arms. I was so alarmed that I forgot for the moment where I was and gasped aloud,

'What's the matter, Frankie? Are you ill?'

I dropped the ink-wells with a tremendous clatter, which I was oblivious of and strained to see Frankie whose head was being lifted by his teacher. My own teacher had come over and was trying to drag me away but I resisted her defiantly and remained looking through the glass partition. Frankie's face was covered with what looked like bright patches and he looked quite ill. By this time Liza had come over to see what the matter was and the rest of the class took the opportunity to break our regimented routine. They crowded round, standing on tiptoe, craning their necks to see Frankie and pulling faces at the boys. Liza and I were too upset to join in the noisy chaos. We were intent on watching Frankie who was being carried out to the corridor by the master. Our teacher was totally pre-occupied, trying to restore order, so Liza and I took the chance thus offered to run out to where he was.

'What's the matter with my brother?' I wept.

'I believe he has a fever. Is your father at home?' he asked.

'Yes, sir, I think so. If he isn't, I know where I'll find him.'

'Run along then and tell him to come at once!'

I was off like a shot. I didn't need telling twice.

I only paused to pick up the flowers, then off I ran home, leaving Liza to wait there. I burst into the house, throwing the flowers on the table and breathlessly pouring out my story to Dad. He hurried along to the school as soon as he heard what was up and I trailed behind, trying to keep pace with him. I noticed that all the boys and girls were seated and quiet when I entered. The schoolmaster had a few words with Dad who picked Frankie up in his arms and then carried him home while I was sent to fetch the doctor.

When he arrived the doctor examined Frankie and said he would have to go to the hospital at once because he thought it was scarlet fever. We waited anxiously for the ambulance and I cried bitterly as he was driven off with Dad. I had to wait for Mum to come home and tell her what had happened, but she eventually came in just as Dad returned alone. I just sobbed as Dad told Mum that there had been no empty beds in the hospital and that Frankie had been taken to the infirmary instead. The worst news was that nobody would be allowed to visit him for a week, until it was discovered whether he had scarlet fever or not.

Dad called at the infirmary each time he passed on his way home from work to inquire how Frankie was. He was eventually told by the matron in charge that he had a very bad chill and that he still had to stay in their care for at least two weeks because he had a high temperature and other complications. I missed having Frankie around very much indeed. I prayed and cried for him every night.

When it was clear Frankie's illness was not infectious, Liza and I had to attend school again, but I wasn't able to concentrate on my lessons. Every time we went out into the playground the other children crowded round to ask about Frankie but Liza had to answer because I was so upset. I was glad when the following Friday, as I was gathering the ink-pots, my teacher put her hand gently on my shoulder and told me she'd given this job to Minnie Taylor. I wasn't sorry; it was a dirty job anyway and I always received a scolding from Mum when I came home with ink on my pinafore and all over my hands. I looked up into her glasses, perched on the end of her nose, and asked about the flowers. She looked surprised, but agreed.

'Yes, you may do that if you wish,' she answered kindly. 'And how is your brother getting along?' she added.

'He's still very ill, miss.'

'Never mind, we'll all say a prayer for him. Now run along and change the flowers.'

Off I went to pick over the flowers and discard the dead ones. I returned home with the others and gave them to Mum for her and Dad to take to Frankie with a get well note from me when they visited him on the next Sunday afternoon. On Sunday I waited at home and prepared the tea for Mum and Dad when they returned. When I looked out of the window, I saw them returning and Mum still carrying the wilting flowers. Why were they home so soon, I thought? I imagined all kinds of things had happened to Frankie in the few seconds before they came in and I was afraid of hearing their answer when I managed to ask how he was.

'He's been put outside on the verandah,' Dad replied.

Apparently he was very pale and the matron had said he needed plenty of sun and fresh air. When Mum had gone indoors the neighbours began to flock round, asking Dad all sorts of questions about Frankie and the infirmary and the nurses and if he had seen so and so in there. Dad elbowed his way through them muttering that Frankie was clean and comfortable. He never had much to do with our neighbours because he thought they gossiped too much, which was the truth, and on this occasion they wandered up the yard noisily speculating on matters of health and illness. With their shawls pulled tightly round their heads and shoulders they formed a ring, and I hovered on the periphery to listen to them, and you should have heard them, nodding their heads and thinking the worst.

' 'E ain't got enough flesh on 'is bones to keep 'im warm,' said one.

'Poor lad. I don't think 'e'll come out agen, do you?' said Mrs Taylor to Maggie.

'I don't know,' she answered, shaking her head.

'Oh!,' wailed another, ' 'e must be a-dyin'.'

I couldn't bear to hear any more from these ragged, ignorant women. The tears ran down my cheeks and I put my fingers in my ears and screamed at them, 'You're a lot of wicked old witches!' then ran indoors.

'What's the matter with 'er?' Mum asked Dad, and I told them.

When she heard what they were saying, Mum made to dash out into the yard but she was restrained by Dad who told her not to be a fool and that it didn't make any difference. Fortunately, when she did get the door open they'd scattered.

Not much was said that night. We had a late tea but I wasn't hungry and Dad didn't go out but read his paper while Mum sat stitching a patch on a sheet. After Liza and I had washed the dishes, I took my candle and went to bed and prayed as I had never prayed before.

'Please, Jesus, save my brother. Don't let him die and please show me a way to go and see him and also forgive these wicked people who are telling lies. Also forgive me if I have sinned. Good-night, O Lord, and God bless everyone. Amen.'

I crept into bed but I couldn't sleep. I kept thinking of a way to see Frankie. I knew children were not allowed in the wards but I also knew that Frankie would be missing me. Whatever would I do if he died, I thought. I imagined the worst. I felt so sad when I pictured him lying at the bottom of our bed. Then I pretended he was still there and I shook up his pillow and tucked him in. Just then Liza came into the room. She too was weeping as she knelt down to pray for Frankie. I looked at her with some surprise. I hadn't thought she cared, but apparently she did because when we got into bed we threw our arms round each other and cried ourselves to sleep.

Next morning, very early, I awoke and lay there puzzling how I could get inside that infirmary when suddenly I remembered the gully that ran along one of its walls. If only I could climb that wall I'd be able to see him and then he'd feel better, I said aloud. I told no one about my plan, not even Liza.

The next afternoon, when teacher let me out early, I made my way to the infirmary. Before I got there I remembered the flowers I was going to give Frankie and I ran home to fetch them. I was lucky, and there was no one in. I sorted out the best ones from the wilted ones but all I found were six daffodils. I didn't want to be seen carrying them because I'd be asked where I was going, so with them under my pinafore I hurried to the infirmary. I found the gully, but each time I tried to climb the wall I slipped back again, taking the skin off my knees. I made several attempts, but my clogs wouldn't grip. I took them off and walked along to where the wall was lowest and, leaving my clogs at the bottom, I scaled the wall in my stockinged feet. Then I was inside the grounds.

I could see several beds outside on the verandah, so I crept over and peered at the faces of the people lying there, but I couldn't see Frankie's until I came to the last bed outside the ward. I stood and looked at his pale face.

'Frankie,' I whispered. 'It's me, Katie.'

But he didn't hear me because he was fast asleep. I was just about to kiss him when a nurse appeared from nowhere and saw me.

'What are you doing here?'

I was afraid then. I threw the six daffodils on the bed and ran towards the wall. I climbed back over as quickly as I could, put my clogs on and ran home. I was disappointed but determined to try again.

The following afternoon I asked my teacher if I could leave early. She said I might but only after I had got all sums correct. This seemed like an impossible task but with the help of an

1. Kate's mother (seated) and eldest sister Mary (standing right) with Mary's daughter and baby granddaughter in 1932

2. Kate's brother Jack (seated far left) in the army in 1914

3. Kate's father (standing fourth from left) outside the 'George and Dragon', Albion Street, 1921

4. Kate's brother Charles holding her first born son, Camden Street, 1922

5. Kathleen Dayus in 1933

6. The Bull Ring was, and still remains after recent redevelopment, the market where Brummies go for a bargain. This shows the view from the High Street looking towards St Martin's-in-the-Bull-Ring as it was in 1895, with the market stalls in the shadow of the church.

7. The heart of Joseph Chamberlain's remodelling of Birmingham was the Council House, seen on the left here. Colemore Row which stretches into the distance was cut through an area of poor housing and its inhabitants moved into areas like that Kate grew up in, immediately to the north and west.

8. Number 1 Court, Camden Drive was identical in every respect to Number 4 Court where Kate's family lived. Five three-floor, three-room back-to-back houses faced the communal toilets and wash houses, across the brick yard.

9. This court at the rear of Holland Street was typical of thousands in the densely-populated central wards. The galvanised iron bath hangs on a hook and the milk churn and barrow suggest that the family had a small milk round.

10. The ground floor living room of a court house like Kate's. The sparse furnishings, small ornaments and pictures over the range are just as the author describes her own house. Ironically, this was probably taken to illustrate how a 'respectable' working-class family might live; few would have been able to aspire to this level of luxury.

11. Black Country hop-pickers at Little Witley, Herefordshire, in 1896. The photograph captures both the community spirit and holiday atmosphere of working excursions like those taken by Kate's family into the countryside.

12. & 13. These ragged, bare foot 'children of the poor' were photographed on an outing by the charitable Cinderella Club to Sutton Coldfield Park. Like Kate, they can have had few opportunities of a good meal or a sight of the countryside.

14. Two women in the Flower Market, one of Birmingham's central markets not far from the Bull Ring, photographed in 1900.

15. Whenever a Victorian or Edwardian photographer set up his cumbersome tripod a crowd of curious onlookers gathered to enjoy the experience of being photographed although they can rarely have seen the results. Here such a group of children and shop assistants are gathered outside shops in Great Hampton Street, one of the main thoroughfares which bounded the area of slums and workshops where Kate's family lived (1901).

17

16. Surprisingly few photographs of Birmingham's metal-working trades have survived. This one of brass bed-stead makers taken in 1905 shows the cramped work space and laborious nature of the job.

17. St Paul's churchyard, seen here at the end of the nineteenth century, was the 'titty-bottle park' of Kate's childhood. The church was designed by the Wolverhampton architect Roger Eykyn in 1777 when St Paul's Square was the fashionable home of merchants and manufacturers. However, long before Kate knew it, the area had declined socially and the houses had been converted to small jewellers' workshops, which they remain to this day.

older girl who sat next to me I did. So off I went to try my luck again at the infirmary. First I peeped over the wall to make sure no one was about, then I took off my clogs once more and climbed over. I couldn't see Frankie anywhere and had no idea where he could be. I was beginning to worry when a young man in bandages on the verandah hailed me.

'Who are you looking for, my dear?'

'My brother. He was here yesterday and now he's gone.' I was almost in tears by now.

'Oh, you're the little lass that was here yesterday. He's been taken into the ward. If you peep round the door quietly before the sister comes you will see him. He's in the last bed on the right.'

'Thank you, sir.' I replied with pleasure.

I wiped my eyes on my sleeve, and peered into the ward. There were about a dozen beds on each side but Frankie's didn't seem to be there. Men and boys were sitting up in bed blocking my view so the only way to see if he was there was to pluck up courage and run down the ward. I saw no nurses or doctors about so I ran in. As I did so my stockinged feet slipped on the polished floor. I skidded, bringing a screen down on top of me. I struggled to push the screen aside and getting to my feet I saw that I was next to Frankie's bed and I slipped quickly in. As I pulled myself together I heard the man in the next bed say, 'Poor little sod,' and he smiled at me as I turned in his direction. The rest of the patients were laughing at my comical entrance but I only had eyes for Frankie, who was sitting up in bed sucking an orange. In my excitement to see that he was well, I jumped on to him, hugging and kissing him. He was happy to see me, too. But the sister and matron were not; they had come to see what the commotion was all about. They had to drag me away from him: I wouldn't let go. Eventually each took an arm and hustled me along the ward. As I was ejected, I could hear Frankie's voice. 'Don't worry, Katie. I'm coming home tomorrow.'

They pushed me outside without saying a word. It wasn't the way I'd come in, but through the front gates. I didn't care. I was happy now. God had answered my prayer and Frankie was coming home again. I still had to walk round to pick up my clogs from where I'd left them, but when I got there, I couldn't find them. Someone had stolen them. So it was with tears in my eyes that I slowly walked home in my stockinged feet. I knew Mum would cane me hard for this. I would make no difference explaining. Still, I thought, it would have been worth it, so it was an added bonus when I met Mrs Taylor.

'Whatever are yer doin' with yer clogs off?' She smiled when I told her what had happened. 'You'd better come with me and see if our Min's old 'uns'll fit yer before yer mum finds out.'

'Thank you, Mrs Taylor,' I said, and followed her.

She sorted them out from a lot of other clogs and boots in the bottom of her cupboard. I tried them on but they were too big, so she packed the toes with paper and that did the trick. Then she gave me a sweet and sent me off.

'Yer better get 'ome now before yer mum misses yer.'

I thanked her again and asked if she wanted any free errands run for her. I don't think anyone ever found out about the clogs: it remained a secret between us.

The next day was Saturday and Mum and Dad got themselves ready to fetch Frankie home, but at the last minute Mum complained of a headache and told Dad he would have to go without her.

'Can I come with you, Dad?' I asked eagerly.

'Yes, but you'll have to wait outside the gates, and you can't take that with you,' he said, pointing at Topsey.

I laid her down on the sofa and tagged along with Dad. He gave me Frankie's clogs to carry, wrapped up in an old comic while he took the clothes. He stopped to have a quick one at the pub, not long , though it seemed like hours to me. I kept looking through the door and calling to him to hurry, but he just ignored me. At last we were on our way and it was not long before we arrived. Dad took the clogs while I waited outside the gates. I walked up and down the pathway to keep warm. I felt tired and hungry but excited in anticipation of seeing Frankie. People passed in and out of the hospital but no one spoke to me. I wished Dad had let me bring Topsey, I thought, at least I'd have been able to talk to her. The waiting seemed to last for ages then eventually I heard the familiar sound of Dad's hob-nailed boots and the clatter of Frankie's clogs coming down the path. I ran towards him as he came through the gates. The visitors turned to look at us and smiled as I threw my arms round his neck and kissed him several times.

'Come on, don't eat him,' Dad said kindly.

I asked Frankie if I could carry his parcel and was curious as to what was inside. 'I'll show you when we get home.' he told me, winking.

It seemed a long walk home from the infirmary and Frankie began to lag behind. Dad looked back and when he saw how pale he was he put his hand into his waistcoat pocket, took out two pennies and we boarded a tram: a penny fare for him and a halfpenny each for us two. Mum was waiting indoors with a roaring fire and the kettle singing on the hob. She greeted Frankie gruffly.

'Well, and 'ow did yer like the nurses looking after yer?'

'Smashing! It was better then here,' he replied without thinking. Mum and Dad glared at him.

'Well, you know what I mean,' he added quickly.

'Yes, we know what you mean,' replied Dad.

As Frankie was untying his parcel I heard Mum whisper to Dad, 'We'll 'ave to get 'im a bed of 'is own now, 'e's too big to sleep with the girls, Sam.'

'Yes. I see what you mean, Polly!'

And so did I and I turned to him. 'Did you really like being in the infirmary, Frankie?'

'Yes, everybody was kind. I didn't have to bath myself and even the patients gave me sweets, fruit and comics. And the nurses tucked me up!'

I asked him what happened to the comics and he reached down his trousers and pulled them out.

'Put them under the bed with the others,' he hissed.

As I went upstairs Mum shouted, 'What 'ave yer got there?'

'They're only my comics,' replied Frankie.

When I returned, Mum and Dad had gone out so we sat in their chairs. They wouldn't be home again until late, so we

69

kicked off our clogs and pushed our feet towards the fire. Then Frankie told me all about what went on in the infirmary. Frankie wanted to be a doctor when he grew up. I told him I thought that would be great, if I could be a nurse too. At least I wouldn't have to climb the wall to get in, I said, and we burst out laughing again at my antics. We were so happy to see each other. We wanted things to stay like that for ever. We had no idea then what the future would hold for any of our generation.

I told Frankie about the wilted flowers and the loss of the clogs, and then our elder sister came in. Mary picked Frankie up and hugged him. 'I'm so glad you're home again.' She had tears in her eyes: in those days hospitals were places to fear.

Frankie had never had so much fuss made of him in his life before. He was lapping it up. I asked Mary where Mum and Dad were.

'They're down the local. We're all going to celebrate your homecoming tonight, Frankie.'

'Where's Liza then?' I asked.

'She's down at Granny's but she'll be home later.'

She sat down in the armchair with Frankie on her lap and began to sing in that sweet voice of hers which we all loved to hear, except Mum of course, who was jealous because Mary could reach the top notes and she couldn't. She was too ill-educated to know that Mary was a soprano and that she was a contralto. Mum was a good singer, but when she tried to reach Mary's top notes she made an awful noise. Mary stopped singing soon after because Liza had come in and she was always off-key when she joined in. She too only had eyes for Frankie.

'Hello, are you better?' she asked, and kissed him too.

He looked surprised and so did Mary. They hadn't expected any fuss from Liza but I thought that perhaps she'd changed for the better. Then Mary began to tell us about what had happened to her when she'd been in hospital herself, but before she'd finished Mum and Dad stumbled in.

'You can all stay where you are,' Dad managed to say as we all jumped up in surprise. Then we all experienced something new. They stood up while we sat down. 'We're all going to have a sing-song tonight,' Dad said.

Dad gave us children some port wine and we all waxed happy and merry. Mary drank stout and Mum had gin. Dad poured himself some ale. Then we each had to sing in turn. It was only on very rare occasions that we sang together – at weddings or christenings and sometimes when our aunty came to visit us, which wasn't very often. On this occasion Mum and Dad were so pleased to have Frankie back that they declared a general celebration. Mum got out the gob-stoppers that were kept on the shelf for special occasions and gave one to Liza in case she joined in.

Mum did 'Nellie Dean', and we all joined in the chorus. Liza joined in as well, off-key. Mum stopped at once and shouted at Mary, 'Give 'er another gob-stopper. I don't know who 'er teks after. Not me!'

As Mary pushed it into her mouth, Liza grinned at Mary and sucked away to her heart's content. Mum gave Liza one of her hard stares before she started again. We all sat quiet while Mum finished her song, then Dad said it was time for Mary to sing a duet with him. She sang her favourite, 'Annie Laurie', and Dad harmonised. It was beautiful to hear their rich voices, Dad's baritone and Mary's soprano. When they'd finished, I asked Dad to sing my favourite.

'What's that?'

'You know, the one you sing in the pub, ''A Soldier and a Man''.'

I always called it 'my song' because I knew the tune and most of the words. I'd heard Dad sing it so often when he wanted a few coppers for a pint.

'Very well,' he said and cleared his throat with a swig from the bottle. Then he thrust out his chest and was about to begin when Mum's fist came down with a bang on the table, causing everything to shake and rattle.

'Now give order! All on yer, while yer Dad sings 'is war song.'

Mum sat down at once. So did Mary. Frankie and I were still sitting on the horsehair sofa and Liza sat on the stairs sucking her gob-stopper. Dad looked at each of us in turn, then rose to

71

his feet, and with his back to the fire he began to sing. I gazed at him, fascinated. He gave the song all he'd got. I would have liked to join him but I didn't dare. I knew what Mum would do to me if I did, so I contented myself with listening to the stirring song.

'A solider stood upon the battlefield,
His weary watch to keep,
While the pale moon covered his mantle o'er
A soldier who needs a sleep.
"Ah me," he cried,
With tearful eyes,
As he called to God above.
"I am far away from my children dear
And the only ones I love."
But as the bugle sounds
He turns once more, amid the shot and shell.'

But he never finished the rest of the song that night. He said it was too sad and brought back too many memories. I always pictured Dad in the Boer War standing on the top of a mountain, alone and sad, and I loved to hear him sing because it always made me weepy. Dad's song ended our evening because Frankie and I were sent to bed. Liza was still sucking her sweet when she joined us soon after. As we climbed into bed Mum shouted up to us, 'Yer can 'ave a lie-in later, being' it's Sunday.'

Then the stairs door closed with a bang. Our privilege was a mixed blessing because if we made use of it we'd miss our meagre breakfast and have to wait until dinner-time to eat.

Next day we went to Sunday school. They were kind and asked Frankie if he was better, making a fuss of him and giving him sweets and cake. I could never understand why people were so generous when a person was ill and had such short memories when they got well.

Monday morning came all too soon and we had to return to school. I watched Frankie with envy as he cleaned his teeth and washed himself with scented Erasmic soap someone had given

him while he was in hospital. I was proud, though, to think he
looked and smelled better than anyone else in our school. We
settled down into our different classrooms, but halfway
through lessons I was eager to see how my brother was faring
on his first day back. So while my teacher was writing on the
board I tiptoed to the glass partition and peeped through. His
teacher was making a fuss over him. I asked myself why he was
having all the attention. I felt sorry for myself because I was
always ignored. Then I heard my teacher's voice boom out so
loud that it startled me. I walked slowly back to my place and
sulked.

'Sit up straight!' she cried out. 'I'll settle with you after
class.'

She turned once more to write on the board and I was aware
of the class's eyes on me. It was then that I had an idea.

'I don't feel well,' I whispered to Nelly, who sat in the next
desk.

'What's the matter, Katie! You look pale.'

I didn't answer. I just lay my head on the desk and pretended I was ill. I thought that if I could convince my teacher, I
might get a little affection and perhaps go to the infirmary. I
lifted my head and whispered to Nelly to tell the teacher I was
feeling sick. I sprawled back on the desk and waited.

'Please, teacher, Katie's ill.'

However I began to be afraid when I heard the heavy tread
of the teacher's feet coming down the classroom towards me.

'Sit up and pay attention,' she said angrily.

I didn't move a muscle. I meant to carry out my plan now at
all costs but when she caught hold of my hair and lifted my
head up roughly, I began to tremble inside. I must have
turned pale in earnest then.

'What's the matter with you!' she asked sharply.

Then I put my hand to my forehead and lied for all I was
worth.

'Please, teacher, my head and throat hurt.'

I tried to squeeze out a few tears but none came. I was even
more frightened now, in case she found out that I'd lied. I
must have been pale because the next thing I knew she called

out to Liza to come to me. She saw that by now I was trembling all over but she did not realise the cause. I wished I hadn't started the deception.

'Take her home, and if she's no better your mother had better call in the doctor.'

With that she turned to the rest of the class and brought the cane down with a loud swish and screamed at the rest of the girls who'd turned round to see what was happening. It was difficult to remain calm and take no notice as I walked slowly out of the classroom with Liza. I must have put on a good show because Liza appeared to believe that I was ill and she put her arm around my shoulder and helped me home. She'd never shown such kindness before. I hoped Mum would be home and I was pleased when I could see the welcoming smoke from our chimney. Then I remembered that today was the day for scratching stew[1] and I began to anticipate it with pleasure. When we entered Mum's first reaction was to ask why we were home so early. I just looked at her, feeling sorry for myself, while Liza told her about my sudden illness and being sent home to see a doctor. When she'd heard all this she turned on me and let fly.

'An' now what's the matter with yow? Don't yer think I've 'ad enough with yer brother being ill an' only one pair o' 'ands 'ere ter do everythink?'

Oh dear, I thought to myself, when's she going to stop. My head really was beginning to ache now and I wished I hadn't started this pretence. But I'd gone this far and had to continue. I began to whimper.

'My throat's sore, Mum, and my head aches.'

'Sit down theea!' she cried out and pushed me down into Dad's armchair. 'An' open yer mouth wide! Wider.'

Trembling with fear I slowly opened my mouth a little way as she returned with something from the cupboard. I regretted trying to deceive everyone, it wasn't worth the trouble.

'Come on, open up agen!' she screamed in my face as she leaned over me. I opened wide, there was no escaping.

'I feel better now, Mum,' I cried, and struggled to get up from the chair. But she prevented me.

' 'Old 'er 'ands down,' she told Liza.

Then I was told to open my mouth again as wide as I could but she had to slap my face before I'd opened it wide enough. I watched her make a funnel with a piece of newspaper; then she emptied some sulphur powder from a jar and blew it into my throat. I coughed and spat it out immediately but she made sure the second time. She held my nose with her finger and thumb, squeezed hard and blew down again. I had to swallow it this time. She blew so hard I was knocked breathless and I thought I was going to choke.

'That'll learn yer a lesson not to play the fool with me. Now get yer dinner 'an then get ter school before I blow some mower down yer.'

I couldn't eat a bite; my throat was really sore and felt like sandpaper. My head hurt terribly and I had to admit to myself that my plan had failed miserably. I determined there and then to run away from home and become a nurse when I was old enough.

NOTE

[1] 'Scratching stew' was made from boiled 'scratchings' – small pieces of fried pig skin. They are still sold in Midland pubs as an alternative to potato crisps.

8
Granny Moves In

Each Friday night Liza, Frankie and I had to stay up later than usual. This was not a treat, far from it. We had to blacklead the grate and the big, iron kettle that stood on the hob, as well as rub off any soot on the enamel teapot that stood beside it. On the other hob was a battered copper kettle which had a hole in the bottom; Mum never threw anything away. She said Dad would mend it one day, but he never did, and we still had to polish it. Jutting out from the top of the grate was a large meat jack which always held our stewpot. I called it a witch's cauldron. We had to scrub the deal-topped table, the stairs, chairs and the broken flag-stones, brown as they were from years of hard wear. The soda we used hardly touched them, the only things that were cleaned were our hands.

Standing each side of the fireplace were two wooden arm-chairs, one for Mum and one for Dad. We children were never allowed to sit in these unless given permission to do so, but we did make good use of them when Mum and Dad were out at the pub. Our usual seat was the old horsehair sofa under the window. Someone had given this to Dad in return for doing odd jobs. It replaced the old wooden one which was chopped up for firewood. Only the legs were spared because Dad said they might come in handy for something one day. Every corner of the house was cluttered up with odds and ends. Our sofa was moulting badly and had bare patches all over. We nicknamed it 'Neddy'.

Beside the table were two ladder-backed chairs, one for my brother Jack and the other for Mary. There had been three but after Charlie and Dad had a row over money, Charlie left home, and Dad burnt the chair. There was also a three-legged stool under the table; on its top stood our large, tin washing bowl. Set into the wall beside the fireplace was a long, shallow, brown earthenware sink. We only used this for putting dirty crocks in because we had no running water indoors. On the other side of the fireplace was an alcove behind the stairs door where the old, rotten mangle was kept; this was a permanent fixture. We had orders that if anyone called we had to leave the stairs door open to hide our laundry from view.

The fireguard, round the fireplace, was always covered with things airing or drying, especially when the lines across the room were full. Around the mantel-shelf was a string fringe with faded, coloured bobbles and on the shelf were two white, cracked Staffordshire dogs and several odd vases which contained paper flowers and pawn tickets. Hanging high on the wall above was a large photograph of our granny. We'd have loved to have got rid of it, but didn't dare. When you

76

stared at it, the eyes seemed to follow you round the room. The effect was heightened at night when the paraffin lamp was lit. This was the only picture in the room with the glass intact. Mum in particular objected to it.

'I carn't see why yer don't 'ave a smaller picture of 'er. It takes up too much room.'

'No!' Dad would reply. 'Nothing's big enough for my mother. It stays where it is.'

'It'll fall down, you'll see, one of these days!' Mum replied.

'Not if you don't intend it to. But I'm warning you, Polly!' He wagged his finger at her in admonishment. So there the picture stayed.

We also had to dust all the pictures and knick-knacks that hung over the walls. There were three pictures, 'Faith', 'Hope' and 'Charity', as well as a print of 'Bubbles' – the advertisement for Pear's soap – and many photographs of Mum's first-, second- and third-born, all dead and gone. Underneath these were the death cards and birth certificates of the others, and photographs of relatives framed in red and green plush. They were so faded you had to squint to recognise who they were. There were even paper mottoes stuck to the wall which announced such sentiments as 'God Bless This House' and 'Home Sweet Home'. I could never understand why they were there, our house or home was far from happy. They were supposed to be Christmas decorations but they were not taken down until Easter, when Mum folded them up and put them away for next year.

On the wall opposite was a picture of Mum and Dad taken years ago on their wedding day. Mum looked happy, wearing leg o' mutton sleeves with her hair parted in the middle. She was smiling up at Dad who stood beside her chair. Dad had one hand on her shoulder and was standing erect like a regimental sergeant-major. His hair was dark like Mum's and was also parted in the middle, with a kiss-curl flat in the middle of his forehead. His moustache was waxed into curls at each end. He held a bowler across his chest. Now as it happened this was the very same hat which had pride of place on the wall, just low enough for me to dust. One night I happened to knock this hat

77

on the floor just as Mary entered. As I stooped to retrieve it she said, 'You'd better put that back on its nail before Mum comes in.'

So I snatched it up and, as I put it back, I replied, 'It's no good. It's going green. About time Mum got rid of it, like most of the relics here.'

'You'd better not let Mum hear you. She happens to be proud of that. It has a lot of memories for her.'

I went on working around the room; then I noticed that Mary was smiling. 'What are you smiling at, Mary?'

'Come and sit down and I'll tell you about it.'

I sat on 'Neddy', but before Mary sat down she peeped round the curtain to see if anyone was coming. Then she began her story.

'Now that billy-cock – ' she pointed towards Dad's delapidated hat, ' – that hat has sentimental value for Mum. About the time when she started having the family . . . I'll tell you all about it, but only if you don't laugh and can keep a secret. Every twelve months Mum gave birth to a baby and when it was a few weeks old Mum and Dad went to church to have it christened. They thought they'd gone on their own. They never saw me watching them. I used to hide behind the pillar.'

Her face was beaming and I was intrigued to hear what was coming next.

'Now when the parson took the child off Mum he'd sprinkle water on its forehead and then it would cry and water would come out the other end. When the parson had finished the christening and handed Mum the baby she'd sit down in her pew and change its nappy. Well, it was then that Dad was at the ready. Taking off his billy-cock he'd take out a dry nappy and put the wet one inside the hat and then when he replaced it on his head, they'd leave the church and go in the pub to celebrate. You see I always followed them, just like you do.'

She gave me a sly wink and we both burst out laughing.

'Phew!' I cried, holding my nose.

Then she left and I finished my chores and although the house looked and smelt better it was not fresh air, it was carbolic soap and Keating's Powder. In the end I was almost too tired to crawl up the attic stairs and fall into bed. I just peeled off my clothes and was asleep immediately. I didn't even say my prayers.

Friday wasn't the only day I had chores to do. Saturday mornings was my day to get up early and be down to riddle the overnight ashes and place the embers in the steel fender ready to place on the back of the fire when it was lit. It was also my job to make a pot of tea and take a mug for Mum and Dad.

Now as the reader can imagine, Mum's temper wasn't always at its longest first thing in the morning. She'd yell at me, 'The tea's too 'ot!' or 'It's too cold!' or 'Not enough sugar in it. You ain't stirred it up!' She'd find fault with anything. This particular morning I was saved from her nagging, but only for a short time. Just as I was about to take the mug of hot tea upstairs, a loud knock sounded on the door. I lifted the corner of the curtain and peeped out. It was only the postman, who was a cheery man with a smile for everyone he met.

'Good morning, Katie, and how are you this bright, cheery morning?'

'Very well, thank you, Mr Postman,' I replied.

If only everybody in our district was as pleasant, life would have been much happier. He asked me to give a letter to Dad and returned down the yard. He'd only just stepped down from our door when Mum shouted, 'Who's that bangin' on the dower this time of the mornin'? Carn't we get any sleep around 'ere?'

She'd forgotten that she woke everybody, singing and banging at the maiding-tub at six o'clock every Monday morning.

'It's the postman, Mum. He's brought a letter for Dad,' I called back from the foot of the stairs.

I put the letter between my lips and turned to get the mugs of tea. It was then that I saw the postman standing under the window, shaking his head from side to side. I heard him tutting to himself as he walked down the yard. Mum shouted down again for the letter, so I hurried up to the bedroom where I found her sitting up in bed. I put the mugs down on the cracked, marble-topped washstand and had the letter snatched from my lips.

'An' about time too!'

'It's for Dad,' I said, loud enough to wake him.

'I know, I know' she repeated. 'An' where's me tea?'

'On the table,' I answered timidly.

I made to go downstairs, but she called me back to read the letter. Mum couldn't read or write. She couldn't even count, except on her fingers and then it always took a painfully long struggle. I always did any reading or writing when Dad wasn't about. Dad could correct my spelling because he was more literate than Mum and he spoke better too. I watched him stir and yawn as I fumbled with the envelope. I was glad he was awake; it was his letter anyway. But he waved me away.

'Oh, read it, Katie, and let's get back to sleep.'

I was anxious myself now to find out what the letter contained but when I'd opened it and read it there was no extra rest for anyone that morning. It was from Granny and although her spelling was bad I managed to read it out.

' ''Sam an Polly,'' ' I read aloud, ' ''I'm not well in elth me ouse as got ter be fumigated The Mans bin an ses Ive gotter move for two weeks so Im coming ter you Ill bring wot bitta money I got an Im goin ter joyn the salvashun army an Ill bring me rockin chare an me trunk so Ill see yer all tomorra so be up early. Hannah.'' '

She didn't ask if she could come, she just assumed she could. When I'd finished reading the jumbled and nearly illegible writing, Mum jumped up with a start.

'Good God above!' she cried, waving her arms about. 'We ain't 'avin' 'er nuisance agen, are we?'

She glared at Dad, who was still lying on his back. He wasn't asleep. Who could be, the way Mum was raving? But he did have his eyes closed. He was thinking about how to deal with Mum.

'Yow asleep, Sam? Dain't yer 'ear wot I said?'

'I heard yer,' he shouted back and opened his eyes wide. 'The whole bloody town can hear when you start.'

'Well, what can we do?'

'It's only for two weeks. Nobody will take her, so we'll have to do the best we can,' Dad replied.

They must have forgotten that I was still standing at the foot of the bed. I watched them both lay back again and stare up at the ceiling deep in thought. Then suddenly Mum shot up out of bed. I'd never seen her move so quickly, nor look so misshapen as she did then, standing beside the bed in her calico chemise all twisted up in the front. I'd never seen her undressed before, or without her whalebone stays. She used to have them laced so tightly she used to look like a pouter pigeon with her heavy breasts pushed up high. I never knew how she got all that flabby flesh inside those stays. She looked so comical that I had to put my hand over my mouth to keep from laughing out loud. As she leant over the bed and shook Dad, her belly wobbled and her bare breasts flopped out of the top of her chemise.

'Sam!' she shrieked. 'Wake up!'

'Stop bawling. I'm not deaf.'

'I wanta knoo where 'er's gonna sleep.'

I thought it was about time to go downstairs before they noticed me giggling.

'Shall I go and make some more hot tea, Mum?' I managed to say.

Suddenly she realised that I was still there and she yelled at me to shut up and clear off as she tried to cover herself with her shift. This was the chance I'd been waiting for, so I fled downstairs, but still strained to hear what was being said.

'Now listen, Polly, and calm down. You know she'll help. She'll bring you some money for her keep and if you don't tell the relief officer we'll be all right.'

'But where d'yer think she's gonna sleep? She carn't sleep with us. It ain't decent.'

'I'll sleep on ''Neddy'' for the time being so don't worry about me.'

This arrangement must have pleased her because I heard a change in her voice.

'Orl right, just as yer like, Sam.'

Now the shouting had died down, I took two mugs of tea up to find that they were still discussing Granny. I stood the mugs on the table and stood anticipating the usual grumbles from Mum but she and Dad just lay there looking snug and warm. She pulled the clothes around her and turned to Dad.

'Do yer think the bed'll 'old us two? She's sixteen stone. I'm sixteen stone an' that meks us . . . er . . . er . . .'

I could see she was trying to puzzle out how many stones they would both be. Suddenly she sat up in bed. Sticking her two hands in front of her face and spreading her fingers apart she began to count. 'I'm sixteen and sixteen makes seventeen, eighteen, nineteen . . .'

'Sixteen and sixteen makes thirty-two,' I said, trying to help.

'I count my way then I know I'm right,' she snapped.

Dad lay back smiling and let her get on with it. Up went the fingers again and she counted on each finger again and again until eventually she yelled, 'The bed'll never 'old us!'

Dad and I collapsed in laughter as she tried with her hands to demonstrate the combined weight.

'Well,' Dad replied, still smiling, 'if you both come through the ceiling we'll have to do a moonlight flit.'

This was not the first time a flit was threatened, but we never did.

'Well, we'd better get up an' goo downstairs an' 'ave an 'ot cuppa. This is stone cold.' She handed me the mugs of tea which they'd forgotten to drink.

I found Frankie and Liza washed and dressed when I got downstairs. I was pleased because I could see that my brother had lit the fire and had put the kettle on to boil. Mum and Dad were not long following. We pulled our chairs up to the table and waited for our breakfast which turned out to be a burnt offering of toast; however, the tea was fresh, as I'd just made some more. Usually the leaves were used over and over again until they were too weak to stand the strain, then they were thrown on the back of the fire. Nothing was ever wasted if it could be reused, not even water or paper. We seldom had enough to eat. Sometimes we sat like three Oliver Twists, although we didn't dare ask for more, In fact, if we ever refused to eat anything that was placed in front of us, it was taken away and we had to eat it next mealtime, by which time we'd be so hungry we'd be glad of it. After our burnt toast, Dad told Mum to get the bedroom ready and he pinched her bottom as she rose from the table. She waved his hand away and warned him not to do it in front of us children. They both seemed happier. He pushed her gently up the stairs and turned to wink at us. I thought, if only they were always smiling or acting this way our lives would be much happier.

As we stood washing up the mugs and enamel plates we could hear the iron bedsteads being dragged along the bare floorboards towards the wall so that Granny wouldn't fall out of bed. This was only the preliminary to a hectic tidying up operation and although we'd cleaned the night before, we had to get out the carbolic soap and begin again. Mum was always one for making an impression when Granny called, but I couldn't see why because Granny's house was far more cluttered than ours. Dad cleared out and Frankie and I were left singing as we dusted and scrubbed. When Liza joined in Mum yelled at her to stop her 'cat warlin'. I think she was expecting another gob-stopper but if so she was unlucky. We all fell silent and I thought maybe Granny would bring a little cheerfulness into our home now she was going to join the Salvation Army.

Very early next morning, before anyone was awake, I heard a loud knock on the downstairs door and before I could get out of bed a louder knock and three taps on the window pane. I woke Frankie and Liza with a good hard shake and told them what was happening. We three got out of bed and dressed quickly. Then we lifted the window to see what the racket was all about. As we leant over the window sill to look down into the yard below we saw Granny at the door, calling and waving her arms in all directions.

'Ain't nobody awake yet! 'Ave I gotta stand 'ere all day? I'm freezin' an' if nobody lets me in I'm comin' through the winda.'

She sounds just like Mum, I thought. Then, before anyone could get down to let her in, she tried to push up the window. Turning to the little man who'd brought her things on a hand cart, she shouted for assistance. He looked too scared to move.

Then Granny saw the bucket of rainwater that Mum kept for washing her hair. She promptly tipped the water away and turned the bucket upside down. Then she pushed the window up and stepped on to the bucket to aid her entry. The reader can imagine what a funny sight sixteen stone Granny was, standing on a rusty old bucket. We were not used to the capers that Granny cut. Suddenly, just as she was halfway through, disaster struck. The sash cord broke and the bucket slipped, leaving Granny pinned half in, half out, by the window frame. She began to kick her legs in a vain attempt to free herself but she only succeeded in showing the neighbours her pantaloons. For the first time we experienced a temper worse than Mum's. She swore till the air was blue. Proof, I thought, that she needed to join the Salvation Army. Then Dad popped his head of the window and called down angrily, 'You'll have to wait, Mother, while I slip me trousers on.'

When he came downstairs and saw the plight she was in, he lifted the window but he was too quick. Granny fell out backwards, rolled over the bucket and landed in a puddle of rainwater.

'An' about time too,' she bawled while he struggled to pick her off the floor.

'I'll get meself up,' she muttered.

By this time Mum's head had appeared at the window and the neighbours too were peering down at the commotion.

''Annah!' Mum shouted. 'Yer'll wake up all the neighbours.'

'Wake 'em up! Wake 'em up!' she shrieked, struggling to her feet.

She turned round and waved her fist at the amused onlookers and bellowed at them, getting redder and redder in the process.

'Look at 'em! The nosy lot of idle sods.'

All the time she'd been carrying on, the little old chap was standing still, waiting to be paid for his labours. Suddenly she turned on him, leaned against the cart and sniffed.

'Don't stand there all day. 'Elp me off with me trunk an' me rockin'-chair. An' mind 'ow yer 'andle me aspidistra.'

84

He couldn't manage the trunk nor the rocking-chair, but Dad soon came to the rescue. Meantime Granny felt inside the bosom of her frock, sniffed a couple of times and pushed a silver sixpence into his outstretched hand. He looked down at it disdainfully and mumbled a barely audible 'Skinny old Jew.'

'What did yer say?'

'I said, "Thank you",' he answered meekly.

'Dain't sound much like "thank yer" ter me,' she retorted.

Scratching his head, he wheeled his empty cart away and said to Dad in a louder voice, 'I feel sorry for yow, mate,' but Dad ignored him.

The neighbours closed their windows. The fun was over for them but for us the trouble was only just beginning. We dressed hurriedly and dashed down to see Granny. She looked huge standing beside the trunk. We hadn't seen her for some time and it was easy to forget her size. She wore a black taffeta frock almost to her feet, black elastic-sided boots and a battered black woollen shawl. Her lace bonnet, also black, was hanging from ribbons on the back of her neck where it has slipped while she'd been trying to climb through the window. Her hair, too, was dishevelled, but what I noticed most was the large raised lump on her behind. I poked Frankie and he whispered, 'Ain't she got a big bum.'

'That ain't her bum. It's a bustle,' I replied as he started to snigger.

Liza too stared at Granny, but Granny paid us no attention until she suddenly straightened herself up to her full height of six feet, pulled her shawl around her and addressed us. 'Don't just stand theea gorpin'. Come an give yer ol' gran a kiss.'

I closed my eyes and lifted my face up sideways for her to kiss my cheek. She must have read my thoughts because she just pushed me roughly away, with a slap and bent to peck Liza and Frankie's cheeks. As I walked off clutching Topsey she asked what I was holding.

'It's the golly you made me, Granny,' I replied.

'I don't remember mekin' that.' She shrugged her shoulders and dismissed me.

'Now, now, Mother. You gave it to her last Christmas. You must have forgotten.' Dad attempted to pacify her.

'Er's always forgettin',' Mum piped up from putting Granny's plant away.

'Put the kettle on, Polly, and we'll all sit down and have a cup of tea.'

This was Dad's favourite tactic when he saw a quarrel brewing. He drew Gran's rocking-chair towards the fire. Granny sat down and rocked in the creaking chair. With hers in the middle and Mum's and Dad's chairs on either side of the fireplace no one else could feel or see the flames. I picked up Topsey and sat with Frankie on 'Neddy' to await my tea. When it was made, Granny's was the first cup to be filled. Then she took a sip and without warning spat it back out.

'What yer call this?' she spluttered, pulling a face at Mum.

'It's yer tea. Like it or lump it.' This was a favourite retort.

'Tastes like maid's water¹ ter me.' Granny could give as good as she got.

We looked at each other; we all knew what Mum's tea was like. The pot had been stewing all morning. Dad told me to make a fresh pot. As I squeezed past Mum to empty the tea leaves into the spare bucket, I heard her whisper to Dad, 'Thank the Lord we've only got 'er fer two weeks.'

During Granny's stay the gas-fitters came to connect the place to the mains. We'd already had the enamelled iron stove and the gas mantle fixed to the wall weeks before. They'd also fitted a slot meter to the wall at the bottom of the broken cellar stairs. It was lovely to see the lighted gas mantle after the paraffin lamp. We still had to keep this relic, along with the others, in case Mum ran out of pennies. We also had to have a candle to light us to bed because, as Mum said, 'It's not safe to have gas upstairs.' I thought it was much more likely that she objected to gas in our bedrooms because she had candles free from Jack's works. He always brought a couple home in his pockets every night. He supplied Granny too. She didn't believe in having gas installed at all, and said, 'When I die I wanta goo ter me Maker in one piece, when me time comes!'

The following Saturday afternoon Mum said they were

going to the Bull Ring² to do the shopping. This was our marketplace, where everything was sold cheap. There was the fruit and vegetable market, the fish market, the rag market and the flower market, all next to each other; and on each side of the street were barrow boys shouting their wares.

Dad asked Granny if she would like to go as well, but she said, no, that it was too noisy, and that there was too much swearing for her liking. I could tell by the look on Mum's face that she didn't want Granny to go but Dad asked anyway.

'No. I can find summat betta to do with me time. Anyway I'm gooin' ter see the Captain of the Salvation Army,' Gran replied when pressed.

'Come on, Sam, before she changes 'er mind,' Mum said irritably.

As he was leaving the house, Dad said, 'Now if you kids behave yourselves I'll bring yer back a little present from town.' Then off they went, slamming the door behind them.

'Things must be looking up,' said Frankie, 'Dad's getting generous.'

'Well,' I answered, 'he's better than Mum.'

'Perhaps.' He shrugged his shoulders.

Granny put on her bonnet and shawl and went off to the Salvation Army Hall without a word to us. We were at a loss for something to do: then our eyes alighted on Granny's trunk. Frankie heaved open the rusty tin lid and we peered eagerly inside to see what secrets it held. We were disappointed to find only a pair of white pantaloons, a long, black lace frock with a bustle, a pair of button-up boots and a pair of whalebone stays like Mum's. We lifted them out to see what was underneath. It was then that we discovered Granny had been in the Army before. There was a tambourine, a uniform, and a bonnet with a red ribbon with 'Salvation Army' written on it. Underneath these was a bundle of old papers tied with string. We were about to start returning these things to the trunk when I hit on an idea to amuse ourselves until the grown-ups returned.

'Let's dress up and pretend we're in the band,' I said. The other two agreed.

Frankie fetched Mum's broom handle and tied the pantaloons on to it to represent a flag. Liza put on the bonnet and carried the tambourine and I put on the long black frock with the bustle. When we were ready we marched up and down the yard. Frankie waved the flag, Liza banged the tambourine and I dragged the bustle behind me. We sang 'Onward, Christian Soldiers' as we marched back and forth. All the neighbours turned out to see what all the noise was about. They joined in too. People sang a lot in those days. The children joined our band and we paraded up and down. Frankie's pantaloons bellowed out in the breeze as Liza's tambourine kept the beat. We were having great fun until Liza gave one hell of a scream, dropped the tambourine and ran into the house. Frankie and I' were scared stiff, thinking it was Granny or our parents come home early. Frankie dropped the broom and followed Liza into the house. I tripped over the long frock in my anxiety to follow them. Everybody was giggling, thinking it was all part of the act. When I did manage to get indoors I saw Liza was standing on 'Neddy' still screaming and pointing at the bonnet. We couldn't understand what she was screaming about until she flung the bonnet violently at Frankie. I stooped down to pick it up when I was startled by a mouse which suddenly ran out across the floor. Liza was still hysterical but Frankie and I tried to catch it; the mouse was too fast for us. Like a flash it ran down a hole under the stairs and was gone. We must have caused quite a commotion because people had gathered round our door to see what all the fuss was about. They disappeared quickly enough when I told them what it was though. I couldn't understand why they were so squeamish; they had plenty of mice of their own.

We managed to quieten Liza down eventually. Then we packed Granny's belongings back into the trunk, but we had a good look to see if we'd left any other little friends behind. Then we fastened down the lid just as we'd found it.

Now perhaps the reader will remember what I've written about Liza telling Mum tales about Frankie and me, so we warned her that if ever she said anything about what had happened we'd put the mouse down her frock while she was asleep. Liza knew that whatever Frankie said he meant, so she promised not to say a word. We'd only just put the things away and set the kettle on the stove when the door opened and Dad walked in.

'Yer been good kids?' were his first words.

Frankie said we had, and warned Liza with a look.

'Well, here you are.' Dad handed me a box. I couldn't believe my eyes when I opened it. There, sitting on some straw, was a tame white mouse with tiny pink eyes.

'Oh, it's lovely,' exclaimed Frankie.

'Thank you, Dad.' I was overjoyed, but Liza didn't look or speak. Frankie stared at her in a meaningful way and she said nothing.

'You're not to let it out of the cage,' Dad told us. 'We don't want any offspring. We've got enough already.'

'I don't know why yer bought it,' Mum snapped.

'I didn't buy it. It was given me,' Dad replied.

'Hm . . . hm . . .' She obviously didn't believe him. 'I've 'eard that before.'

Just at that point I opened the cage to stroke it. Liza gave an enormous scream when she saw, and jumped on a chair.

'Don't be a babby,' Dad told her. 'It ain't going to hurt yer.'

'It ain't going to get a chance,' she retorted, climbing gingerly down from the chair.

I really thought she'd tell Dad our secret now so, as Dad turned to the fire to light his pipe, Frankie whispered in her ear, 'I'm warning you. If you let on, this is the one I'll put down your neck.'

She went pale and we didn't hear another word from her for the rest of the day.

'Where shall we keep it?' asked Frankie.

'We'll keep it on the attic shelf, away from Pete,' I answered.

We asked Dad what sex it was, but he said he didn't know so we called it Snowy to be on the safe side. Each night before we went to bed we fed it on breadcrumbs we'd saved and watered it on cold tea in a cocoa-tin lid. Frankie and I were so proud of our little pet and we showed it to all the kids in the yard, but we didn't let them touch it. As the days went by, Snowy looked well and happy running up and down his cage, standing on his back legs or washing his face; until one morning when we went to give him his tea and crumbs the cage was no longer on the shelf. There was a scuffle on the floor and there we saw the cage with Snowy still inside and Pete trying to get his paw between the bars. I shouted in alarm to Frankie but before I could rescue the mouse a clog came flying across the room. Pete was not deterred by this though. He only retreated under the bed from where he watched, ready to pounce again if the opportunity offered. As I bent down to reach for the cage I caught Liza out of the corner of my eye grinning all over her face. She lay back quickly and hid under the bedclothes. Then I guessed how the cage came to be on the floor. Frankie had guessed, too. He snatched at the cover and dragged her out and accused her. He was just about to strike her when we heard Mum's heavy tread on the stairs.

'What's all that racket and what yer all doin' out of bed?' she demanded. 'Get back, the three o' yer, before yer feel the back of me 'and!'

I crawled out from under the bed where I'd been keeping Pete at bay. Liza lay on the floor whimpering and although we tried to explain, Mum wouldn't listen. She made us bare our bottoms and slapped us hard and pushed us on to the bed. She seemed to have the strength of a tiger when she was roused. We were really scared and so was Snowy, who was running madly round inside his cage. We sat watching Mum nervously, wondering what she was going to do next. She struggled to get down on her knees to reach under the bed for the cat.

'Come on out. I know yer theea!'

But Pete sensibly stayed put. He was used to Mum's rough handling so he remained where he was hiding under our comics. However, after fumbling around she eventually managed to grab his tail. Then, as she tried to pull him out, we heard hissing and spitting. This had its effect on Mum who was afraid he would fly at her. So she let go and Pete, his fur standing on end, flew down the stairs. Mum heaved herself off the floor with considerable effort and, seeing Snowy's cage, she snatched it up.

'Not another word from any of yer!' she yelled, and with that marched downstairs.

We knew very well what Mum's temper was like and we were sure she'd get rid of the mouse. Without waiting to dress, Frankie and I ran down the stairs two at a time and peeped round the corner into the living-room. Mum was nowhere to be seen but there on the table was the cage with Snowy still tearing round inside it. Pete had also plucked up his courage to make another attempt to catch him and was sitting glaring at the mouse. We made a dash for the table but Mum must have loosened the catch because, when Pete clawed at the cage, the door flew open and like a flash Snowy fled down the same hole as Granny's mouse before either of us could grab him. I began to sob, but I stifled my crying when I saw Mum standing in the doorway. Silently she reached for the cane but we were saved from a thrashing when the door opened and Dad walked in. 'Now what's going on here?' he asked. 'What yer doing standing there in yer underclothes.'

We didn't get a chance to explain. Mum told the story her way and ended by pointing out the hole that our mouse had disappeared down. 'An' that's the larst of that,' she added. 'Yow never ought to 'ave bought it. I'll get rid of the cat as well, fer all the good 'e is.'

'All right. Calm down. Don't keep on about it. Anyway it'll be happy enough down there with the rest of them. And get back upstairs, you two, and put some clothes on before you catch yer death. Go on, GET!'

There was nothing else to do but obey, but as we climbed slowly up the steep flight Liza pushed past us on her way down, fully dressed.

'I'll pay you out for this, you wait and see,' Frankie hissed.

'It's all her fault,' Frankie grumbled as we were dressing.

I agreed with him, and tears began to trickle down my cheeks again.

'Even Granny pretends to be deaf when we tell her anything.' I nodded my agreement.

For weeks after, when nobody was about, we'd wait by that hole in the hope of catching a glimpse of our Snowy. We even pushed scraps into the hole so he wouldn't be hungry. Little did we know it was the worst thing we could have done. Still, we were happy knowing he would have Granny's mouse down there to play with. Each night I mentioned Snowy in my prayers and asked Jesus to watch over him because Frankie and I missed him so much.

NOTES

[1] Outmoded slang for wine.

[2] The Bull Ring was the centuries-old daily marketplace. Nearby where the wholesale fruit and vegetable and fish markets. The old markets were demolished in the late 1960s and have been replaced by a new complex. The modern Bull Ring is an enormous covered shopping centre which straddles Birmingham's inner ring road.

9
Mums Decides to Take Us Hop-picking

Almost everyone in our neighbourhood thought it was best to steer clear of Granny when they saw her coming towards them down the street. She was a holy terror! But all the kids, especially her grandchildren, loved marching along with her when she was in her Salvation Army uniform singing in the band. Sometimes she let me carry the tambourine while she waved the banner and we all sang 'Onward, Christian Soldiers'. You'd have thought that Granny really was 'marching as to war'. Everybody looked out to see her with her head held high and her voice above all the others. She knew they were watching, but didn't care a jot, she just gave them a haughty stare and sniffed between hymns.

I was never able to keep pace with Granny's big strides and

when I fell behind she'd snatch the tambourine from me and urge me on. 'Sing up, little soldier,' she'd cry and tap me on the head with the tambourine.

Soon, I'd grow too tired to stay in the band, and cold and hungry as a rule, I'd wander back home. On this particular occasion it was getting dark, and when I got indoors I found Dad dozing in his chair by the fire. There was no other light in the room, just the flickering flames of the burning coals. I tiptoed quietly towards him and whispered in his ear. 'Are you awake, Dad?'

He sat up and yawned. 'I've been waiting for one of yer to come and put a penny in the meter.'

I was scared to go down the dark cellar, but I asked him for the penny and tried to be brave. As soon as I reached the meter and heard the penny drop I was up those stairs three at a time. I lit a paper spill Dad always kept in the fender for lighting his pipe, then lit the gas.

'Where's the other two?' he asked, meaning Liza and Frankie.

'Still with Granny in the band,' I answered.

He twisted round in his chair and told me to get the bottle off the shelf and fetch him a pint of beer.

'And hurry yerself before yer gran comes home. You know how she sees the beer bottles about.'

'Yes, Dad,' I replied. He handed me tuppence and I ran off to the pub. The lamplighter was just about to enter and noticed me.

'That for yer dad?' I nodded. 'Very well, I'll get it, littl'un.'

I waited outside and kept a look-out for Granny but there wasn't a soul about. At last he emerged with the pint bottle. I thanked him and he gave me a humbug and told me to hurry home before the froth went off it. I hurried, but it was for a different reason. However, as bad luck would have it, I spotted Granny in the distance. My heart nearly stopped beating. I doubled back around the square to get indoors first. I stumbled inside the room, nearly dropping the bottle which must have had a good head of froth by now.

'Quick, Dad!' I blurted out, 'Granny's coming up the street.'

He snatched the bottle from my hand and took a quick gulp, then hid it in the sink behind the curtain. He flopped down in his chair and I sat cradling Topsey on 'Neddy'. We were both hoping and praying that she hadn't seen me, but she had eyes like a hawk's and must have spotted me in the street because she came into the room sniffing the air and made a dive straight for the sink, hauled out the bottle and held it away from her as though it were about to explode.

'What's this?' she cried out and waved the bottle with the remainder of its contents under Dad's nose. Dad just shrugged his shoulders and said it was cold tea.

'Don't yer tell me more of yer lies!' she shrieked. 'Yer wicked, the lot on yer. Yer'll never goo ter 'eaven. 'Ell's the place fer yow.'

She kept on and on, still waving the bottle at him. Dad let her carry on. He never said a word until she began pouring the beer down the sink. Then he lost his temper. Jumping up from his chair he stood beside her and shook his fist.

'Now look here, Mother, I've just about had enough of your tantrums. Now I'm warning you. While you're in my house you'll behave or you can go back to your own bloody house now!'

All the time Dad was shouting at her she kept marching up and down, waving her arms in all directions and knocking over everything in her way. I thought she was going out of her mind, but she stopped dead in her tracks when Dad caught her by the shoulders and began to shake her. When he released her, she straightened her bonnet and walked to the door with her head thrown back.

'I'm gooin' back ter the Mission Hall and pray ter the Lord ter wash yer sins away,' she declared.

'Yer better ask Him to wash away yours too while you're at it. Don't think I ain't seen yer sitting on the stairs having a sly drag from my pipe. Mission Hall my foot!' he shouted after her as she disappeared into the yard.

I felt sorry for Granny because I'd seen tears in her eyes while Dad was shouting at her, so I ran outside and caught her up.

'Where're you going, Granny?'

'In the churchyard an' wait fer me Maker,' she replied.

'Can I come with yer, Granny?' I pleaded.

'No yer carn't. Yer as bad as 'im for fetchin' it,' she said, pushing me to one side, and looking down her nose at me.

But that didn't deter me, I intended following at a safe distance. She turned down the street, passing the churchyard and the Mission Hall. I packed quickly into a dark doorway when I saw her look back. Then I couldn't believe my eyes – she marched straight into the pub! I was really surprised at Granny going into such a place, particularly after her recent argument with Dad, as she always condemned pubs. Anyway, I waited for about half an hour for her to emerge but I was shivering with cold, and when it began to rain I returned home to tell Dad.

As soon as I got indoors I blurted out what Granny had done, that she hadn't gone to the churchyard or the Mission Hall but to the Golden Cup instead.

'Yes, I know,' he answered calmly. 'She's there washing away her sins with gin.'

'But Granny's religious, Dad.'

'You'll understand one day. Now get the bottle and fetch me another pint before she comes back.'

Just at that moment Frankie and Liza returned home and Frankie volunteered to get it. When he came back, Dad gave us our lighted candle and told us to get to bed before Mum or Granny came in. We took our bread and dripping and did as we were told. We ate our supper as we were undressing and jumped into bed. I was too tired to say my prayers even. It wasn't long before we were all asleep.

Next morning I told Frankie about the quarrel and how I'd followed Granny and what I'd seen. But Frankie only smiled.

'She carn't help what she says or does. Not really. She's a bit doo-lally, tapped,' he said.

'What's that mean?' I asked.

'Don't yer know? It means she's a bit funny in her head.'

95

He pointed his finger to his temple.

'I don't believe yer.'

'You ask Dad, then. Mum knows too. That's why she keeps out of Granny's way when she can. But you carn't help laughing at her some of the time.'

I couldn't see anything to laugh about and I didn't really believe him. I still made up my mind to ask Dad about it the first chance I found.

When Dad had an extra drop of drink he always talked to himself. Two nights later my opportunity arose. Dad was sitting in the chair by the fire dozing off, when I whispered nervously, 'Can I fetch you another drink, Dad?'

'No,' he mumbled between yawns, 'I've had enough tonight.'

I could tell by his voice and the smell on his breath that now was the time to ask about Granny.

'Why is our granny like she is? You know, quarrelsome all the time.'

I edged away from him in case I was sounding too inquisitive. He started to mumble under his breath but I couldn't catch all the words because he kept nodding off to sleep. But I nudged him and kept him awake.

'What yer standing there for?' he asked, smiling at me.

'I was listening to you talking about Granny. Did you have a dad?'

He stared hard at me, no doubt wondering whether to tell me about his family or not. He could probably see how interested I was, and after a bit he said, 'Make me a nice cup of tea.'

I made the two mugs of tea and watched Dad light his pipe, then he told me to sit on Granny's rocker. I was pleased with myself. I hadn't annoyed him and when I handed him his tea he told me the story in between puffs of his pipe.

'Now, Katie, I hope you'll understand why your granny is like she is. Your mum knows, but she loses patience with her. My father joined the Salvation Army band when we were very young.'

'Who's "we", Dad?'

'Me and my two brothers. Now don't interrupt.'

He stopped to yawn before continuing. 'He asked your granny to join with him but I remember her saying she didn't believe in "blood and fire" praying. She was just happy to stay at home and look after us. But one night he went out and never came back.'

He sounded sad and his voice drifted away and began to nod off to sleep again. So I gave him another nudge to rouse him once more and he opened his eyes blankly. 'Oh yes,' he said, 'you might as well know the rest. Anyhow you'll find out one day. Your granny went to the Captain and asked if anyone had seen him. But he told her the sad news that Dad had run away with a Sister called Agnes. My mother never really got over the shock. She loved Dad and so did us three boys. He was our only breadwinner and although the Captain came round to try and help us, yer granny was very proud and stubborn. She wouldn't accept charity from no one. So when her savings had gone she had to let us go to the workhouse. She even joined the Salvation Army and travelled from town to town trying to find him, but she never did.'

'What became of your brothers, Dad?'

'Arthur went to Australia, and George died when he was ten,' he answered sadly, and a tear appeared in the corner of his eye. I had tears flowing from my own and I couldn't ask him anything else. We were both upset but I hoped he would tell me more some other time.

'Now think what I've told you and be kind to your gran. And you'd better clear the table and get up to bed before she or Mum come home.'

I kissed his cheek after fetching him his tea and wished him good-night. Frankie and Liza were still out playing so, as I had the bedroom to myself, I decided to say a private prayer. I prayed, 'Dear Lord, please find my Dad's brother and Father for Granny.' I also asked Him to make her better and help her mend her ways, then I crawled into bed and cried as I tried to picture my grandfather and piece together what Dad had said, but I was too young to grasp what it all meant.

By the following morning I'd forgotten the previous evening; it was Dad's pay night and he gave us each a penny to buy sweets with.

Dad and Granny must have settled their differences because they seemed to be in a better mood when we sat down to breakfast. Mary and Jack had already left for work when there was a loud knock on the door.

Mum jumped up from the table exclaiming loudly, 'Now who can that be this time a mornin'? Bloody pest, whoever it is.'

'Well, go an' see,'' Dad told her.

Shrugging her shoulders, she shuffled to the window and lifted the curtain to peer out. 'It's Mrs Nelson, Sam.'

'Well, call her in then, don't leave her standing there.'

Now Mum was a real artist, she could change her mood whenever it suited her. She opened the door and greeted Mrs Nelson cheerily, 'Good mornin', Mrs Nelson. An' 'ow are yer? Come in.'

As she came in Granny called out, 'An' who's Mrs Nelson?'

'I don't think yer know 'er, 'Annah. This is the kind lady what organises trips an' outin's.'

'Oh,' said Granny, and carried on munching her toast with toothless gums.

Mrs Nelson lived over near the churchyard and did a lot of work for local charities. She was also better off than most and helped those in need. She was small and round as a barrel.

'Good morning, everybody,' she bellowed to us in her deep, manly-sounding voice.

We all returned the greeting, except Granny who looked up and merely grunted. Dad drew up my brother's chair and wiped it with his newspaper.

'Please sit down,' he said.

Mum smiled at her and asked if she'd like a cup of tea, 'just med it 'ot'.

'No thank you, I carn't stay. I have more calls to make.'

'Suit yerself,' Gran piped up, but Mrs Nelson ignored her.

'Would any of you be interested enough to go hop-picking for a few days in the country? I believe the change and the fresh air will do the children good while they're away from school. Transport's laid on and meals and sleeping accommodation's free.'

We all looked at each other, but I could see that Mum had already made up her mind. 'I'll 'ave ter let yer know,' she answered pleasantly. 'An' thank yer fer askin' us,' she added.

'I must have yer answer this evening at the latest,' Mrs Nelson told her, and then rolled out.

As soon as she'd gone, Mum turned to Dad, beaming all over her face. 'It'll do us the world of good. Don't yer think, Sam?'

'You can go, and the kids, but not me?'

'Well, yer carn't, can yer? You've got yer job ter goo to.'

Then, banging her mug on the table Granny exclaimed, 'An' who d'yer think's gonna look arta 'im an' me?'

'Now, now, Mother, don't worry.' Dad reassured her, patiently. 'Mary'll see to our needs. Anyway, it'll do us good to have a change.'

'Yes, you can come too, 'Annah. You can earn as well as mek yerself useful.'

Granny mumbled under her breath, but Mum ignored her and rushed out of the house without stopping to take off her apron or put Dad's cap on.

'I shan't be long. I'm gooin' ter tell Mrs Nelson we're gooin',' she called back over her shoulder.

While she was out Dad gave us three a lecture. 'Mind yer manners, and don't forget to address the farmer as "sir", and no climbing trees or scrumping apples. Anyway, I don't have to tell you how to behave. Yer mum and granny'll see to that. And, you, Katie, if you don't like it, just write me a note and I'll fetch you back.'

'Yes, Dad. But I wish you were coming.'

'Some other time. Anyhow, I might jump on the train and come and see how you're all getting along. The country air will put some colour in all yer cheeks. Now be off and play, the three of yer, while I have a talk to yer gran.'

He didn't seem too cheerful. In fact he looked a bit down in the mouth as we ran out. We rushed along the yard to tell the other kids we were going hop-picking with them. They'd all been before, either potato-, pea- or hop-picking, but this was a new experience for us. I used to envy the kids when they went

away each summer and returned with lovely brown com-
plexions. They always bragged about what good holidays
they'd had.

All our neighbours and their kids were busy as bees, dodg-
ing from place to place, getting the clothes off the line and
fetching their buckets and bowls from the wash-house. Everything in our district was done on the spur of the moment; you
were never given a date. It was 'make up yer mind' or 'it's now
or never'. That was why Mum dashed out of the house the way
she did. However, we weren't sure whether we were going or
not until we heard Mum call us indoors to tell us we'd have to
start getting things together for ten o'clock in the morning.

'She might have given yer more time,' Dad said.

'She couldn't, Sam,' Mum replied, 'Mr and Mrs Goode 'ad
a bad cold an' she 'ad ter 'ave somebody ter fill their places.'

'Oh, I see, a makeshift. Well I hope yer know what yer
doing. And I'm warning you – look after them kids!'

And so with those sharp words Dad went out, slamming the
door behind him. Mum began at once snatching down the
clean clothes from the line around the room and giving out
orders to us to fold up what we needed.

'Come on, 'Annah, get a move on,' she shouted at Gran,
who was trying to do her best but badly.

'Oh, back-peddle!' Granny shouted back, and threw down
the towel she was trying to fold and stormed upstairs. Mum
retrieved the towel and threw it to Liza.

'Silly ol' fool. I s'pose she'll tell yer dad I've bin on to 'er
agen. Mek a cup of tea an' tek it up to 'er, Frankie.'

While Frankie put the kettle on to boil Mum handed me the
list Mrs Nelson had provided, with all the instructions printed
on it. First on the list was a towel, followed by soap, clean
clothes, cups, frying-pan, bucket, bowl and other articles that
we'd need. And underlined at the bottom was 'NO PETS, CATS
OR DOGS'. We were happy tying labels on each article with
string to identify them as ours. Just as we were doing this,
Granny came downstairs.

'I thought we goin' 'op-picking!' she said when she saw the
jumble of utensils on the floor. 'I ain't carryin' none of them,'

she added, pointing to the bucket and bowl.

'Don't worry yerself, Granny. The kids will carry 'em.'

Just as that moment Mrs Taylor called in the door. 'What time are we going, Polly?'

'Ten o'clock in the mornin', prompt. An' if yow ain't ready, Mrs Nelson said she'll leave yer be'ind,' Mum replied.

'We'll be ready.' She ran off to tell the others.

While us children were doing our best to help, Mum was losing patience with Granny. She wanted to wear her uniform and take the tambourine along too. But after sharp words, Granny got her way. I managed to smuggle Topsey inside the bucket and covered her with Liza's clean knickers. When everything was ready and pushed into a corner for us to pick up next morning, Mum flopped down into her armchair.

'I'm done in,' she puffed.

Just then Dad and Mary came in. I could see Mary was upset and so could Mum. 'What's the matter with yow?'

'Nothing's the matter with me,' Mary answered. But she glared at Mum. 'It's what's the matter with you. Dad says you're taking the kids hop-picking. You must be mad. It's no place for them.'

'Now, now, Mary,' Dad said calmly, 'It's all arranged, so calm down. Anyhow, I'll be able to get a bit of peace when they're gone.'

'They won't like it, Dad. They'll soon want to come back.'

'If they do, Katie will write and let me know. Now let's have something to eat. I don't want to hear any more about it.'

But Mary wouldn't have any supper. She gave Mum one last frozen stare and flounced up to bed. Frankie, Liza and I ate our pig's trotter and followed her. Mum was not the only one 'done in' and we soon fell asleep.

Dad, Mary and Jack had left the house early before Mum called us downstairs.

'Come on, get a move on. An' yow, 'Annah. Unless yer want ter stay be'ind.'

We jumped down the stairs two at a time. A few minutes later Granny came down already dressed in her uniform and bonnet with her tambourine clutched in her hand.

'I said I'd wear 'em, dain't I, Polly?' She grinned, and gave Frankie a tap on his head with the instrument. Mum didn't answer but Frankie yelled, 'Save it for the trip, Granny, we'll need a bit of community singing.'

We each had something to carry. I hung on to the basket and Frankie and Liza carried the tin bowl and the other odds and ends. Granny, true to her word, just carried the tambourine. We had our mugs tied with string round our necks. We each had the labels I'd written round our necks as well, in case we lost them.

After Mum had taken a last look around to see if we'd forgotten anything we were ready to join the others in the yard to wait for the cart to pick us up. With us was Mrs Taylor and the little twins, Joey and Harry, wearing their everyday suits which had been starched and mangled. Mrs Buckley was dressed up to kill in her dusty, black velvet coat with a hat that looked more like a plate of withered fruit. Every time she moved her head, I thought it would fall off. She had her eldest girl and boy with her who were busy scratching their heads. Then there was Mrs Jones and 'Pig's Pudding Face', her son. She was gossiping with Mrs Phipps who was one of Granny's neighbours. She kept getting out of line to show off her moth-eaten fur coat which she always wore on special occasions, no matter what the weather. This day promised to be hot, the sun was already shining and Mum saw an opportunity to get in a dig.

'Where yer think yer gooin', ter the North Pole?'

They all turned to stare at Mrs Phipps's coat, but she threw her head back proudly and breathed defiance.

'It's real skunk!'

'Smell's like it, an' all,' Mum shouted back in triumph, and held her nose.

'Yer only jealous!'

'Jealous? Of that? I wouldn't be seen dead in it.'

Just then Mrs Nelson intervened. 'Now then, you two!' she yelled out like a sergeant-major. 'Get in line, all of yer, and let's have some order!'

But they went on pushing and shoving although after a bit Mum's temper cooled off and she helped Mrs Nelson form some sort of straight line. Granny helped too by tapping the kids' heads with her tambourine and shouting, 'Get in line, little soldiers, get in line.'

Mum smiled at Granny and said, 'That's come in useful after all.'

Then Mrs Nelson spotted little Billy Bumpham and Maggie. She hadn't noticed him before, as he was hidden from view behind Maggie's large, battered and well-worn picture hat.

'In line, you,' she bawled, but when he didn't move she grabbed hold of his shoulders and shook him. As she did so his little terrier jumped out from under his coat where he'd hidden it.

'Didn't you read the list I gave out? No livestock!'

' 'E carn't read. Please let 'im tek 'is little dog,' Maggie pleaded.

'No. *You* know the rules even if 'e carn't read.'

As she walked to the front, Billy came running forward with the dog in his arms. 'Can I tek 'im?' he pleaded, pushing the dog into her face. 'Look, 'e's a nice little dog. Ain't yer, Rags? 'E'll be no trouble I'll promise yer.'

'I'm sorry. No.' She'd calmed down by now and told him that there were two sheep-dogs on the farm.

'You wouldn't like them to eat him for their supper now, would you?' she said kindly, but Maggie shook her fist and shouted, 'Well, if Rags ain't gooin', we ain't gooin'.'

'Please yourselves,' replied Mrs Nelson as Maggie and Billy walked off.

Everybody was feeling a bit down in the mouth by now because we all knew Billy would have entertained us after his fashion. Mum and Granny pushed everyone closer together and got us three to the front of the queue so that we'd get in the cart first. Just then we saw two shire horses pulling a farmer's cart down the street. I wondered how we were all going to get in but we did, with a squeeze. Mrs Nelson urged us to hurry and the driver dismounted from his high perch and tied the reins to a lamp post. He looked a typical farmer with a old dusty cap, corduroy trousers, a fat face and wiry, grey hair like a halo. He gave a jolly laugh and scratched his head as he spoke to us.

'Well, what a motley crew.'

He dropped the back end of the cart which looked like one I'd seen in a book describing the French Revolution. Some sat on the floor, some stood. It smelled like a pigsty and he apologised for not having had time to clean it out. I don't think any of us minded much really. We were all too happy to be on our way to the country. Granny was the last on board and stood looking at the cart sniffing.

'I ain't gooin' in theea,' she protested to the driver.

'Well, by the look of yer, you'd better sit up front with me.'

This pleased Granny. She beamed, but when she tried to climb up, she slipped backwards.

'Let me help,' the driver said, and got down to assist her.

'I can help meself up,' she snapped back.

Everyone was tittering as they watched her capers. Several times she tried to lift herself up into the passenger's seat, but failed.

'Come along, Grandma, we'll be here all day,' he said, getting behind her and heaving her bottom up with his shoulder. Eventually she flopped on the seat, and the farmer got back into the driver's seat. Granny gave him a dirty look for pushing her that way, but he just sat there gathering the reins and the whip.

At last we began to move. The rest of the people in the yard waved us goodbye and shouted ' 'Ave a good time,' and 'We'll look after yer animals,' and we in turn waved and shouted our farewells. By the time we'd reached the end of the street we'd begun to sing, even Liza. And Mum only put her hand on her shoulder and said, 'Yer'll 'ave ter yell, I'ain't gooin' back for no gob-stoppers.' Everyone seemed happy, even Granny who was banging her tambourine. As we passed the Golden Cup the draymen rolling the barrels off the drays turned and waved, and the shopkeepers swilling the pavements stopped to cheer us on our way. Even our local bobby turned to smile as we sang merrily along into the unknown.

It seemed hours before we saw any country lanes or green fields and, when we did, I thought it was a wonderful sight. I wished I could go on riding forever. However, our journey nearly ended in tragedy. As the horses trotted along, they relieved themselves and Mrs Phipps remarked what a waste it was and how she could have done with that on her window box. At this, Granny turned round from her high seat to register her disapproval and was only just saved from falling into the road by the driver grabbing her coat. He pulled the horses up and after seeing that Granny was all right he climbed down to retrieve her tambourine, mumbling grumpily all the while.

By this time we were getting restless. Most of us thought it was time we got down to stretch our legs, or that was what we said! However, the driver wouldn't stop till we reached a water trough where we could water the horses. Luckily we rounded a bend and came upon a public house which had a trough outside. The farmer spurred the horses on with the whip which made Granny hold on for dear life, because when the horses saw the water glistening in the sunlight they broke into a gallop, throwing us all on top of each other. Mrs Phipps and Mrs Jones swore at the driver when he came round to unfasten the chain, but he ignored then and dropped the side of the cart for us to tumble out, much relieved, or about to be! The little twins began to bawl as they'd wet their trousers but nobody paid them any heed. They were too concerned to rush behind a hedge to do what nature intended. Granny, I noticed, looked down at us in disgust but even she had to join us eventually. I saw the driver glance back and indicate to the boys to follow him into the inn, but they couldn't wait either, and peed up the wheel of the cart. When our immediate needs, had been satisfied we stood around on the grass verge waiting for the farmer to come back. It wasn't long before I saw him returning, carrying a large enamel jug.

'Get this down yer!' he cried, and handed us the jug filled with cider. 'Then let's be going.'

Mum was the first to drink. Then the other women followed and finally it was the turn of us children. I noticed that the farmer didn't give the jug to Granny who was staring hard at him all the while. We kids unfastened our mugs from round our necks and had them half-filled in turn, but when Frankie's had been filled Granny snatched the remains of the cider from his hand and, pointing at her Salvation Army uniform, said angrily, 'Don't let these fool yer, mista. I've gotta swolla as well!'

And with that she emptied the rest of the jug.

Frankie was told to take the jug back to the inn and when he returned we were pushed back into the cart and Granny was once more heaved up next to the driver; and so we continued our long, cramped journey. I was hot, hungry and drowsy and before long I began to nod but I couldn't sleep. I was restless like everyone else. Joey, one of the twins, was tugging at his mother's skirt.

'I wants me titty. I'm 'ungry,' he protested.

'Later,' his mum snapped back.

'Gi' 'im some an' shut 'im up,' Mrs Buckley retorted.

Everyone was getting on each other's nerves. I looked down at Mum dozing on the floor with Liza's head in her lap, thankful that, for a change, she wasn't interfering with me. Then Mrs Taylor managed to squeeze down between Mum and Mrs Jones and, pulling the twins towards her, exposed her breasts for all to see. Harry decided he wanted some too and she lay there he and Joey helped themselves to whatever they could get. It was a pitiful sight to behold. There was nothing there to satisfy them, but they sucked away and hoped. After this slight comfort they fell asleep.

After a while everybody had dozed off, doubtless suffering from the effects of the cider. I strained to keep awake, because I was inquisitive to know what was happening and where we were going. After a while the driver turned the horses sharply to the left and they broke into a trot and we rocked from side to side. I held on to the open lathes until the driver pulled the horses to a dead stop and I could see we'd arrived at our destination. We were in a farmyard.

'We're here!' I screamed. 'We're here!'

There were ducks and chickens running in all directions to

avoid the rattling wheels of the cart. I noticed the pigs and cows in the field had stopped to stare, wondering, no doubt, what was happening. We all tumbled out of the cart, dishevelled, dirty and hungry, with an avalanche of tin bowls, mugs and buckets. We were glad to roll out of the old jalopy after our tiresome journey. Mum, Granny, Mrs Buckley, Mrs Phipps and Mrs Taylor with the twins dragging behind made a dash to sit on a low wall that ran along the side of the farm-house. Frankie, Jonesy and Annie ran off to explore, with Liza tagging behind. I was too bewildered to move. I'd never seen a farmhouse or a farmyard – especially one with live pigs! The only ones I'd seen were dead ones hanging outside the pork-butcher's shop. Then there were the cows, which I was pleased to see were in the distance because I was more afraid of them than I was of the horses. I watched the driver lead the horses to the water trough, then he went off across the field to look for the farmer. I was fascinated by everything. I spotted a water pump and realised how thirsty I was. I ran towards it, took the mug from round my neck and pumped for dear life. But when it came, the water gushed out so quickly that I was soaked to the skin. I put the mug on the ground and held my head under the tap so that trickles ran into my mouth. It tasted like wine. When I'd had enough I pumped again and again until the stone basin was full. Then, taking off my woollen stockings and clogs I stood in the water, happily bathing my feet.

I looked round to see if Mum was watching but everybody was fanning each other with their hats and paying me no atten-tion. I was so happy jumping up and down in that cool, clean water that I didn't notice two black and white sheep-dogs and several ducks waddling towards me, followed by a lame pig. They'd decided that they were thirsty too. When I saw them I hopped out of the basin, afraid of what they might do to me, but they were friendly enough and seemed more interested in drinking than they were in me. So I helped them and pumped some more. Then suddenly they scattered. They'd seen the farmer and our driver coming towards us. I had no time to dry my feet or put my stockings and clogs on before Mum came running towards me.

'Goo an' find yer brother an' Liza!' she shouted, and pushed me along.

I ran down the yard. The cobblestones were hot and covered with the muck of farm animals, and slipped as I tried to find the clear spots to put my feet on. When I eventually got to the end of the lane, I saw Frankie and the rest coming along.

'Come on, you lot!' I yelled. 'Mum's sent me for yer. The farmer's here an' yer know what that means.'

But they weren't interested in what I was saying. They were only interested in telling me where to go scrumping later!

10
Our First Day in the Country

We all gathered round the farmer to hear our instructions. I realised from the likeness that he and our driver were brothers. Later, we found out that the driver had a farm a mile down the road. The farmer introduced himself as Farmer Onions which caused some tittering amongst the boys. Mum soon put a stop to that by giving them one of her black looks and raising her hand. But it didn't fall because the farmer gave a warning glance and told us to go and wash ourselves before going to the kitchen.

I'd never seen them move so quickly. We all took turns pumping, but most of them only splashed their faces. Granny was last but she was too busy shooing away the ducks to have much of a wash. Master Harry, Farmer Onions's brother, came over and told us we would find his brother a good man to work for if we did as we were told. However, he said his wife was a tartar who we ought to steer clear of. With that, he gathered his horse and cart and went on his way. We didn't see him until a month later under very different circumstances.

Farmer Onions emerged from the house just then and told us our meal was ready. We followed him into the kitchen where the first thing we saw was a large, stony-faced woman of middle age staring through us all as if we weren't there. But she couldn't outface Mum who went boldly up to her and, putting on her best tone of voice with aitches in the wrong places, said, 'Good hafternoon, Mrs Honions.'

Jonesy started to giggle. 'What's the matter with 'er? Showing off agen? Silly old fool.'

His answer was a resounding slap across his face from his mother. Mrs Onions said nothing, but her eyes spoke volumes. She beckoned us to follow her into a larger kitchen where we could smell bread baking. I glanced around and saw several hams and strings of onions hanging from the ceiling. The shelves around the kitchen were full of all kinds of stone jars of homemade jams, honey and preserves, labelled with dates written on. There were slabs of cheese and butter and lots of other good things to eat. In the middle of the red-tiled floor stood a white wooden table with cheese scones, chunks of new bread, butter, pickled onions, cakes and buns together with a large jug of cider. We stood drooling as we waited for the word to start. First, Mrs Onions dragged a long wooden form from beside the wall and gave the boys an icy stare. They understood and jumped to help her. At last in a gruff voice she spoke.

'Be yer gypsies?'

'No, we ain't!' piped up Granny and gave her a filthy look.

'Well, whatever yer be, I hope yer be better than the others we've had here.'

We all wished she'd hurry up and tell us to sit down and eat, but Granny would have the last word.

'What yer staring at? Me uniform? Or me? 'Cos I'm as good yow any time!'

'Now, now, 'Annah. Mrs Onions is only being kind,' Mum chimed in.

Mrs Onions said no more but beckoned us to be seated and left us to help ourselves.

'An' about time too,' Granny said ungratefully.

We all made a mad dash for the food. We didn't even wait to sit down. We were ravenous, for we hadn't eaten all day and it was now late afternoon. We soon made up for lost time, though. What we couldn't eat we filled our pockets with for later. Mrs Taylor even found room for some down the twins' trousers.

Shortly after we'd cleared the table, except for a few crumbs. Mrs Onions came back carrying a large enamel jug of warm milk, straight from the cow. It was delicious. I'd never tasted anything like it before, neither had the twins. Their mother had to take it away from them when she thought they'd had enough, but they wouldn't let go until she had given them a couple of smacks. The farmer's wife looked on and frowned as she stood beside the table with her arms folded across her heavy bosom.

'Well if yer be ready, farmer is outside waiting to give ye all the instructions.'

We all filed out. I was fascinated by the kitchen and the food and because I was looking round I was the last to leave. Just as I was going through the door I turned round and looked into that stern face and said, 'Thank you, Mrs Onions,' and ran out scared.

The farmer gathered us altogether and asked us all if we'd had enough to eat.

'Yes, sir. Thank you, sir,' we chorused.

'Now it's too late to go picking tonight so I want each of yer to take a sack, and two for you,' he said, pointing to Mrs Taylor who had the twins. 'Then follow me.'

We picked up our sacks from a pile that stood against a wall and followed behind. Frankie and I looked at each other wondering where he was taking us. We had the idea we'd be sleeping on the logs in the farmhouse, but he was leading us to a large barn across the meadow. Inside it was very warm and stuffy. There was only one small window to let in the light, which was dusty and dirty and covered with cobwebs. At the top end of the barn were piles of clean straw, a broom and a long, heavy rake. There was also a clock and a ladder which hung from hooks on the wall. Overhead was a loft with more hay and straw.

'Now, Sunny Jims,' the farmer yelled out to Frankie and Jonesy, 'get the broom and clear a space for yer mothers and fill yer bags with straw.'

They fetched the broom and swept the dust from the stone floor into the corner while the others began filling their sacks. We were bustling about merrily until Granny turned to the farmer.

'What's the bags gotta be filled for?'

'They're yer sleeping bags to sleep on,' He snapped. 'An' that's where yer sleep!' he added, pointing to the bare floor and snatching the broom from Jonesy who was leaning on it like a crutch. But Granny grabbed it from him at once.

'I ain't sleepin' on no straw. I'm gooin' 'ome.'

'Please yerself, old woman,' he answered, and walked out and left us to our fate.

This was our first disappointment. We all thought we were to sleep in the house but we were a long way from the farmhouse and miles away from home. I was getting homesick already. I wanted to see Mary, Jack and my dad and all my friends I had left behind. This was the first time in my life I'd been away from home. But I tried not to dwell on these thoughts and busied myself helping people fill their sacks. It was too light to sleep, although Mrs Taylor had already bedded the twins down, fully clothed, and they were soon asleep. I sat on my straw bed beside them and remembered what Dad said before we left.

'Yes,' I said to myself. 'I'll write tonight when they're all asleep and I can post it in the morning.'

Suddenly I heard Granny throw her tambourine at a mouse that scurried across the corner where the rubbish had been swept.

'I never ought to 'a' come,' she sobbed.

Mrs Jones and Mrs Phipps went over to her and tried to comfort her, but she pushed them away.

'It's all yower fault. Yower used ter this. I ain't!'

They shrugged and left her to it, but Mum managed to calm her down by telling her that things would seem better in the morning and that the country air would do us all good. I hoped so too. However, as it turned out things didn't get better. In fact they got worse from that night onwards. By this time it was six o'clock by the dusty clock on the wall and the sun still hadn't set. We'd all been so busy picking out our places to bed down that we'd forgotten we still had our hidden surplus food. Then Mum took charge and called us together, all except Granny, who was snoring loudly.

'Now,' Mum began, sitting on an upturned bucket, 'I want yer all ter be'ave yerselves, an' let's 'ave no mower arguments.'

I smiled to myself for it was always Mum who started the arguments and the present occasion was no exception. She stood up and went across to Mrs Phipps and Mrs Jones who were always in league together.

'I wanta ask yow two what 'appens now?'

'Whatya mean, Polly?' returned Mrs Phipps.

'Yow know what I mean!' Mum flared. 'Yow've both bin 'op-pickin' before, ain't yer?'

'Yes, but not on this farm,' answered Mrs Jones meekly.

'But yer know the ropes, don't yer?' Mum snapped angrily. 'What I mean is, when do we start eatin'? An' 'ow do we get our grub?'

'The farmer will tell yer that when he wakes us up in the mornin'. I know we'll 'ave ter mek our own tea an' buy our vittles from the stores.'

'What with?' Mum interrupted sharply, losing her temper.

'With the money we earn pickin' the 'ops,' Mrs Jones yelled back equally annoyed. 'An' if yer wanta know any mower ask the farmer!'

Mum cooled down for a while, but not for long.

'Don't we get any grub from the farm'ouse?'

'Oh, no,' Mrs Phipps replied. 'Only yer first meal, what we've already 'ad.'

Mum looked amazed. So did Mrs Taylor. Then all of a sudden Mum burst forth, hands on hips.

'Then in that case yer betta empty yer pockets an' let me 'ave the grub yow all 'elped yerselves to.'

'What d'yow want it for?' Mrs Phipps ventured meekly.

'What d'I want it for?' Mum was getting angrier. 'It's to keep it safe in case we goo 'ungry.'

'Why carn't we keep it?' asked Mrs Buckley, who'd been quiet until now.

112

'No! An' above all not yow!' Mum snapped back.

'Oh, very well,' she grumbled. And she began to empty her pockets.

'An' the other one!' Mum said waiting beside her.

Reluctantly she emptied them both and so did Mrs Jones and Mrs Phipps, for they were really afraid of Mum. We were hoping she'd let us keep ours, but she didn't wait to ask us; She helped herself. When she'd collected the broken buns, cakes and lumps of cheese, she placed them on a towel which she'd laid on the floor. Then Mrs Phipps piped up, 'What about Mrs Taylor and 'Annah?'

'Gimme time. I'm coming to them next,' Mum snapped back.

She went across to Granny who was still snoring on her straw bed. She bent down quietly to see if she was really asleep. Then, she lifted Granny's frock and from the secret pockets sewn inside she took lumps of cheese, buns, cakes and a lump of butter. Granny had good pickings. I sat with bated breath in case Granny woke up and caught Mum robbing her of her treasures. However, Mum took everything and then pulled down Granny's frock, and Granny still continued snoring. Then Mrs Taylor handed Mum her share but Mum told her to keep it.

'Yow keep yowers. Yer'll need it fer the babbies.'

'Thank yer, Polly,' she replied and after putting the food in a box, she lay down beside the twins.

Then Mum gave Granny a couple of pokes and rolled her on to her side to stop her from snoring. It didn't work for long.

Mrs Taylor was a meek and mild woman and always fell in with other people's plans whether they suited her or not. So Mum knew she'd have no trouble there. Freddie and Annie Buckley were timid too, and scared of their mum and ours, but when they were out with us they let themselves go. However, I couldn't abide Jonesy or Pig's Pudding Face. He was cheeky and always swearing. The twins were different, though. I loved them. They were only a little over three years old and although Joey was bow-legged and Harry was crosss-eyed I took them nearly everywhere with me.

113

We pushed all our utensils into a corner until we'd sorted ourselves out and, while I was shaking out the worn, grey army blankets to cover us, everyone shook out their straw beds.

'Frankie, bring me that bucket an' bowl,' called Mum.

Suddenly I thought of Topsey hidden beneath the clean knickers inside the bucket. Before Mum saw me I snatched her out but then Jonesy grabbed the bucket and bowl and threw them across the floor to Mum. They clattered to her feet and Jonesy shouted, ' 'Ere y'are, yer greedy old sod!'

At this Frankie gave him such a hard clout that he fell over backwards, nearly landing on top of Granny.

'Shut yer mouth, Pig's Pudding Face!'

This started a wrestling match. His mother didn't take an eyeful of notice, but Mum came to the rescue at once and parted them. As she did so, she gave Jonesy a sly dig in the ribs with her elbow.

'That's fer yer cheek,' she hissed in his ear.

Just then Granny woke up and moaned about getting no sleep and the twins began to cry. I lay down beside them and gave them my Topsey to hug it and it wasn't long before they dropped off to sleep again. I sat up and watched Mum untie the bowl from the bucket. All eyes were on her. She was in a real temper and doing things at double pace. She threw the clean knickers across to Liza who could take the credit for thinking of packing them. Then she gathered all the broken food together and rolled it up in a towel, placed it in the bowl and stood the bowl in a corner of the barn, away from us all. She took the bucket and placed it upside down over the bowl of food. Next she marched off into the yard and returned a few minutes later with the biggest and heaviest stone she could carry. This she dropped heavily on top of the bucket. Then she slapped her hands together with satisfaction.

'That'll keep the grub safe from the rats until we need it.'

We all smiled at Mum's performance, and she smiled too when she surveyed her handiwork.

'Now I think we all gotta goo out an' explore. It's too light yet an' too early ter get ter bed.'

Granny was first to respond, for she was wide awake now.

'Yow ain't leavin' me be'ind.'

Mrs Taylor said she couldn't leave the twins in case the rats nibbled them.

'Rats don't eat everything that's moovin',' Granny replied. 'Any'ow, what's the other kids dooin'? Carn't they mind 'em?'

So us kids were left behind to look after them. In any case we all knew where our mums were going to 'explore'. They were looking for the nearest pub which, as it turned out, was the one our driver had stopped at earlier, the Pig and Whistle.

Granny, still clutching her tambourine, marched out on Mum's arm. I'd hoped she'd leave it behind so that I could play with it and use it to scare the rats and mice away. But I had to settle for a rake to shake at them. Mrs Jones and Mrs Phipps followed them out with their heads together and fell in step with Mrs Buckley and Mrs Taylor. They soon caught Mum and Granny up and I watched them all go arm in arm down the lane and out of sight. After they'd gone the boys decided they were going to scrump some more apples. This left only Liza, the twins and myself. So Liza and I decided to look around outside while the twins were asleep. It was still very light. According to the clock, it was seven o'clock, so there was plenty of time to explore.

When we got outside we noticed a large shed with a stove-pipe coming out of the roof. We looked inside and saw a rusty, round iron stove in the middle of the floor. Against the wall was an old, worn, marble-topped table and an earthenware sink like ours at home. In the opposite corner were a lot of baskets piled one on top of the other. There was dust and bits of straw everywhere. Someone had been here recently, as the kettle on the stove was still warm and there were half-burnt pieces of wood in the tin at the bottom.

'This must be the place where we've got to cook our meals,' I said to Liza.

'Well, let's clean it up,' she replied.

Liza began sweeping and I looked around and found a rusty tin bowl behind some baskets, and a wet rag, and then ran down the yard to the pump. I kept my eyes on the cows across the meadow while I filled the bowl and then hurried back. When we'd finished sweeping the dust away, we decided we'd better look for Frankie and the others. However, I remembered the twins and decided to stay with them while Liza went off. The twins were still sleeping, and I was scared to be left on my own, and was startled by noises like the rustle of Woodbine packets in the rubbish so it was with great relief that I heard Frankie and the rest running along the gravel path. I was never so happy to see them and threw my arms round my brother and burst into tears.

'What yer cryin' for?' he asked. 'Look what I brought yer.'

I wiped my eyes on the back of my hand and watched him pull up his gansey to reveal several red, waxy apples. His pockets were bulging fit to burst. The others had plenty too, which they shared out. What we couldn't eat there and then we hid under our straw beds for later.

By this time it was beginning to grow darker. The night was very warm and still, and Liza said she thought we were in for a storm. We searched around and found a piece of candle but we had no matches. I started to get nervous again and imagined all sorts of things that could happen to us. Then I heard the sound of heavy footsteps on the path outside. I crouched behind Frankie who'd taken hold of a rake in readiness. At that moment a deep voice boomed out, and into the barn strode the farmer.

'No need to be afraid of me. I've brought you a lamp.'

We watched him light it and climb the ladder to fix it high on the wall, out of reach. Then he asked where our mothers were.

'Gone for a walk,' Frankie replied quickly.

'Well, Sunny Jims, tell yer mums or whoever's in charge, there's only enough paraffin in the lamp to last another two hours. See you're all up early in the morning,' he said abruptly. He paused as he went off and called back, 'I see someone's been busy in the shed next door. And mind yer all behave until yer mums get back.' Then off he went into the darkness.

We could only just see our beds in the dim light. I glanced

116

up at the clock again. It said five past nine and Frankie, Liza, Annie and Jonesy had all stretched out for the night, fully clothed. I was hoping and praying Mum and the others would return soon. I was so afraid I dared not go near the door to listen for them now that the others had gone to sleep. So after a while, tired of listening for any kind of sound outside, I lay down beside the twins hugging Topsey for comfort. As I nodded in the dim light, all I could hear was the tick of the clock and the rustle of paper beneath the rubbish. I suppose I dozed off at last. Suddenly I was awake again, and could hear voices in the distance. Plucking up courage, I got up and felt my way quietly to the door. I opened it a little way and put my head outside into the darkness. To my great relief I heard Mum's voice singing above all the others.

'My ole man says folla the band', rang out, followed by a chorus of 'An' don't dilly-dally on the way.' I could hear Granny's tambourine distinctly, keeping the beat. They were all drunk; I could tell by the way they were all laughing. I'd been amused by their capers when I was younger, but now I was nearly ten years old, and I no longer found them funny. They all looked stupid, and I hated to see people like this, especially Mum.

I quickly rushed back inside the barn and lay on my straw bed, pretending to be asleep, because I knew if Mum found me awake she'd have pestered me with all kinds of questions and given me odd-jobs to do. I wasn't going to tell her how long the paraffin in the lamp would last. Fortunately, there were no arguments. They were all too drunk even to undress and they just picked their places and went to sleep.

Mum lay at the top end of the barn, Granny next, then Mrs Phipps, Mrs Jones and Jonesy, Mrs Buckley and Annie and Freddie, Frankie and Liza, Mrs Taylor and the twins, and finally me. It was very warm and stuffy and there seemed to be no air at all. I closed my eyes and tried to sleep but Mrs Taylor woke me up to look at the twins who were still asleep. Then she turned over on to her side and it was no long before she too was snoring. I wept. I felt so unhappy and miserable. I wanted to be home with my dad and Mary. Then I remembered what

117

Dad had said to me about writing. I determined to write a letter and with that thought in mind I felt better and, hugging Topsey, I fell asleep.

I was woken by a loud crash of thunder and several flashes of lightning which illuminated the whole barn. Mrs Phipps and Mrs Jones sprang up at once. Mrs Jones was evidently frightened because she ran round the barn crying and crossing herself.

'Mother of God, save us all!'

'Shut up, yer stupid fool. Yer wanta wake up all the rest?' yelled Mrs Phipps.

'Let's get some sleep! We gotta goo ter work in the mornin',' Mrs Buckley cried out and pulled Mrs Jones back on the bed.

Everybody was restless now. They tossed and turned but eventually when the thunder died away they all fell sound asleep again. Mum and Granny took up their snoring in contest where they'd left off and I lay back with an arm across the twins and tried to sleep. However, the storm returned with a vengeance. There was lightning and thunder, and hailstones that hit the corrugated roof so hard that I thought it would fall in. Mrs Taylor was wide awake now, and I was very happy to hear her voice.

'You afraid, Katie?'

'Yes,' I replied. And I meant it.

'Never mind. You'll feel betta in the mornin'.'

There was another loud crash and a third which seemed to shake the barn – at that point everybody woke up. I watched Mum between the flashes of lightning as she fumbled around for the candle and matches. Swearing, she lit the candle and placed it on the stone that stood on the bucket. Granny too was cursing and saying she wished she hadn't come. Mrs Phipps were feeling all over her body to find her sleeping pills.

'I know I 'ad 'em. Yow seen 'em, Mrs Buckley?'

'No! But I could do with one meself.'

'I'll gi' yer all one when I can find 'em. Then p'raps we can all get some sleep.'

'That's a good idea,' Mum said, and joined in the search.

Frankie and Liza got up and took the ladder down from the wall, propped it against the loft and climbed up into the darkness out of everybody's way. Then, after knocking the candle over and nearly setting fire to the straw, Mum found the bottle of sleeping pills.

'I'll tek charge of these,' Mum said. 'Or you might tek too many. Anybody like one?'

So Mrs Buckley had one, Mrs Jones followed suit and so did Mrs Phipps, but Granny refused. She said she wanted to 'die natural'.

Then Liza shouted down from the loft, 'Can I 'ave one?'

'I know what you'll get one of if yer don't goo back ter sleep!' Mum shouted back crossly.

Mrs Taylor didn't want one in case she was asleep when the twins needed her. Mrs Phipps was watching Mum hide the bottle down the front of her blouse but she couldn't argue with her because Mum's word was law. She stepped over everyone and blew out the candle and lay down once more. After a while the storm abated and all that I could hear was the sound of snoring once more. I lay there thinking about Dad and what I should put in the letter, and what with these things on my mind, the heat and the lack of air, I couldn't sleep until Mrs Taylor turned over and whispered that she'd open the barn door to let a little cool air in. I didn't answer, but she knew that I was awake. She opened the door a few inches and lay down again with a sigh. Soon she too was snoring and with the light breeze on my face I finally drifted into an exhausted sleep.

11
Settling In

It was just breaking dawn when I heard a cock crowing in the distance. I sat up and rubbed my eyes and looked up into two big brown doleful eyes looking down at me. I fell back and screamed for all I was worth, waking everybody. Mum was the first to my rescue, treading over everyone, before she could push the cow through the door. But it wouldn't leave. I clung to Mrs Taylor who was guarding the twins. She was as scared as I was. We stared, horrified, as Mum tried to get the cow to budge but it only glared at her and mooed loudly. I started to cry, trembling with fear.

'Shut yer blartin'!' Mum yelled, and began rolling up her sleeves as if she really meant business. 'I'll soon settle 'im.'

She wasn't afraid of the cow but nor was the cow afraid of her. They faced each other. Mum 'shoo-shooed', and the cow 'moo-mooed' back. They were holding quite a conversation but the cow had the advantage of size and with an extra loud moo it stepped closer. Mum ran back to the corner of the barn and grabbed a rake. By now the rest of us were giggling, but I didn't think there was anything to laugh about. I was too frightened of what the cow might do to her and me if she used the rake. Luckily, she didn't have the chance because just as she was about to attack, the barn door was flung wide to reveal the farmer standing there with a stout stick in his hand. Glaring angrily at Mum, he snatched the rake from her and bellowed, 'Cows won't hurt yer!'

Then he hit the beast hard on its rump and it backed slowly out to rejoin the others. The farmer looked around the barn and informed us gruffly that he'd lit the fire in the shed and told us we could get water from the pump and milk from the farm. The baskets for the hops were in the corner of the shed and we were expected in the field 'when yer ready'. With that he turned and stalked out.

Mum told me to follow him to make sure he was out of sight, then she really took over. She called the boys down from the loft and we got ready to leave. She gave us orders to pile up our straw beds on top of each other in the corner ready for the evening. By the time this task had been accomplished we were beginning to get fidgety for the toilet but no one seemed to know where one was. Little Jonesy was crossing his legs and Joey pulled the hem of his mother's dress and complained, 'Me wants a two-two.'

Frankie and Jonesy had already vanished after complaining of belly-ache, evidently the result of all the sour apples they'd eaten the previous evening. Mrs Taylor picked up the twins, one under each arm, and went outside. I followed. There, at the back of the barn, we found a long wooden shed which I hadn't noticed before. There was a door at each end of this structure with a wet cardboard notice on each which read 'MEN' and 'WOMEN'. These must be the toilets. I looked round to tell the boys but they were nowhere to be seen. So while Mrs Taylor was holding out each twin in turn over a piece of newspaper, I entered through the door marked 'WOMEN'. There was a stone floor covered with wet lime, the result of water leaking through the roof. From one end to the other was a long wooden seat in which were three round holes. Behind the seats was a tarpaulin sheet which, although I didn't realise it, parted the three holes on our side from the three holes on the other. Curious, I lifted the sheet to see what was behind it but I dropped it quickly with shock because what I saw were the two bare bottoms of Jonesy and my brother. They both turned round and, when they realised that it was me, burst out laughing. I went all hot and felt so ashamed. I ran out, nearly knocking Mrs Taylor over. She was on her way to dispose of the newspaper parcel. I watched as she disappeared through the door of the boys' side but I was too late to tell her. I waited to see what would happen, when all at once I heard Jonesy say in loud voice, 'Yer can come an' sit on the 'ole next to me if yer like.'

'Yer cheeky bleeda,' was her startled reply.

The next thing I heard was a loud slap. Then she chased him outside, still with his trousers round his ankles. Needless to say, he made his escape. I held my head with shame as Mrs Taylor came over to me.

'Come now, Katie.' She took my hand. 'There's nothing to be ashamed of. We've got to put up with what we find on a place like this.'

'I wish I was home,' was all I could say.

'I wish I could goo 'ome too. I wish we'd never come,' she answered sadly.

I told her I was going to write to my dad and tell him everything and that when he collected us perhaps she and the twins could come too.

'We'll see,' she whispered softly.

I liked Mrs Taylor. She was the only one who ever really talked to me and she'd helped me when I'd lost my clogs.

As we made our way back we could see the others waiting their turn. Mum was first as usual. She announced that she was closing the door and that they'd have to wait. However, Granny managed to squeeze past her sideways. At this further example of high-handedness, the others began to grumble. I felt very uncomfortable and hoped Mum and Granny would hurry. I couldn't see Liza or Annie anywhere and hopped from foot to foot.

Then Mrs Taylor whispered in my ear, 'You go through the men's door. I'll watch out fer yer.'

Reluctantly, I entered. I thought no one would see me but there, sitting on the same two holes as Frankie and Jonesy, were Liza and Annie. So I lost my embarrassment and dropped my bloomers and with great relief sat next to them on the vacant hole. They were giggling and whispering together but I didn't know what about until they stood down from the seat, pulled their bloomers up and then deliberately lifted the sheet and pointed to Mum and Granny sitting next door. But when Mum turned and saw them they dropped the flap and it swung against Mum and Granny's bare bottoms with a thwack. I sat there, afraid to move in case I was blamed. Meanwhile, Liza and Annie rushed outside. I could hear Mum after them. When I'd fastened my bloomers I ran out too. Liza was half-way across the meadow with Mum calling after her, 'I'll deal with yow later! Yer brazen little bugger!'

As Mum turned she saw Annie hiding behind her mother's skirts and she was promptly dragged out with cries and yelps. Granny began laying down the law to Annie's mum but she didn't bat an eyelid. Mum put Annie's head between her legs, pulled down her bloomers and gave her three hard slaps on her bare buttocks in front of all of us.

'Now, 'ow d'yer like everyone ter see yower bare bottom?' Annie went screaming to her mother.

'Serves yer right fer bein' cheeky. An' stop yer snivellin' or yer'll get some mower off me!' And she pushed Annie away.

At last the commotion died down and they got their turn in the toilet. We then went into the shed to wash and get something ready to eat. But before we could do this, Mum said we had to pool what little money we had. I gave the only penny I'd been saving for some sweets. Mrs Taylor said she'd only got the rent which had to be paid when she returned home, but she would willingly give some of that until they did. However, Mum restricted her levy to half a crown whilst the others placed a few coppers on the table. Granny hesitated to give her share until she saw Mum glaring at her, then she threw a shilling down on the table.

'An' I want it back!'

Altogether there was four shillings and twopence three farthings. Mum called Annie to her because I was busy washing little Joey, but Annie, remembering their recent confrontation, backed away. However her mother pushed her towards where Mum was sitting by the table.

'She ain't gooin' ter bite yer,' she snapped.

Mum gave Annie a pencil and paper and told her to write down what we wanted from the general stores down the lane.

' 'Alf a pound a cheese, 'alf a pound a marg, three loaves, an' don't forget the mek weights. A quarter a bacon, an' see it's lean. Two ounces a tea, a pound a sugar, an' a tin a 'andy brand.'

'What yer want tinned milk for when we can 'ave fresh from the farm'ouse?' Granny wanted to know.

'It's ter shove on the twins' dummies ter keep 'em quiet,' Mum snapped back and she began to count on her fingers how much the food would cost: but after getting herself into a muddle she pushed Annie away and called for me to reckon it up. I told her it all came to one shilling and three halfpence.

'That's right,' she answered, defying the others to deny her ability to add it up herself. But she hadn't a clue whether it was right or wrong: she could only trust to her fingers. I was still standing, waiting while she sat fumbling with the money in her lap as though she didn't want to part with it; then after a while she told me Annie could fetch the food while I went to the farmhouse for the milk. I didn't wait for any more orders.

Grabbing hold of the twins, I dragged them after me as I rushed out of the barn.

It was a lovely, warm, sunny morning and the cobbled path looked clean and fresh now that the heavy rain had washed all the animal dung away. I skipped along happily with the twins following closely behind. Turning round to check on them I saw Frankie and Jones at the water pump. I hoped the twins hadn't seen them, but they had, and Joey called out, ' 'Ello.' I shook him because I wanted to avoid the boys, but Frankie called me over. He looked rather shamefaced, no doubt remembering the toilet incident. I walked over to him.

'What yer want?'

'Here, take these apples and 'ide 'em.'

I took them and turned away. I put them down my bloomers but I hadn't gone more than a few yards when the elastic gave way and the apples rolled down into the gutter, I looked around for my brother but he had disappeared. Before I could pick them up I felt a tug at my frock and when I turned round the twins were trying to attract my attention to a little pig with a limp and some ducks approaching us. I became nervous again for I remembered what Granny used to say when we ate pigs' trotters at home.

'Kids who eat trotters or cows' meat are 'witched. An' animals are like elephants, they never forget.'

She often said she never ate meat of any kind but we knew she did if she thought no one was watching. She also used to frighten me with the story that cows tossed you in the air if you wore red drawers. As a result, I was terrified of almost any animal with four legs. With this in mind, I picked up one of the apples and threw it at the pig. It was a good aim and while the pig stopped to eat the missile I grabbed the twins and ran towards the farmhouse as fast as I could.

However, it didn't take the pig long to swallow the apple and come running after me for more. I quickly lifted the twins on to a wall and pushed their dummies into their mouths, and told them to sit still until I returned with the milk. Then I dashed off, only slackening my pace after I'd run some distance. When I looked back I could see the pig had dropped behind so, I reached the farmhouse safely. I knocked on the door, and the farmer's wife came almost at once.

'Please. My mum has sent me for some milk,' I said timidly.

She looked down at me and asked if I had something to put it in. I'd forgotten to bring any kind of vessel, so I told her Mum hadn't got a jug and would she please lend one. She disappeared into the dark depths of the kitchen and returned a few moments later with an enamel jug filled with milk, still warm from the cow.

'Here yer be,' she said, handing me the large jug. 'And tell yer mum to let me have the jug back.' She didn't seem to look as stern as when I had first seen her. She really smiled broadly and asked if I was getting on all right. I nodded, and then asked her boldly what was wrong with the little pig's trotter.

'Yer mean Hoppity. There's nothing wrong with his leg now, but he did cut it on some barbed wire. My little granddaughter plays with him sometimes and wraps a rag round it.'

'What for?'

'She thinks his leg still hurts and that's why he hops.'

'Is that why he's called Hoppity?'

'Yes. Now be off with yer before the milk gets cold,' she said, returning to her sharp manner. 'I'm busy.'

I thanked her for the jug and went off to pick up the twins but when I looked over to the wall they were nowhere to be seen, nor were the ducks and nor was Hoppity. I thought the worst. There was only one place to look: the pigsty. And that is where they were. They were sitting in the midst of the filth, still sucking their dummies and stroking Hoppity. I rushed in and hauled them out and dragged them across to the shed where I knew Mum would be waiting impatiently for the milk. But before we'd gone three strides Hoppity began to follow. I picked up one of the previously discarded apples and threw it at him but he merely swallowed it and continued to wobble after us. We ran and arrived back to find Mum in an awful temper. She scolded me for being so long but I knew it was hopeless trying to explain. I glanced across at Liza and could see from her red eyes that she'd had her punishment. I was lucky to have avoided a similar fate!

Mrs Taylor snatched the twins away from me and began to wash them down while the others sniffed the air. This didn't stop them continuing to eat their bacon sandwiches. Mum was cooking my pieces of bread in the bacon fat. Mrs Taylor filled the twins' titty bottles with the rest of the milk. I was surprised that they guzzled it so readily because I wasn't aware that they'd ever tasted cow's milk before. I thought it would be a good idea for us to have a cow, but I knew this was only wishful thinking. Anyway, where would we keep it? I knew Mum wouldn't keep it in the yard for the neighbours to help themselves, and it was probably as well we couldn't afford one because I always wore red flannelette bloomers.

When we'd all finished eating, the farmer came along with his horse and cart to take us to the hop field. The cart was similar to the one we'd come in, but larger, with plenty of room for us and all the baskets. The farmer threw the baskets in first and then told us to jump up after. We all climbed in one by one, except Granny. She wanted to ride up on top with the farmer, but he wouldn't hear of it and insisted that she had to ride with the rest. So after a few moans and groans Mum pulled her inside and they embarked on their first trip to pick hops.

It was decided between Mum and Mrs Taylor that Liza and I should stay behind to look after the twins. So we waved the others out of sight and returned to the shed to clean away the crocks. While we were busy, Liza told me how Mum had taken down her bloomers and smacked her bare bottom in front of everybody.

'Not in front of Frankie?' I said, shocked.

'Yes. And Jonesy,' she replied. 'They didn't even look away. They just laughed. But I'll get my own back when they return,' she said darkly.

I could see plainly that she was still upset but I was soon able to cheer her up when I told her about the twins and Hoppity.

'I'd forgotten until now about writing to Dad so while Joey and Harry were playing around on the floor, I turned to Liza and said, 'I don't like it here, do you, Liza?'

'No. I wish I could go home,' she answered.

Then I told her I was going to write to Dad to fetch us home.

'When?'

'Now. As soon as I can find the pencil and paper he gave me.'

After fumbling in my pockets I found the paper and envelope and a stub of pencil. While Liza was getting the twins to sleep, I began to write. My letter went something like this.

Dear Dad,

We are all very unhappy here. Will you come and fetch us home? Mum and Granny and Frankie and the rest have gone to the hop field and left Liza and me to look after Mrs Taylor's twins. Liza is trying to comfort them while I write this letter. Please, please fetch me back home or I shall run away. I'm afraid of the cows. One came in the barn this morning and if the farmer hadn't come in when he did, the cow would have tossed Mum in the air. And there's a little pig here called Hoppity and he follows me everywhere I go. So please come and fetch me home as soon as you can. I don't know this address, only that the farmer's name is Onions. Mrs Nelson will give you our address.

love, Katie

This was the first letter I'd ever written and I was hoping it sounded convincing. Liza read it and put in the envelope and addressed it.

'Where's the stamp?' she asked.

I fumbled around again in my pockets. Then I realised Dad hadn't given me one. 'Now we carn't post it,' I told Liza.

'Yes we can,' Liza said. 'But we'll have to take a chance whether Dad gets it or not.'

She held the envelope and in the top right-hand corner she pressed her wet, dirty thumb.

'There you are,' she said, smiling at her handiwork. 'The postman will think the stamps's fallen off. If he don't, Dad'll have to pay when he gets the letter.'

We were both pleased with this idea, and hoped it would work.

'We'd better not tell Mum you've written to Dad or we'll cop it,' she warned me.

'I'll have to, Liza. she'll find out soon enough.'

'Well, we'll wait until she's in a good mood before we decide, then maybe if she's had a few drinks . . .'

So we decided on our approach, gathered together Joey and Harry, and went off to post the letter in the letter-box outside the stores. We'd only gone as far as the toilets when Joey decided he wanted to go.

'Yow would, yer little pest,' Liza snapped and began to shake him.

'I want a two-two,' Harry joined in.

We both lost our patience then and pushed them into the lavatory, but they couldn't reach the seat and we had to help them. We took their ragged trousers down and held them over the holes. I had to put the letter in my pocket until Harry had finished. Then, as he was pulling his trousers back on, I saw that Liza was holding her nose and had released her grip on Joey. Quickly I grabbed him by the feet just as he was vanishing down the hole. Liza came to the rescue and we hauled him out just in time. I shudder to think what he would have looked or smelled like if he had fallen in. We started on our way again down the lane, then suddenly we looked at each other and burst out laughing, hysterically.

'Oh, what a calamity that would have been. He nearly went down the hole,' Liza giggled.

'Yes. And it could have been worse,' I answered.

At last we reached the collection box and I slipped the letter in. Then we gazed into the shop window. There was almost everything imaginable there to make your mouth water, or so it seemed – cakes, jam tarts and all kinds of sweets. But we hadn't got a halfpenny between us – at least we thought we hadn't until Joey said, 'Me got penny, Tatie. To buy yoo sweeties.'

We didn't bother to find out where he'd got it from, but grabbed it from him and entered the shop. Once in the stores, we had no hesitation in asking the lady behind the counter for two liquorice laces.

'Let's see the colour of your money first,' she said, peering accusingly at us.

Liza showed the penny and she promptly gave the two long strips of black liquorice. She glared at us all the while.

'Where yer from?'

'Onions's farm,' snapped Liza. 'An' we want a coupla bull's-eyes with the change.'

Bull's-eyes were what Mum called gob-stoppers, and gave to Liza when she tried to join in the singing. When we left the shop, the twins were chewing on the black strips and we followed behind sucking a bull's-eye each. I always liked these sweets because they lasted a long time. While we sucked them we took them out of our mouths now and again to observe their changing colour. So we left the shop a lot happier than when we entered. Liza and I skipped merrily down on the lane and the twins followed up behind with more liquorice around their mouths than in them.

It was a very hot day and the bad weather of the previous night had quite disappeared. We didn't know what to do or where to go, so Liza suggested we go exploring. We walked along the quiet lanes for about a mile and didn't meet a soul, only the cows in the fields. Soon the twins grew tired and decided that they'd had enough so down on the grass verge they flopped. I must say I was surprised Joey's little bowed legs had carried him that far. Liza and I wanted to go on, but we couldn't leave them behind to get lost. So we pick-a-backed them, but we soon wearied of this. They were small for their three and a half years, but they were still heavy if you tried to carry them as we were doing. We decided that we'd have to return to the barn. Just then we heard a lot of hammering and saw sparks flying overhead from somewhere nearby.

We sat the twins on the verge and told them to stay put. Then we went to investigate the noise. As we rounded the corner of the lane we saw a large, well-built, muscular man outside what we realised was the blacksmith's. He was hammering out a red-hot horseshoe on the anvil. The red sparks were shooting in every direction as he hammered out the metal. We didn't speak to him, and as he had his back to

us, he didn't see or hear us. We stood fascinated by his move-
ments and the sweat dripping from his body. After watching
for a while we remembered the twins and wandered back to
collect them and make our way back to the barn.

12
The Hop-pickers

After our long walk we were tired and beginning to feel
hungry. On top of that, we realised that we hadn't allowed for
the return journey. The twins were still sitting where we'd left
them, sucking on their dummies, which always conveniently
dangled from strings round their necks. We took them by the
hand but still had to carry them at intervals. Unfortunately, we
were too young to have much sense of direction, and instead of
keeping to the same lane, we must have turned off at some
point. All the lanes looked the same to us. There was nothing
but fields and meadows – not a house or a human being in
sight. Soon we were completely lost, afraid and on the verge of
tears. My clogs had rubbed holes in my stockings and made
blisters on my heels. Liza was complaining about the heat. We
decided to sit down by the wayside, remove our clogs and rest.
Perhaps someone would come along and show us the way. The
twins began to grizzle.

'Me is 'ungry, Tatie.'

'An' me's wet me trousers.'

Soon we were all in tears together. We were hungry, tired,
lost, and not a little miserable. We endeavoured to pacify the
twins with a lullaby but they continued to sob until eventually
they fell asleep. Then Liza decided to take a look to see what
was round the bend in the lane. I didn't want to be left
because I was still afraid the cows might come and I was
beginning to panic. Liza promised she wouldn't go far, but I
was determined not to be left alone. But Liza pointed to the
twins who were still sleeping and told me not to leave them.
They soon woke up though, they must have sensed we were

considering leaving them. Just as I got to my feet, they stirred. So it was impossible for me to leave. I stayed, but I was praying Liza wouldn't stray off for long.

While she was gone, I was more scared than ever. I was aware of every little sound and I imagined everything I heard was a cow or a pig that was about to pop out of the hedge. What would I do? 'Please, Lord,' I prayed out loud. The twins renewed their wailing and we hugged each other for comfort. I hummed a tune to them and they fell back to sleep and I dozed off myself after a while. I don't know how long the three of us slept, but we were awakened with a start by Liza's voice.

'Wake up! Look what I've got!'

I rubbed my eyes and rose to my feet and looked at what she was carrying in her pinafore. I could hardly believe my eyes. Her pinafore was full of rosy red apples. She must have been running because she was out of breath, but when I looked up the lane I could see no one had been chasing her.

'Where did yer get them from?'

'Shush,' she whispered. 'Never yer mind. Yer 'ungry, ain't yer? Well, eat.'

We all made absolute pigs of ourselves. Then, when we'd devoured the lot, we huddled together on the verge and slept. We must have been there for hours because the next thing I knew was a horse neighing and loud voices. Then somebody was shaking us.

'What yer all doin' 'ere? Wake up. Wake up, the pair on yer.'

I can't remember being so happy to see and hear my Mum bawling at me. Liza and I quickly got to our feet and the twins were snatched up by Mrs Taylor.

'Oh, my poor little babbies. Whatever are yer dooin' 'ere?'

But we were too relieved to answer her and we just gazed at Granny and the rest of the hop-pickers who were standing among the baskets on the cart. They all looked surprised to see us, even the farmer.

'Come on,' he called. 'Jump in, all of yer. I'm late already.'

So Mum pushed us roughly aboard the cart and told the farmer that she'd walk, and off she went with Mrs Taylor and the twins. It was then that it dawned on us. We were only a few yards from the farm and we hadn't realised it. In our panic we must have walked round in a circle.

The farmer dropped us off, and then went over to Mum and paid her the hop-picking money for her and the rest of the women. This provoked a lot of grumbling from Granny and the others because Mum was in charge. But they needn't have worried. She shared it equally amongst them – all except Annie and the boys, who had to be content with a penny each for their troubles. Mum called me over to do the counting. When I'd completed this by a feat of mathematics, she wasn't satisfied with her share which she'd already calculated on her fingers, so I was ordered to do it all over again.

'All bloody day for two bob each?' she asked Mrs Phipps.

'Well, we do get twopence more than the other farm we worked at, dain't we, Mrs Jones?' she asked. 'An' we do get paid every day.'

Mrs Jones nodded her head in reply, but Mum wasn't satisfied. She shouted across the barn to Granny and the rest, still glaring at her two shillings.

'We worked like bloody Trojans for this!' She spat her words out with contempt. 'If that bloody farmer thinks I'm pickin' 'is 'ops all day for two bob, 'e's off 'is rocker.' She was livid, and paced up and down.

'Yow tell 'm, Polly, I ain't doin' any mower! I want ter goo back 'ome,' Granny sobbed, and sniffed and blew her nose.

'We'll think about that, 'Annah, after we've 'ad summat ter eat.'

Mum collected sixpence off each person to buy some food from the stores and Mrs Taylor walked over to get some food from under the bucket for the twins. When she yelled out in surprise we all went to look.

'It's gorn. The rats 'ave 'ad it.'

Mum pushed us all out of her path and strode over to see for herself. She examined the bowl and then turned and glared at us each in turn. Placing her hands on her hips, she snarled angrily, 'They're two-legged rats 'ave 'ad it. Come on, who's the varmint?'

The Hop-pickers

We looked from one to another, waiting to see who was going to own up. I knew it wasn't Liza, the twins or me. But all eyes were on us because we were the only ones left out of the hop-picking party. Mum dragged Liza and me over to the corner where the bucket and bowl were. She raisd her hand high but we both vehemently denied having been in the barn. Then, just as she was about to bring down her hand, Mrs Phipps piped up.

'Wait a bit, Polly. What about them two? They dain't pick 'ops all the time. They ran off part of the afternoon.'

Mum turned to question Frankie and Jonesy but there was no need. They had both fled. Mum and Mrs Jones made a dive for the barn door but Granny cried out, 'Yer won't catch them two. Send somebody to the stores and let's 'ave summat ter eat. I'm clammed. I wish I was back 'ome. I was allus sure of a pot of stew.'

'Oh shut up, 'Annah! We're all clammed,' Mum snapped back. 'Anyway, let's goo to the shed an' 'ave a cup a tea while one of yer fetches some food.'

'I'll goo,' Mrs Jones volunteered quickly.

'No!' shouted Mum. 'I don't trust yer.'

So Liza and I had to go instead, and by the time we returned the tea was ready in the pot. I still had to go to the farmhouse though, as we had no milk. I'd hoped to avoid the twins but they tagged along behind before I could fetch the jug and dash off. Most of the time I loved their company, but other times they could be a couple of pests. They dragged along after me and there was nothing I could do without hurting their feelings. Before we'd gone very far we saw little Hoppity in front of us. I tried to edge past him because I was still nervous, but Joey and Harry ran up and stroked him. They thought he was a kind of dog and they tried to climb on his back. I tried to call them away because I was afraid the pig might turn nasty. But they didn't turn a hair; they were enjoying themselves and so apparently was the pig. It was then I found enough courage to stroke him myself. He was just a friendly little pig. I noticed that the dressing had come loose so I wrapped it back on for him and from that moment we became friends. He trotted along behind us and when we got to the farmhouse the farmer's wife told us not to encourage him or he would follow us everywhere. I smiled, and thanked her for the milk and the pig followed us back along the path towards the shed. But didn't come in. He stood outside and, would have nothing to do with anybody else, only the twins and me. In the end the only way I could get rid of him was to throw an apple as far as I could and hope he wouldn't return for more.

It was about eight o'clock and the evening was still warm and light. We had our share of fried bacon, mugs of cocoa and fried potatoes. Mum, Mrs Phipps, Mrs Jones, Mrs Buckley and Mrs Taylor washed and combed their hair ready to go to the pub again. The other kids had already vanished across the field to do their scrumping. I knew I would be left alone, but I didn't mind being left with the twins as long as someone else was there in the barn with me. Mrs Taylor could see that I was apprehensive and on the verge of tears so she agreed to stay behind with me. I threw my arms round her waist and almost cried for joy. She bent over me.

'Come on now. Wipe your eyes and we'll go back to the shed and clear up the crocks and pans and then we'll go for a walk.'

I felt happy then, but not for long. Mrs Taylor was the only one who seemed to notice me when I was unhappy or miserable, and I was too young to realise that she was only using me. She washed and cleaned up the shed and I helped her to wash and dress the twins. Then, while she took them into the barn, I filled their two empty medicine bottles with what was left of the cow's milk and fastened the teats on the ends. I took them to the twins who were already bedded down for the night. I lay down beside them and they sucked their milk while I sang a lullaby until they fell asleep, then I rose to my feet and crept quietly out of the barn so as not to disturb them.

Mrs Taylor was already standing outside and I could see how restless she was to be off. She took me by the hand and quickly hurried me along the lane. I felt that the twins shouldn't be left, but when I told her Mrs Taylor snapped, 'Don't worry yerself. They'll be orl right.'

134

I could see that she wasn't happy either, but I was too innocent to realise that it was the pub she was eager to get to, I asked where she was going.

'Only to the pub. I'm garspin' for a drink,' she replied.

But I wasn't prepared to accompany her.

'I'm going back to the twins. They might wake up and cry for us.'

'Please yerself,' she said smiling, and left me to return to the barn by myself.

She hurried off in the opposite direction and I retraced my steps. The twins were still asleep, sucking their empty bottles. I tried to remove them but they held them too tightly, so I gave up and flopped down beside them. I felt so unhappy and miserable that I considered running away. But where could I have gone? I was miles from home and I couldn't even walk to the farm to ask the farmer's wife if I could stay with her because I was too afraid of the cows. I could still hear their lowing in the fields. All kinds of things crowded into my mind, but above all I thought I must not leave the twins. I put my arm round them and cuddled them until we all dropped off to sleep. This didn't last long. Liza and Annie and the lads woke me up when they came bounding in and dropped their pile of apples and carrots on the floor. I heard the farmer approaching with his dogs and we pushed the loot under some straw. When he'd gone by we retrieved the fruit and vegetables, and gorged ourselves before our mothers returned. But I knew they wouldn't be back before closing time.

When the boys had had their fill they climbed the ladder to the loft and settled down for the night. Liza and Annie made their beds on the other side of the twins. It was really dark now and I could only just make out the time by the dusty clock on the wall. It was ten thirty. Soon after this I heard the farmer enter and hang the lamp on the wall but he didn't bother to check who was there.

His departure marked the beginning of a night I shall never forget.

It was very warm in the barn with the door closed and very humid as well. So I tiptoed to the door and opened it to let in some air. As I did so I heard singing in the distance, and I was relieved to hear Mum's voice way above the others. But as I stood in the doorway waiting for them to arrive I became aware of male voices too. For some reason I assumed that it must be my dad and felt immensely happy that he'd come in response to my letter. However when they all drew nearer I could see, in the dim light of the lantern, Mum, Granny and the rest arm in arm with four men we'd seen earlier in the other hop field. I was disappointed and frightened when I saw the state they were in. The smallest of the four was holding Granny up, while the other three were trying to push past Mum into the barn. They were disshevelled, ragged and swearing loudly and they each brandished a bottle of beer. I was scared when they tried to get into the barn, but Mum pushed the first one outside.

'Thank yer fer seein' us 'ome. But that's as far as yer goo,' she said firmly. But they wouldn't budge. The leading one stood there and seemed most aggrieved. 'What d'yer tek us for, missus? We've treated yer all night. Come on, let's open a bottle inside.'

Then he pushed his way inside and the other three followed, waving their bottles in the air. I ran to the twins to protect them in case they were trodden on, but they were difficult to miss because they were screaming their heads off. Liza and Annie were awake too, and seemed to be perplexed about what was happening. Then the little bearded man grabbed Granny round the waist and dragged her on to the straw, nearly landing on the girls as they rolled about. Mrs Phipps, Mrs Jones and Mrs Buckley were also struggling to free themselves from the other men and Mum was giving a right and a left to the other fellow's belly. Before he could get a grip on her, she lifted her heavy foot and landed a kick in his groin. He let out a yell and fell to the floor, clutching his private parts and, as he laid there groaning, the contents of his bottle poured out beside him. Mum clapped her hands and grinned.

'That's number one settled.' She smiled, as she stepped over him to help the others on their way out.

Mum was really enjoying herself and so were the boys, who

were laughing fit to burst in the safety of the loft. However, Liza and I were scared. We were in the thick of the skirmish and didn't think it was funny at all. We crouched in the corner with Mrs Taylor and the twins, who were still crying loudly, and watched as Mum caught hold of the little man by his beard and dragged him off Granny, down whose throat he'd been trying to pour more beer, Mum held him firmly and then threw him through the door. He was probably glad to leave! While Mum was dealing with these two, Mrs Phipps, Mrs Jones and Mrs Buckley were still struggling with the other two burly fellows. These blokes obviously had no intention of leaving the women and things seemed to be getting rougher. As Mum made to help, the men lashed out at her and she fell over Granny who was lying on the straw exhausted, but with sufficient energy to cry and swear at the interlopers. Mum was unable to get to her feet. Each time she got up she was pushed down again. I shouted out to Frankie to come down and help, but he was already sliding down the ladder with Jonesy and Freddie close behind. They jumped on to the largest fellow's back and pummelled him and they were soon joined by Mum who'd struggled to her feet. Meanwhile Mrs Jones was standing in the corner, crossing herself and praying. 'Mary, Mother of God, save us!' she kept crying out.

Meanwhile the second man was chasing Mrs Phipps and Mrs Buckley round the barn, when suddenly we were all plunged into darkness. The lantern and our supply of paraffin had burnt itself out. Liza, Annie, Mrs Taylor and I were still crouching out of the way, afraid for our lives. But as the man chasing Mrs Phipps passed us for the second time I lifted my foot and kicked for all I was worth. Unfortunately I missed my target. Mrs Phipps yelled out and fell, with the man on top of her. When I realised what I'd done I dodged behind Mrs Taylor, out the way of retribution. Just then the big fellow shouted, 'Come on, George. We'll settle this lot tomorrow night.'

Mrs Buckley crawled to the up-turned bucket and lit the only piece of candle we had left. When we could see where we were and what we were doing we could see George getting to his feet. Mum rushed at him, but his friend came to his rescue; but Mum was afraid of no one, not even the devil. She lunged at them both but we could see that she was getting the worst of it. However, we were too frightened to interfere. She knocked one fellow down and then Frankie tried to come to her aid with the hay-fork. He rushed at them but the fork was too heavy an he tripped over the chap on the floor. He pulled himself to his feet and when he saw that Mum was not going to stop he dashed outside and at last the big fellow decided he'd had enough, too. He helped the first fellow Mum had floored, who appeared to have fallen into a drunken stupor, to his feet, and they limped out. Mum slammed the door and pushed its wooden bar into place, and slapped her hands together, in a gesture of having polished them off.

'Well, that's the end of that!' she cried in triumph.

Frankie and Jonesy climbed back into the loft and we emerged from our hiding-place. The barn was a shambles. Straw and empty bags were strewn about amongst the broken beer bottles. We all set about refilling our beds but it was impossible to see, so we girls clambered up to join the lads in the loft. The women below began to quarrel. I could still hear their efforts to scrape together some straw when I heard Mum's voice.

'I wish to God we 'ad a light in 'ere to see what we're doin'.'

Suddenly her prayer was answered. The farmer stood in the doorway with his lantern lighting up the whole barn. He gazed at the scattered straw and then looked at us all hard in turn.

'What's been going on here?'

Mum put on her look of surprised innocence.

'Nothin', sir,' she replied, giving him the benefit of one of her smiles.

'What do you mean nothing? I want an explanation!' He was angry. 'The place is a shambles and I could hear the noise all the way down the lane. Come on, who's going to own up?'

No one spoke. We all stared at him, afraid of what he might do. Then after a few seconds he spoke.

'Very well. You all leave in the morning.'

But as he turned to go, Granny burst out with sobs.

'It worn't us, sir. It was them men from the other field who followed us 'ere.'

Mum stood in front of Granny and said she didn't know what she was saying. 'A bit funny in the 'ead, sir,' she said, putting her finger to her forehead. He glared at Mum and passed out of the way.

'I'll talk to you lot tomorrow. And see that you've all got yer belongings ready to clear out!'

When he went off, leaving us in the dark again, the quarrelling started in earnest.

'Yer dain't 'ave ter tell 'im, 'e'd 'ave found out anyway. The way yow carried on with all yer 'ootin' an' ravin'.'

'Oh, lie down, yer silly ole fool, an' get ter sleep!' Mum yelled.

Then Granny laid down on the straw again and Mrs Phipps asked, 'Do yer know who kicked me on the shin, Polly?'

' 'Ow do I know? I was too busy tryin' to defend yow lot! Get ter sleep, all on yer. Any'ow, I'm tired if you're not.'

I was pleased to know that no one had seen me kick out in the dark and I was not fool enough to own up either. Soon everybody was snoring but I just lay there praying that my dad would fetch me home as quickly as possible. It was pitch dark now and quiet but for the sound of a steady succession of women using the bucket. Then I resolved to run away as soon as it got light and with that thought I must have drifted off to sleep.

13
Our Last Day on the Farm

I was woken by Frankie shaking me. I looked around sleepily and realised that it was long past dawn, in fact it was ten o'clock by the clock on the wall. When I was fully awake I could hear that there was a storm overhead. It was thundering and lightning and raining in buckets. All thought of running away was out of the question. We couldn't even get to the shed to see if there were any scraps or leftovers from the previous evening. Instead we set about rousing our mother who made loud complaints about the weather and their headaches. Granny was the last to rise and was the loudest complainer.

'I want ter goo 'ome. If nobody comes ter fetch me I shall die 'ere!' she sobbed.

'Don't cry, Granny. I've written a letter to Dad to come and take us home,' I confided in her. This seemed to pacify her and she pulled me to her.

'God bless yer, me wench.'

But I recoiled from her. The smell of stale beer on her clothes made me feel sick. I felt miserable because the rain had prevented me from running back to Birmingham, but I consoled myself with the thought that Dad might come after it had stopped. By now everybody was up and the twins were yelling to be fed, but their mother couldn't be bothered with them. I looked away. I knew how they felt; I was hungry too. It was then that I remembered the apples and carrot I'd hidden under the straw the night before. However, when I looked the apples had gone and only the carrot remained. I could see no sign of rats or mice so I guessed that the culprits must have been of the two-legged variety, but it would have been no use arguing about it. Nobody would have owned up. Anyway, I felt too drained to pursue it so I took the carrot and after wiping it on my frock, I bit a piece off and gave the rest to the twins.

'Do 'em good, Mrs Taylor. 'Elp 'em see in the dark,' Frankie piped up, when he saw them munching their carrot like human rabbits.

She was not in a pleasant mood, however.

'They've seen an' 'eard enough, yer cheeky little sod!'

Mrs Taylor was not the only one in a temper. Everybody was in the same mood. They were getting in each other's way as they tried to clear away the half-empty bags of straw. We were really fed up, particularly with the rain, and every few minutes someone would stick their head out the door to see if it was easing off.

After a while Mum asked Granny and the rest to pool what

money they had left to buy some more food from the shop.

'I carn't, Polly,' said Mrs Jones, 'I've only a few coppers left.'

I saw Mum, hands on hips, glaring at Mrs Jones and it was then that I noticed for the first time that Mum had the biggest black eye I'd ever seen – and I'd seen a few in my time! There were always drunken brawls in the street. I don't think Mum herself knew that she had it, because there were no mirrors in the barn, and although the others had seen it they were too afraid to mention it, but I couldn't stop myself glancing at it every now and then. Mum grew red in the face giving out instructions.

'All on yer!' she commanded. 'Yer'll 'ave ter doo yer share! There's no 'ops ter be picked terday in this rain. An' another thing. We've got ter get our chattels together. Yer knoo what the bloody farmer said.'

To which Granny responded, 'Talk a the bloody devil an' 'e'll be bound ter appear.'

At that, all eyes turned to the barn door and everyone lost their tongue in amazement as they saw the farmer standing there. He gave them all an icy stare before he broke the silence.

'Well? And what have you all got to say for yourselves?'

No one answered. Not even Mum. They were all looking very sheepish and feeling sorry for themselves. Then he called us to him and continued in a gentler tone.

'Now I want you to listen carefully. All of yer. I been over to my brother's farm and I've found out what happened last night. Now if you'll promise not to go to the local I'll let things pass. But I warn you all, if you do go you'll be sorry! The men you tackled last night said they won't forget you lot in a hurry, so I'm putting you on your guard to keep away.' It was then he caught sight of Mum's face and saw her black eye and his face broke in a broad smile. 'Well, I see you won a medal too!'

Mum smiled, but she didn't know what she was smiling at until Granny told her later. The farmer gave us another black look and stroked his whiskers.

'There'll be no picking today. The ground's too wet. But see you're up bright and early in the morning. I want double-pickings tomorrow.'

As he reached the door he turned and looked at Frankie and the boys.

'And you lads don't sleep in that loft any more. You'll sleep on the floor with the rest.'

With that, he picked up the ladder and took it out with him.

We felt a bit happier now we knew we weren't going to be turned out in the rain. Mum turned again to collect the few coppers the others had placed on the table. Liza and I knew we'd have to go to the shop, so we went out to the closet and as we went we could hear Mum shouting, 'Don't yer be all day. We're starvin'.'

When we got back, Mum and the others were waiting for us. I jotted down the items as Mum dictated them, and Liza found an old basket to carry them in. We also took two sacks to cover our heads and shoulders from the rain. Then, carrying the basket between us, we skipped along the lane. When we arrived at the shop we peered through the window and saw two gaunt-looking women and a down-and-out-looking man inside. The man was small with a goatee beard. I immediately recognised him as the man who'd held Granny down on the straw bed the previous evening. I was scared stiff and too afraid to go in but I had to, or face Mum. Liza wasn't frightened though.

'Come on,' she whispered, 'follow me.'

She pushed open the door. The bell tinkled overhead and all eyes turned towards us. We edged to the counter. They'd stopped talking and backed away from us as though we had some kind of disease. Liza glared boldly at them and pulled me after her.

'I want these,' she said abruptly to the women behind the counter, and put the note down in front of her.

Timidly, the shopkeeper asked the man something but we couldn't make out what she said. We felt sure that they were talking about the events of the night before, and we could tell by their attitude that they were hostile.

'Yow ask 'em, missus.'

So the shopkeeper asked us who we were.

'Be yer 'op-pickers from Onions's farm?'

'Yes,' said Liza, imitating the woman, 'we be the hop-pickers from Onions's farm. So what about it?'

At that the man and the two women left, giving us extremely hostile looks and leaving the woman behind the counter to serve us. She seemed to be very nervous and apparently wanted to serve us quickly and get rid of us because she didn't take the list to reckon up the goods, she just slapped them down on the counter and when she weighed the bacon it bumped the scales but she didn't stop to take any off like she had before, so we got good measures. She didn't even count the money Liza gave her. She put it straight into the drawer.

'Thank yer,' she managed to mumble. 'Will that be all?'

We could see that she was on edge, wanting to be shot of us, but Liza nudged me and then gave her a hard stare before replying, 'Where's the jar of jam?'

Down came a two-pound jar of blackcurrant jam which Liza put in the basket with the other things. We'd no sooner got outside than we heard her shoot home the bolt and saw her pull down the blind. We took the sacks off our heads and I turned and said, 'Why did you ask for jam? That wasn't on the list.'

She smiled artfully. 'She was too nervous to see the list or count the money, so it was payment for talking about us.'

'But what will Mum say?'

'She ain't ter know. I'll tell her she gave it to us for being good customers.'

'But that's a lie, and you're sure to be found out.'

'Not if yow don't tell 'er. Anyway it's the truth. She did give it to us, didn't she?'

I thought for a moment. 'Yes, I suppose you're right.'

When we got back to the shed everybody was doing something, even the kettle was boiling on the stove and the pan was ready with a lump of lard melting, to fry the bacon. The table was laid ready with tin plates and mugs. The twins were seated on up-turned boxes, rattling away at the mugs with their spoons. After a while we sat on the floor – there wasn't enough room to sit at the table – and our meal, which Mum had rationed out, was presented to us. There was only enough food for breakfast and we still had the rest of the day to get through before we could pick more hops and earn more money. Liza explained to Mum about the jam and it was put with the leftovers for later.

It was still raining hard and so there was nowhere any of us could go. We couldn't even play outside and the only time our mothers ventured out it was to make a journey for some straw.

'I hope they don't get splinters in their bottoms,' someone said.

After a while everybody, except Mrs Taylor, the twins and me, left the shed to return to the barn. I stayed behind because I wanted to wash the boys. I was glad when I'd finished because while I was drying their pants in front of the stove the wind blew the smoke down the pipe into the shed nearly choking us. At last we went into the barn and sat with the others. Mum, Granny and the rest were stretched out taking an early nap, and Liza and the children were playing a guessing game. At about seven o'clock it stopped raining and since it was still light we decided to end our boring game and go out while the adults were still sleeping. We didn't get far enough, because Mum woke up and called to us, 'Where do yer think yer all gooin' to?'

At that the other kids ran off, leaving me. I only wished I had the courage to follow them, but I was timid and very afraid of Mum so I stood still.

'Yer better goo to the farm'ouse an' get the milk,' she ordered.

I collected the jug from the shed and looked around to see if I could see Frankie and the others but they'd fled. I was feeling very miserable. None of them seemed interested in me until there was a job to be done. I took the jug and trudged reluctantly to the farmhouse, hoping that at least I might meet Hoppity, but he too appeared to have forsaken me.

Mrs Onions was sweeping pools of rainwater away from the door as I approached. She looked up when she was aware of me and fixed me with a glare.

'Well!' she said sharply, 'I see you've come for some more milk.'

'Yes, please,' I replied timidly, and handed her the jug. I didn't like the look of her when she returned with the jug full.

'This is the last yer get without money. Yer better tell yer mother I want paying at the end of the week.'

'Thank you,' I whispered, but as I was creeping away she called me back and was smiling.

'Just a minute. You wait there while I wrap a parcel for you.'

I wondered whatever it could be. Some leftover clothes, I supposed, and while I was guessing she returned with a parcel wrapped in newspaper inside a large paper bag. She also gave me two rosy red apples which I was tempted to eat there and then. However, I put them in my pocket for later. I couldn't really understand Mrs Onions. One minute she snapped at me, the next she smiled and handed me a present. I thought I'd never understand grown-ups.

'Off yer go now and don't forget the money for the milk.'

I thanked her again and hurried back to find a bustle of activity as the table was prepared for tea. Mrs Taylor took the milk from me and I handed the parcel to Mum.

'What yer got there?' she wanted to know.

'I don't know. Mrs Onions gave it to me and she says she wants paying for the jugs of milk.'

'Well she can wait till we goo to work tomorra,' she snapped and the rest, who'd gathered round to watch her unwrap the parcel, nodded in agreement.

'If it's 'er left-off clothes, she can keep 'em,' Granny grumbled.

Everybody's face changed and their eyes lit up. So did mine as Mum placed on the table a dozen buns, a big lump of cheese, a lump of best butter, a slab of currant cake and a piece of fat bacon.

'She ain't so bad after all,' Mrs Phipps said as she stared hungrily at the contents of the bag.

I thought so too. Grown-ups were changeable creatures when they wanted to be. They all bustled about like busy bees, getting everything laid out in apple-pie order. Mum told me to call the other kids in and while she wasn't looking I managed to grab one of the buns for my trouble and contrived to find a corner to gobble it down. I spotted the other kids coming over the field, their pockets bulging with booty which they'd managed to hide in the barn before we left. They could hardly believe what they saw on the table. It was laid out with everything we had, even the jar of blackcurrant jam was there. And when we'd eaten, we thought it was the best feed any one of us had had for a long, long time. We even had the best butter on our bread with thick jam on top, and a bun each as well. The adults had fried bacon and cheese sandwiches. They'd been warned off the Pig and Whistle, so the kettle was boiling and the pot brewing all night. It was still light and Mrs Taylor asked me to go for a drop more milk. I told her what Mrs Onions had said about paying but she insisted.

'Well yow tell 'er it's for the twins. They won't sleep without their bottles. I'm sure she'll let yer 'ave some till I can pay 'er.'

With that she pushed the empty jug into my hand. I looked up at Mum for some support, but she only stared blankly back at me.

'Goo on! Do as yer told. An' 'urry yerself!' she bawled.

I began to weep. How could I ask for more milk when the woman had been so kind and given me all that food? I was too ashamed to go to her door. In the end I decided what I'd do. I'd take my time and pretend I had been and tell them a lie and say that there was none left. So I began to walk slowly when I noticed a van drive up towards the farmhouse and stop near the door. I stood and waited to see what was happening but when I saw who got out I dropped the jug and ran as fast as my thin little legs would carry me; because it was my brother, Jack.

'Jack! Jack! Oh, you've come to fetch us back home!' I cried out and tears welled up in my eyes.

'All right, let goo.' He smiled at me clinging to his trouser-legs. I let go and hung back while he knocked on the door.

'Anybody in?' he called out, but there was no reply.

He knocked again to make sure, but there was no one about but Hoppity who came running towards us on his three legs. I was happy and excited, telling my brother that this was

Hoppity who followed me wherever I went.

'Funny little pig,' he said, lifting his flat cap and scratching his head in wonderment. 'What's the matter with his leg?'

I told him the pig had been cut on barbed wire while he petted it.

'You've got him tamed all right,' my brother said, smiling.

Nevertheless I didn't like the look he gave Hoppity when he said, 'You'd look nice on the table, Hoppity.'

I was very shocked when I realised what he was saying.

'Don't look so worried. I'm only kidding. You know I wouldn't do that.'

But you never knew with my brother Jack. However, I was so happy to see him that I forgot how he looked and what he'd said for the time being anyway.

'Jump in the back and show me where you're staying,' he said.

'It's the first big barn at the bottom of the field,' I replied, and leapt in the back of the van.

Hoppity followed along behind us. He knew I had another apple, but when I saw that he couldn't keep up with us I threw it back to him and watched him stop and munch it.

As Jack drove up to the barn I jumped down and while he parked it at the back I ran to tell Mum the good news. Mrs Taylor was the first person I ran into, but she wasn't interested in Jack. She only wanted to know about the milk. I was glad I didn't have to lie as I told her nobody was in. Then I ran to Mum who was sitting on a box near the table.

'Mum, Mum!' I cried excitedly. 'Our Jack's outside. With a van. He's come to take us home!'

Mum jumped up, knocking the box flying against the wall and rushed outside to meet Jack. She threw herself at him and, with her arms round his neck, almost smothering him, she kissed him. But he tried to hold himself aloof. He always did when she tried to kiss him.

'Where've yow sprung from?' she cried out.

Jack replied in his usual joking vein, 'Well, old 'un. I've come ter fetch yer 'ome.' He very seldom called her Mum or Mother.

147

'Thank God y've come. I've 'ad anough of this 'ole,' she declared, indicating the farmyard in general with an expansive gesture.

It was then that he noticed her black eye.

'Who give yer that?' he asked, pointing at her face.

'I fell over in the dark an' 'it it on the wall,' she lied.

Granny jumped up and screamed out, 'No she dain't! Tell 'im the truth!'

Mum walked away, giving Granny a filthy look, but Granny always had to have the final word.

'Yes. I'll tell 'im an' all. An' why dain't 'e come? 'E never answered Katie's letter.' She paused to draw breath. 'Any'ow, it's about time too. Somebody's come to fetch us at last.'

I was scared now and hoped Mum hadn't heard Granny mention the letter but she'd began quietly putting things away. She seldom listened to Granny's outbursts. Then Mrs Buckley asked how everybody was at home and if her husband and children were all right, but before Jack could answer Mum butted in, 'How's yer dad, Jack? An' 'ows Mary an' Charlie and 'ow's everybody coping with the rest of the kids?'

'They're all doing fine. Maggie an' Billy have been looking after 'em,' Jack replied, 'but Dad wants you all back 'ome.'

While they were all trying to get a word in edgeways, I put the kettle on to make Jack a cup of tea but when he noticed what I was doing he said he had something better in the van. He went out and came back with a pint bottle of whisky. All eyes were on him now. So were Frankie's and Liza's. They'd only just entered and were obviously surprised to see him. The women's eyes were glued to the bottle. Nobody wanted tea now. He poured them half a mug each but there wasn't enough to go round so, to our surprise, Jack went out to the van and returned with another bottle. Frankie and Jonesy were hoping Jack would give them some too, but Jack was adamant. They were too young and the whisky was too precious to be wasted on them. So the tea came in useful after all. We kids drank it.

I noticed Mrs Taylor putting some of her whisky into the twins' milk and when she saw me watching her she put her finger to her lips and whispered, 'Shush. It'll mek 'em sleep. They was awake 'alf the night with the row.'

After a while, when all the chatter had died down and the crocks had been cleared away we retired to the barn.

'Mower room ter move about in theea,' Granny said.

We led the way and when Jack entered he began fuming. 'What a bloody place to sleep. I'll have a bloody word with the farmer.'

'It's better than some barns we've slept in, ain't it?' said Mrs Phipps.

'Yes, that's right,' Mrs Jones replied, trying to look indignant. 'Anyway we ain't gooin' 'ome till the end of next week.'

'You please yerself what yer do.' Jack was annoyed. 'I'm teking my family out of this place first thing in the morning.'

Frankie piped up. 'I want to stop with Jonesy. I like it here.'

'You'll do as you're told.'

With that Jack gave him a good back-hander that made him sulky for the rest of the evening. I would have loved to tell Jack a lot of things that had been going on, but I knew I'd better be quiet while Mum was around, so I cuddled up next to the twins and watched Mrs Taylor making their bottles up. I knew that whisky was the wrong thing to give them, but I could do nothing; I had to do as I was told. Anyway, I thought, they'll get a good night's sleep. She handed me the bottles and I gave them one each to suck and soon they slipped into sleep. It was not long before the others were dozing off too. What with the commotion the night before, the slap-up meal, and the whisky, it was no wonder they all slept so soundly. Just as I was dropping off, I heard Jack and Mum talking.

'Where yer gooin' ter sleep, son?'

'I'll muck down in the van. Now, don't forget.' His voice dropped to a whisper. 'I'm going to have a drink at the Pig and Whistle. Get some sleep and I'll wake yer when I get back.'

'All right, son, an' mind 'ow yer goo,' she whispered in reply.

I heard the van drive away; then Mum lay down and went to sleep. Everybody was quiet now. I got up off my bed and tiptoed over to Frankie and whispered in his ear, 'Are you awake, Frankie?'

'What yer want?' he mumbled, and struggled up.

'Shush,' I hissed, looking around to see if anyone had heard him, but they didn't stir.

'Jack's gone to the Pig and Whistle and I'm afraid the men might set on him, Frankie.'

'Oh, go to sleep! He can take care of himself. Anyhow I don't care about him any more.'

And with those words he turned his back on me. I could see there was no use arguing with him while he was in that mood, so I curled up beside the twins again. I took Topsey from them. I felt so unhappy I wanted to cry. My mind was like a maze. I imagined all sorts of things were going to happen before Jack could get us safely home. I tortured myself, asking all kinds of questions and getting only black answers. What if he didn't come back? But he had promised and although he didn't always keep his promise I hoped he would this time. Anyway, Frankie was right. He could take care of himself. He was six feet tall and as strong as three men. I still wished I was back in my bed at home. Dad had said the country air would do us good but it only seemed to have made us all quarrelsome and miserable. That was how my mind wandered. Then after I'd said a little prayer, I drifted off into a troubled slumber.

I don't remember how long I slept, but I woke up and could hear voices in the barn. I thought my prayer had been answered. I could see Jack lighting the candle and crossing the floor to where Mum was sleeping.

'Are you awake, old 'un?' I heard him whisper.

'Is that yow, son?' she replied.

'Yes. Are yer dressed ready?'

He wasn't to know that none of us had been undressed since we arrived. It was cold at night and we only had sacks to cover ourselves. I watched Mum get up and, carrying her button-up boots, she followed him outside in her stockinged feet. I closed my eyes quickly when they turned to see if anyone was awake. They needn't have worried, the women slept on, snoring in different tones. I was fascinated to discover what was going on and why they were acting in such a conspiratorial way, so I got up and crept to the door to listen to what they were saying.

150

'Come on, old 'un. We ain't got all night. I want to get away before it gets too light.'

I could tell he'd had plenty to drink by the tone of his voice.

'There's only a few more things to get out in the van now,' I heard Mum reply.

I ran back quickly and lay down again and only just in time because they came back to collect the rest of our chattels. They seemed to be a long time whispering together but I didn't dare listen again. After a while, they both came back and looked around to see if anyone was stirring. Then I heard Jack tell Mum to get some sleep and he'd wake her up at dawn – and not to forget the pills.

'Yer betta 'ave 'em now,' Mum whispered, and I saw her take Mrs Phipps',s sleeping pills from her pocket.

'Only give 'im one,' I heard her say.

'All right. Now get some sleep before the others wake up,' he answered.

Then he put the candle out and disappeared. I couldn't think what was going on. What were they plotting? I tried to puzzle out what they'd been talking about, but I couldn't. My eyes ached and at last I fell asleep again. It was just breaking dawn when I woke again in time to see Mum and Jack carrying armfuls of straw and empty sacks out to the van. Then they returned and whispered to Gran to get up and go to the van.

'What's 'appenin'?' she mumbled as Mum led her outside still half asleep.

'Hush. We're tekin' you 'ome. We don't want to wake any of the others.'

I jumped out of bed quickly, thinking they were leaving me behind. I grabbed Topsey in one hand and my clogs in the other and ran outside and stood by the van. They weren't leaving without me, even if I had to hang on the back. Even though Granny was only half awake, she still made sure she had plenty of room and she stretched out on the straw to finish her sleep.

'I'm glad you're up and ready,' Jack said. 'You can keep an eye on Gran while we go and get Liza and Frankie.'

There was no great need to watch Gran: she was already

snoring. After a couple of minutes, Jack came out with Frankie who was still protesting about having to leave, but when Jack raised his hand to him he soon scrambled aboard. Mum and Liza were the next to climb in and I followed before Jack closed the door. Then he mounted the driver's cab and we slowly pulled away. Only Mum and I were awake but I closed my eyes and tried to let the rocking motion of the van going over the ruts send me to sleep. We hadn't gone far when Jack stopped the van and opened the doors and Mum got out. I pretended to be asleep.

'Come on, old 'un,' Jack hissed, 'we'll have to hurry up before it gets too light.'

Mum jumped down and followed Jack in the direction we'd just come from.

They've just gone for a wee, I thought. But after they'd been gone quite a time I began to worry. Then at last I heard their footsteps and I feigned sleep again. When the door opened I could see Jack with Hoppity in his arms fast asleep.

'Where yer found him?' I managed to splutter.

'I've bought 'im off the farmer for yer.'

I stared at him wide-eyed as he continued, 'He told me he was always running away and getting lost and said you might like him. Now move over while I put him down.'

I moved across to accommodate the pig and Mum, but apparently she was riding up front with Jack. I was glad of that. But I wasn't very happy about the pig beside me. I liked him well enough when he ran to me for apples, but I couldn't bring myself to be too friendly because I was really nervous of him. However, I consoled myself with the thought that I would now have the opportunity to become more fond of him. Anyway, Jack placed him on the straw and whispered, 'Now listen carefully. I don't want anyone to know I've bought him. Not even Liza, Frankie or yer gran. This is our secret. I'm going to hide him until he wakes up. Then we'll make him a sty in the yard. Promise me now that you'll keep our little secret.'

I believed every word he told me and crossed my heart and hoped to die. Still I couldn't make out why we had to keep it secret and as Jack swung the doors shut I whispered, 'Jack, I

152

wasn't asleep last night when you and Mum were whispering. Did you give Hoppity a pill?'

'Yes, two. To keep him from waking all the other pigs up. Now lie down and don't forget your promise.'

I nodded my reply but I still couldn't understand why it was necessary. He started the van and when we reached the open road we speeded up. I tried to sleep, but between dozing off I could hear Granny's snores and the pig's grunts. Liza and Frankie slept on like the babes in the wood. It was still very early in the morning and the lanes were misty and quiet. All I could hear was the occasional noise such as the bellowing of cattle, and later the clanging of a tram bell in the distance. At last the van halted in our yard. Jack opened the doors and whispered instructions to me to make no sound. I watched him lift the sleeping pig in his arms and carry him into the house. Mum followed behind with an armful of straw. Jack lifted the old bit of sacking off the cellar grating and carried the pig down into the darkness. I stared and wondered. Why were they hiding him in the cellar if they'd bought him? It didn't make sense. I assumed they'd explain to me later, and in any case the cellar was the only spare room we had.

14
Our Homecoming

There was no other at home when we arrived and the house was cold, so I was soon busy chopping sticks to make the fire with. Then I put the kettle on to boil while Mum covered the cellar up with the sack and woke the others up. They rushed in to the fire to warm themselves. I was itching to tell them what Jack had bought for me, but Jack guessed that I was about to tell Frankie and he shook his head at me. I didn't have time to say anything further because Mum began bustling about, making a meal. She asked Jack to reach up to the cupboard to find out what was there. He found some eggs, cheese and sausages but this didn't please Mum. She moaned at the way Dad had spent all the money so there was none left for other household expenses. But, as Jack pointed out to her, there was nothing we could do now except eat what he'd purchased. So we sat down to our breakfast – all, that is, except Granny. She was sniffing and sneezing in the corner and seemed to have a bad cold.

'Come on, Gran,' Jack chivvied her, 'yer breakfast's ready.'

But as she tried to stand up, she swayed and was only saved from falling into the fire by Jack's timely intervention. We were concerned, but Mum, predictably, was unmoved.

'I 'ope I ain't gooin' ter 'ave 'er bad on me 'ands. I've enough ter do round 'ere as it is.'

'Don't be too hard on her, old 'un. She's caught a chill,' Jack said, as he steered Granny to bed.

'I know I ain't wanted,' Granny cried between sniffs. 'I'll be gooin' back to me 'ouse in the mornin'.'

But she didn't leave the next day, nor the next, nor the one after that. Jack was firm with her and Dad told her she was to stay until she felt well again. Jack had changeable moods, like Mum. Sometimes he'd be kind and jolly, and others he would be bad-tempered. A lot liked him though, especially the women. He always seemed to be pestered with lady friends wanting him to take them for walks, and of course he always tried hard to oblige! On Saturdays and Sundays he looked very smart with his freshly pressed suit, highly polished boots, flat grey cap and white starched muffler. He looked extremely handsome, or so I thought, particularly when he brushed down his sideburns with burnt cork. It was my job to procure these on my numerous errands fetching and carrying. Jack would give me a penny for every six I collected, and cheap they were if you remember the number of errands I had to run to get them.

Granny was quite ill and I was given the job of looking after her, but she was far from being an ideal patient. One time when I took her bowl of gruel she refused to eat it. When Mum found out, she determined to see that she did eat it, cold for her next meal if necessary. I was only too happy to let Mum take over.

Anyway, to return to the day of our return – we finished our meal, and Frankie and Liza went out to play and Jack returned the van after I'd helped him clean out the bits of straw. I could see he was in one of his better moods when he smiled at me and handed me a silver sixpence. I could hardly believe my eyes and stared at the coin in amazement.

'That's for being a good girl,' he told me. 'But don't forget our secret.' He winked. I nodded but I wanted to tell some-one, Frankie for example, because I knew he could keep a secret. But I had crossed my heart and promised. I dropped the sixpence down my stocking and went indoors. I knew it was no use asking Mum to explain why it had to be a secret. She was busy combing her hair and arranging it in different styles to hide her left eye, which had now turned yellowish. She turned round from the cracked mirror and glared at me.

'Don't stand gorpin'! Call Liza to come an' 'elp fill the copper. I want ter get the washin' done before yer dad gets 'ome.'

Liza was nowhere to be found as usual, so I took the bucket and went to the tap in the yard to fill it. This was Monday morning – Mum's washday, and most other women's too. Maggie was standing by the tap with her own bucket as I approached.

' 'Ello, Katie,' she greeted me – in some surprise I thought. 'When did yer come 'ome?'

I told her we'd arrived early that morning.

'All on yer? But where's Mrs Taylor and the others?' she asked. 'They ain't bin ter collect their kids they left be'ind yet!'

I explained that we'd returned alone, and this aroused her curiosity.

'How's Jimmy?' I said to change the subject.

'Oh, 'e's bin as good as gold. But I carn't say the same fer the other little varmints.' She didn't say any more because she'd seen Mrs Huggett hurrying down the yard. 'What d'yer think, Nell?' she said. 'The others ain't come back yet.'

She turned to me again for an explanation as though it was my fault. I was about to reply when I saw Mum dashing towards us. I could have laughed out loud. She looked so

155

comical, marching along with Dad's flat cap pulled well down over her left eye. She just snatched up the half-filled bucket and marched back towards the wash-house, glancing back over her shoulder and calling out, 'They're stoppin' a few more days if yer want ter know. We've 'ad enough of it!'

'An' so 'ave we 'ad enough!' Maggie shouted back at her. 'It's took me an' Billy, an' the rest of the good people round 'ere to feed 'em. Let alone tryin' ter keep 'em out of trouble,' she continued, looking to Mrs Huggett for support.

But Mum wasn't listening. So they went off to the neighbours to spread the news and gossip about it. 'Never agen!' I heard one of them say. 'The little buggers 'ave eat us out of 'ouse an' 'ome.'

This was the first Monday I'd seen Mum washing alone at the washtub. The women always did their washing in pairs, but on this day the rest were too busy pulling everybody to pieces. Mum was pleased because it gave her more time to get the clothes dried and into the pawnshop before Dad returned for his meal. Once or twice I went upstairs to keep an eye on Granny, but she was fast asleep and peaceful. I also ventured down the cellar stairs to see how Hoppity was. He too was asleep and although I did think he might be dead I could see the rise and fall of his belly and knew he was sleeping peacefully. Then, just as I was about to return upstairs, I heard Liza above. She was looking for her whip and top and when she'd found them she left, and I re-emerged into the room. But I had a sudden thought. What if my little Hoppity woke up and wanted a drink? So I emptied the soapy water out from the only tin bowl we had, and filled it full of fresh water for him.

Later, in the warm of the late evening, I helped Mum fold and mangle the dry clothes and while she was away at the pawnshop I set to and peeled the potatoes. We were having a treat that night – corned beef and mash. I placed a clean newspaper on the table and arranged the tin plates. The potatoes were already cooked when Mum came in with her apron full of goodies. Two loaves, margarine, a tin of condensed milk and, of course, the corned beef.

Mum counted the plates and then said to me, 'Mek yer gran

156

some more gruel. Do 'er more good while she's in bed.'

I made it, and when I took it upstairs I found she was still sleeping soundly. So I left her meagre meal on the marble-topped table in case she woke and was hungry. I felt sorry for my gran. She seemed to be unloved, just like me. I could see that Mum was going to send her packing when she was well and I hoped she would send me away too. But I knew that this would never happen, not yet anyway, not until I was older. At the moment I was too useful. Someday, I thought, when I'm older, I'll alter things around here or clear out completely. I was in the middle of these musings when I heard Jack's footsteps outside the door.

'Wipe yer feet!' was Mum's greeting.

When Jack saw the cap over her eye he burst out laughing.

'Yer better put it on straight before the old man comes in. He'll notice it anyway. Yer carn't hide an eye like that.'

'Sit down, an' stop yer staring, all on yer!'

She was in an awful mood. Mary wouldn't be home till late, so I sat on her chair next to Jack. Frankie and Liza sat on the other side of the table and we waited for Dad to come in. We were never allowed to have our meals without Dad because he always said grace. Soon we heard him scraping his boots on the mat and Mum began slapping mashed potatoes and paper-thin corned beef on to the plates. When Dad entered he looked at Jack first and said, 'Have much trouble getting home, Jack?'

'No, Dad,' he answered, smiling.

Then Dad looked round at us all and said, 'I'm glad you and the kids are home, Polly. I've missed you all.'

Mum was careful to present her unbruised cheek for him to kiss for obvious reasons, but his attention was caught by the cap. 'Yer want to get yer cap straight, Polly. You look like an out-a-work navvy,' he teased.

'Navvy am I now?' She straightened herself to her full height but her quick temper had found her out again because Dad saw her eye for the first time.

'How did yer get that?' he demanded.

'I fell down,' she snapped back at him. 'Now sit yer down

157

an' get yer supper before it's cold.'

He left it at that, and went to the sink to wash his hands.

'Where's the bowl, Polly?' he asked.

'On the stool under the sink where I always keep it,' she answered impatiently.

It was then that I forgot my promise and blurted out 'I'm sorry, Mum. I took it down the cellar to give Hoppity a – ' But I didn't get any further. Jack gave me such a hard dig with his elbow that I screamed with pain.

'What's going on here?' Dad demanded of Jack as I began to weep.

Mum tried to change the subject and told Dad to get on with his dinner while she fetched it.

'No yer don't! I want to know what's going on first.'

He stood beside the table in his shirt sleeves waiting for an answer. He was in a temper by now. His face was red and he banged down his fist like a crack from a gun. The potatoes jumped into the air and rolled on to the floor. Mum moved away from the table and sat in her chair beside the fireplace weeping into her apron. She realised, and so did Jack, that I'd given the game away. I hadn't meant to, but it was too late now. Dad was waiting for an answer but no one spoke. Frankie and Liza looked puzzled but they didn't know what the row was all about. At that moment there was a knock at the door and voices called for Frankie and Liza. They could see that something unpleasant was about to happen, and although they were curious they guessed that they were better off out of it, so they ran out before anyone could stop them. I stayed behind because I wanted to see what Dad was going to do with Hoppity when he found out about him.

'What's all the secrecy about the cellar, and why did Katie take the bowl down there? You may as well tell me because I intend to find out.'

Jack and Mum looked at each other, but neither of them said a word. Dad could see that they weren't going to speak so he went to the door and peered down into the murk.

'What's that down there?' he asked. 'It lookes like a pig!'

'That's right, Dad, but it's all right,' Jack began to explain.

158

'Now don't yer soft-soap me.' Dad was still overcome with surprise.

'Well, Dad, it's like this.' Jack kept stealing a glance at Mum for support. I could see how nervous they looked. 'I was going along the lane to have a drink at this pub, the Pig and Whistle, when I saw this little pig.'

'So it is a pig then, is it?'

'It's only a little one. He was hurt. Some one had put a rag around his leg so I picked him up and put him in the van and drove down towards the farmyard and left him there. But when I came back he was standing outside the barn, and when I called Mum out we decided then to put him in the van and bring him home with us. But when he started to scream I decided to . . .'

'Go on. You decided what?'

'To give him a couple of sleeping pills. You know the rest.'

I jumped and began to pummel him furiously with my fists.

'You lied to me! You lied to me! And I promised . . .' I screamed. And the tears streamed down my face. Dad lifted me into the air and flopped me back into the chair.

'Now you be quiet. I'll hear what you have to say later.'

I'd never seen Dad in such a bad temper, but after he'd paced up and down a few times he seemed to calm down and then he turned on Jack.

'And what do you intend to do with it?'

'I thought we might 'ave 'im for the table or sell him.'

At this, Dad brought his fist down again with a thump and Jack and Mum went visibly paler. 'Have yer gone mad?' he bawled. 'I don't want any part of yer thieving ways. I'm warning you, if that pig or whatever you call it ain't out of this house when I come home tomorrow night I'll throw you out with it . . . for good!'

'Don't be too 'ard on 'im, Sam. 'E was only thinkin' of us,' Mum said, weeping some more.

'You can turn yer tap off, Polly. I suppose you've lied as well about that black eye,' Dad said. He turned his back on her.

Then Jack promised he would ask his gaffer to lend him the van again and make some excuse to take the pig back as soon as it was dark.

'Who else knows about this, Polly?' Dad asked.

'Only me, Jack and Katie.'

'What about Frankie, Liza and Mother?'

'No. They don't know. They just slept in the van,' she replied, wiping her eyes on her apron.

'Well, where's Mother now?' Dad wanted to know.

'She's upstairs asleep.'

Dad stared at her. 'I suppose you've given her a tablet, too?'

'No,' Jack answered for her, shaking his head. 'I took her upstairs. She's got a bad cold.'

'I don't wonder at it. I warned yer not go in the first place, but I never thought you'd do this.'

Jack tried to calm him down and repeated that he'd sort things out. Dad was still very angry. 'Don't yer forget what I've told yer. That pig goes back to the farm.'

Dad didn't say another word but sat down in his chair and, picking up his glasses and paper, began reading. Jack didn't say anything. He just gave me a look good enough to kill, then banged the door behind him, and rattled the window frame. This demonstration had no effect on Dad, who read on. Mum told me to fetch the bowl up from the cellar. The water was untouched and Hoppity was still sleeping, so it seemed I'd taken the bowl and the row had happened to no purpose. I bent down and spoke to the pig.

'Poor little Hoppity. I thought you was mine for keeps. What's going to happen to you? Anyhow, you'll be happier with the other pigs.'

But I had my doubts about his future. My brother Jack had lied to me before, and he could easily lie again. I thought how foolish I'd been to believe him. I could only console myself with the thought that he'd promised Dad he'd return him to the farm. I picked up the bowl and climbed back up the stairs. I went into the yard for some clean water and put it in the sink for Dad to wash his hands. As he was doing this, he turned round and looked at me. His face was still grim and he told me to sit in the chair.

'Now, Katie, I want to hear what you know about this.'

I was facing Mum, but Dad had his back to her. He turned

and told her to bolt the door. 'What for?' she asked, surprised.

'I don't want Frankie or Liza in until I've got this trouble straightened out.'

Mum sat back in her chair facing me after she'd shot the bolt home. Dad asked me again what I knew.

'I don't know much, Dad. Only what Jack told me.'

'That'll do for a start,' he said, keeping his voice low. Then I began my tale.

'That's all, Dad. I only know what Jack told me.'

'How did yer mum get that black eye?'

I began to weep and looked across at Mum. The sight of her screwed-up lips and warning eyes made me very careful about what I said.

'Well, I'm waiting,' he said slowly.

'She fell down,' I answered, and the tears flowed faster.

'Where? In the street?'

'In the barn. It was dark.'

'Very well,' he said more gently. 'Dry yer eyes.'

I felt enormously relieved when he didn't ask any more about Mum because I wasn't very good at lying, especially to Dad.

'Now, yer sure Granny nor Frankie nor Liza don't know about the pig?'

'Yes, Dad, they were fast asleep.'

Dad unbolted the door and called out for Frankie and Liza to come indoors. They both looked puzzled and wondered what had been going on, but they were used to quarrels and few secrets remained secrets very long in our close little yard so they weren't very bothered.

I got the small brush and shovel that were kept in the fender and cleared up the mess. There was only a bit of potato mash left. Our cat had eaten what was left of the corned beef. While I emptied the remains of our meal on to the fire, Liza helped Mum to prepare some cheese and onions. Mum didn't say a word but instead she slapped everything down on the table until Dad could stand it no longer and warned her to make less noise and let him read his paper in peace. Liza was treated to his watchful eye to make sure she did her share, and Frankie

161

was given some hard looks as he dragged the chairs about noisily. When we'd all eaten our supper of dry bread and cheese Frankie and Liza went to bed, leaving me to clear away the supper plates and lay the table for the morning. I was about to reach for my piece of candle and follow the others when Dad stopped me.

'Before you go I want another word with yer.'

What does he want now, I thought? I stood at the foot of the stairs wishing I was in bed. Butterflies fluttered about in my stomach and I was scared.

'Don't look so frightened,' he said. 'I'm not going to eat yer.'

I walked across to his chair.

'Now, Katie,' he said quietly, 'you're sure that no one knows about this pig?' I could see that he was really worried.

'Yes, Dad. Cross my heart.'

'No need for that. Now sit down and listen to what I have to say.'

Mum sat down too but I had my back to her this time and I was glad. I couldn't face her again without getting frightened. Dad stood over me and told me to say nothing of what he was going to say nor to repeat it anywhere. 'Now, Katie, I want you to keep this a secret – about your brother and this pig.' I kept nodding my head as he continued, 'Jack'll take it back to the farm where it came from or he'll be put in prison if he's found out. So you understand why you're not to tell a soul, then no one will be any wiser.'

'Yes, Dad,' I nodded. Then suddenly I remembered how Hoppity was always getting lost.

'Dad, I think Jack'll get him back before he's missed because he was always wandering off and getting lost.'

'How do you know?' Dad asked.

'Mrs Onions, the farmer's wife, told me.'

Dad smiled and said he hoped Jack would get him back in time. Then he told me once more to remember what he'd told me and with that I was told to go to bed. I turned to bid them good-night and Mum actually smiled as she wished me

162

good-night, and reminded me to take Gran her gruel. When I was halfway up the stairs I could hear her talking to Dad but I couldn't catch all she said. I only heard Dad reply, 'Yes, she's the best of the bunch. At least she can be trusted to tell the truth and I believe her.'

I didn't hear any more, but took the gruel in to Gran, who was fast asleep. I peered at her and thought to myself, I wonder if Mum has given her a sleeping tablet? She was sleeping so soundly it didn't seem natural. Then I spotted that her bowl was empty so she must have wakened at some stage. So I put the other bowl on the table and after kissing her lightly on the forehead I made my way to the attic.

Frankie and Liza were asleep. I sat down on the bed to undress. Then, as I removed my stocking, I discovered the tanner Jack had given me. I placed it on my hand and wondered if I should give it back. But I took a second look at it and resolved to keep it as payment for the lies I'd been told. As bad luck would have it, as I was blowing the candle out the sixpence fell and rolled down a crack in the floorboards. There was nothing I could do in the dark, so I crept into bed and wept. I felt sorry for myself; everything seemed to happen to me, but I consoled myself with the thought that I might find the sixpence in the morning.

I was first down in the morning after Dad and Jack had gone to work. I lit the fire and filled the kettle ready to put on the hob. Then I went down to the cellar to take a last look at Hoppity. I was sorry for the little pig and wondered what would happen to him. When my eyes grew accustomed to the dark I could see that Hoppity wasn't there. All that was left was the straw he'd lain on. Jack must have taken him in the middle of the night, and I was glad really for all our sakes. Perhaps there would be no more rows now. And there was none, for a while at least. No more was heard of Hoppity and, as Dad and Jack weren't on speaking terms, it made two less to snap at each other. I was glad about this. Anyway, we carried on as though nothing had happened. Mum carried on with her normal moaning and Granny with her aches and pains. Evidently she was recovering. So life went on until the return of the hop-pickers.

Along a little alleyway, not far from our house, was a small whitewashed house which had been turned into a fish and chip shop. It was owned by a Mr and Mrs Gingold, who were Jews. Everyone on our yard used to heave their shoulders and call them 'skinny'.¹ But I didn't think so, neither did Liza. Mum had a little job there once a week for two hours in the afternoon, helping to clean out the stale fried batter from the chip pan. When it was time for Mum to finish, we always found our way to play outside the shop window, hoping Mrs Gingold would see us. Then she'd give us a paper of scratchings. She even put salt and vinegar on them as though she were serving a customer. We'd sit on the step of an empty house and crunch away to our hearts' content and when we'd finished we'd drink the vinegar from the paper so as to get the last drop of flavour. After that we waited for Mum to catch us up.

It was on an afternoon such as this, not long after our return from the country, that we entered our yard to be greeted by a tremendous commotion. There in the middle of the yard were Mrs Phipps, Mrs Taylor, Mrs Jones, Mrs Buckley, Mrs Huggett and Maggie and a few more besides from the next yard, all nattering away, nodding their heads together. Jonesy and Freddie, the twins and Annie, were running around listening to the conversation as they played. However, as soon as they heard Mum's heavy tread they turned their heads and stared at us. Mum seemed to know at once that they were talking about us. They moved away when she marched up to them. Standing with her hands on her hips, her head thrown back, she shouted out for them all to hear, 'What yer gotta say, yer say it to me face!'

All the kids scattered when they saw Mum but none spoke. Everything went dead silent as Mum waited for someone to speak. Then Maggie moved away from the rest and said from the safety of her doorstep, 'Do yer really want ter know, Polly?'

'What yer think I'm waitin' for?' she replied angrily.

'Well, these lot 'ave told me yow've pinched a pig but I don't believe 'em, Polly,' she stammered.

Mum glared at her, knowing she was as big a gossip as the rest, but Maggie went on to finish what she had to say. 'An' the farmer's goin' ter 'ave yer all arrested.'

It was clear that Mum had to deny it there and then to save us from prison.

'Yer must be mad, the lot on yer! They can come an' search my 'ouse as soon as they like. We ain't got no pig. 'Ave we?' she said turning to me.

I noticed how pale she'd gone but I kept up the act.

'No, Mum,' and Frankie called out, 'Yow lot 'ave pinched it and are trying to blame us.'

Mum shut him up with a clout across his face but that didn't stop him sticking his tongue out at them. Then Mrs Phipps spoke up for all the others.

'Well, Polly,' she began timidly, 'what was we to tell the farmer? You left while we were fast asleep. Dain't they, Mrs Jones?'

'Yes,' came the reply. 'And yower Jack made sure we would get to sleep when he give us that whisky.'

'Believe what yer like!' Mum shouted back.

But as we turned to enter our house, Jonesy shouted out, 'I bet it's yower Frankie that's pinched the pig!'

At this there was a scuffle and a fight broke out, as Frankie pitched in and soon they were rolling on the ground. Mum stepped in and dragged Frankie off because he was holding Jonesy down and it was obvious he'd had enough. But that didn't stop her giving Jonesy an extra sly dig before parting them.

The reader will no doubt remember that neither Frankie nor Liza knew what all the fuss was about. They had no idea why we should be accused of stealing the pig, but they were too frightened to ask Mum while she was in such a temper. I was glad they didn't ask me, but then they had no reason to suspect that I knew any more than they did.

News travelled quickly in our neighbourhood and when Mum gave me sixpence to go to the grocer's to get some vegetables everyone glared and whispered as I passed. When I entered the shop it was full of women chatting about this and that. I stood just inside the door and watched them and listened to snatches of their conversation. No one saw me, they were too busy talking to each other and I soon gathered what the subject of conversation was.

'Common lot, them 'op-pickers,' I heard one say.

'Wonder who they were?' said another.

'Don't yer know? They live up the top end.'

'I hear they stole a pig.'

'Yes, an' it only 'ad three legs.'

'Somebody told me they'd tried to chop the other one off!'

'Did yer know the police are goin' ter arrest 'em?'

'Shame.'

'Serves 'em right. They ought to get life.'

I was so scared I didn't wait to hear any more but backed quietly out of the shop and, still clutching the bag and the sixpence tight in my hand, I ran crying back home. I tumbled through the door and began gabbling my story. Mum looked pale when I told her word for word what had been said.

'It's that Mrs Phipps and the Joneses that's got all this about.'

She was wiping the tears from her eyes. This was a great surprise to me because I'd never seen Mum so upset. I noticed how calmly and quietly she was talking to me, which also surprised me.

'Now listen to me, Katie. Jack's took the pig back during the night. The farmer is sure to find 'im an' nobody will be any the wiser. So if anybody asks yer about it, yer don't know anythink. Understand? If you don't we'll all goo ter prison.'

'I won't say a word, really I won't. Really,' I sobbed.

'Now wipe yer eyes before the others come in. And give me the sixpence. I'll goo ter the shop meself.'

I noticed that she didn't snatch the money away from me or dash out of the house as she normally would've done, but moved slowly and told me to make two cups of tea. Then she went off with the bag under her arm. I hoped and prayed that afternoon that my brother really had taken the pig back to the farm, but I had my doubts. You could never tell if he was telling the truth, he had such a way with him when he turned on the charm. Nevertheless, I kept my promise and no one ever knew the truth except Jack, Mum and Dad.

Two days later, Mum said she had to do some shopping. This made me curious because she always asked me to run errands. She saw the look of surprise on my face and said she'd fetch things until the trouble had blown over. I didn't know whether she was trying to be kinder to me or whether she couldn't trust me to remain silent if I was questioned. She asked me to write down the article she wanted and how much they'd cost. Then she left, leaving me alone in the house. Frankie and Liza were out playing somewhere and Granny was at the Salvation Army Mission practising for the Sunday afternoon march. I busied myself tidying up the house when I became aware of Mrs Jones talking outside the door.

'That's the house. They live there, mister.'

There were three loud raps on the door. I went to the window and lifted the corner of the curtain. I saw a policeman and a man in plain clothes who I later discovered was a detective. He wore a collar and tie and a bowler hat, like Dad's on the wall. I trembled when I realised who they were. Slowly, I dropped the curtain and crept down the cellar to hide, but they continued knocking. I was terrified they'd find me and take me away, so I crouched in the darkest corner I could find. I was so scared by now that I'd wet my bloomers. Then I heard the door open and a deep voice above.

'Very well. We'll call again.'

I heard the door close and their heavy tread on the cellar grating as they walked away from the house. After a while I came out of the cellar and could hear the neighbours and their kids outside our door. Off down the broken stairs I went again, too scared to cry. I crawled to the far end and peered up the grating and saw Mrs Phipps looking down at me.

'There's someone down theea,' she squealed.

'I bet they're too frightened to come out,' Mrs Jones suggested.

Yes, she was right. I was frightened and I wasn't coming out not until Mum came back home. Soon I heard the door open once more.

167

'Are yer there, Polly?' Mrs Jones called.

'I wonder where she's gone?' Mrs Buckley said.

Just then, I heard Mum's voice bellow out, 'What's gooin' on 'ere?'

'Two policemen 'ave been to see yer,' Mrs Buckley informed her, smugly.

'What yer bawling about? Clear off before I throw this bucket of water over yer all.'

There was the sound of general scattering footsteps. They knew well that Mum meant what she said. Then the door slammed and I came up to find Mum slumped in the arm-chair, crying into her apron. I felt so sorry for her because she wept so infrequently. I asked her why she was upset and when she heard my voice she sprang up from the chair with fright.

'Where've yow sprang from?' she asked. 'Yer nearly frightened the daylights out of me.' I backed away from her immediately. Then, quite unexpectedly, she did what I'd always wanted her to do; she drew me to her and hugged me, and with our arms round each other we both wept. I was weeping because I was happy and felt safe at last in my mother's arms, but I knew she was weeping over Jack. She told me he'd been arrested and would be tried the next day. I plucked up courage and asked what was going to happen to us. I pressed her to assure myself that everything would be all right.

'But, Mum, he did take Hoppity back to the farm, didn't he?'

'I don't know,' she replied. ' 'E said 'e did when I spoke to 'im last night.'

'What are we going to do to help him, Mum?'

' 'E's goin' to deny 'e ever seen the pig, and I think that's the best way out.'

I looked at her, surprised.

'But, Mum, he did,' I exclaimed. 'You know he did and I know he did. It will be worse if he tells lies.'

Then she sat me down in Dad's chair and faced me. 'Now, Katie, listen to what I'm goin' ter say. Jack is your brother and my son an' we've talked this over before he was arrested. That's the best thing to do an' he might well get away with it.'

Yes, I thought, he could, knowing how he could turn on his charm when it suited him. What I couldn't understand was why Mum was making so much fuss of me. She'd never spoken this way to me before, nor could I remember her ever taking me in her arms.

'Now, Katie, promise me you won't say a word about this to anyone.' Her eyes were full of tears as she pleaded, but I didn't ponder too much on the significance of what was happening. I was too happy and felt on top of the world at the thought that Mum really loved me, so I promised. Then she sat me on her lap once again and kissed me.

'Yes,' I said again. 'I'll even lie if I have to.' I felt I was really wanted at last and would have done anything. 'Shall we have a cuppa, Mum?' I asked, as though we had been this close for years.

'Yes. Mek a pot. Yer gran'll be in soon.'

While I was busy humming a tune and waiting for the kettle to boil, Granny came in. She flung the door wide open and demanded in a loud voice, 'What's all this I've 'eard about our Jack's stole a pig? Is it true, Polly?'

'No it ain't! An' don't yer start yer tantrums. I've 'ad enough from the neighbours,' Mum shouted, her face going red.

Granny could see what a bad temper Mum was in, so she went out, saying she'd come back when Dad was in. At the tender age of nine I couldn't understand the moods and foibles of grown-ups. If I ever asked for an explanation I was told that children should be seen and not heard. I think that's why I was so nervous and afraid of adults.

Dad came home later that evening looking like thunder. He neither spoke nor appeared to notice us, but flung himself into his chair. When I went out into the yard for a bowl of water for his wash they must have started arguing. I heard, 'It ain't my fault the gaffer's put our wages down and put us on short-time,' then I entered. 'Anyhow,' he continued, 'I'm luckier than some. They've been stopped altogether.'

I stood back and watched Mum's eyes raised to the ceiling. Then she erupted.

'Oh my God! Double trouble!'

Dad sat down calmly, lit his pipe, then asked me to give him his specs and began to read his paper. Mum went red in the face as she tried to control her temper.

'Yer don't care, do yer? An' what about poor Jack?'

'Poor Jack!' he burst out. 'I've heard all I want to hear about poor Jack from my workmates. I hope they send him to prison for life. And I'll tell you another thing. He don't darken this door again while I'm here. Now, I don't want to hear any more about poor Jack.'

'But, Sam, he took the pig back,' she pleaded.

'Hmm . . .' was all Dad said.

I thought how unkind and hard he was to talk to Mum this way. I felt so sorry for her, she was very upset. She'd been crying on and off all day. I tried to say something, hoping it might help, but I couldn't get my words out and began to cry too. My eyes were sore and my head ached and I didn't want to be around when Granny returned home because I knew there'd be more trouble. So I told Mum I didn't feel well and asked if I could go to bed.

'Yes, Katie. An' be up early in the morning,' she replied pleasantly.

Then I wished them both good-night. I saw Dad glance at Mum over the top of his paper. He looked surprised when he heard Mum's soft words instead of her usual bawling. I went upstairs and began to undress. Then I realised that my bloomers had dried on me. It was just as well. I couldn't have a clean pair until the end of the week.

I lay on my back staring at the ceiling wondering why Mum was being so kind to me. Things were suddenly changing in unexpected and inexplicable ways and I was no longer being beaten and shouted at. I tried to fathom it out, and then suddenly everything fell into place like pieces of a jigsaw puzzle. I sat up in bed. Yes, that's it, I thought. Mum knew I'd been awake that night in the barn when they were planning what to do and that I'd heard them scheming to drug Hoppity with sleeping pills. Then I felt very miserable again. I also knew how she'd come by that black eye. Yes, that was why she was so nice to me. She was afraid I might tell Dad the truth. But while I kept my promise she would think twice now before hitting me again. The knowledge of this secret between us made me feel happier and with this comforting thought I fell asleep.

NOTE

[1] A corruption of skinflint, meaning they were considered to be mean.

15
Our Jack's Trial

After Dad had gone off to work next morning we got ourselves ready to go to the courts to see my Jack's trial. I watched Mum in the mirror putting on her Sunday best, her stiff, starched pinafore, over her shabby alpaca frock. Then she twisted her hair into a bun on top of her head and reached for Dad's flat, grey cap that was hanging behind the door. She put it on the bun and glanced in the mirror to see how she looked. All at once she snatched the cap off and slung it across the room.

'That don't look right,' she said, completing her preening.

Granny too was busy getting dressed. After she had put on her uniform she tied on her bonnet. Mum saw what she was doing. 'Yow ain't gooin' in that get-up. Put summat else on.'

'No!', Granny shouted back, 'An' yer carn't mek me. An' I'm gooin'. I'm one of the witnesses.'

Mum didn't answer, she just shrugged her shoulders, tut-tutted and shook her head. Liza and me were already waiting to go, but Frankie too had to give a finishing touch to his wiry hair with a dab of dripping from the basin. Then off we went, closing the door behind us.

The reader will appreciate that we knew everyone in the district, and they knew us, so the incident of Jack and the alleged theft of the pig was the topic of the hour. However, we never expected the scene that greeted us outside. All our neighbours were there dressed to kill and waiting to follow us to the courts. There was Mrs Phipps with the same old moth-eaten fur coat which was supposed to be real skunk. She also had a flat cap on. She was talking quietly to Mrs Buckley who had her black, dusty velvet coat on which brought her in steady income from the tuppence fee she charged when she loaned it out for funerals, and she had her old, flat straw hat with the wax fruit on top. Mrs Jones wore a boater on her red hair and a brown, coarse-looking frock which dragged to the floor. All the while she chatted with her two friends, she kept swinging an orange coloured boa round her neck, and the loose feathers flew everywhere. They stopped whispering when they saw us. Mum stared at them.

'Yow lot ain't comin' with us,' she cried out haughtily, throwing her head back.

'But we're witnesses. Yer carn't stop us. The copper came an' told us we 'ad to goo an' give information on what we know. Dain't 'e, Mrs Jones?'

'Yes,' said Mrs Jones meekly. 'An' if we don't 'urry we'll be late.'

'Plenty a time,' Granny told them. 'Yow can goo in front.'

I could see she didn't want to walk with them either. Nor did I. It wasn't because they looked like freaks – they thought they looked lovely. But to my mind they were three gossiping, spiteful old women and I was scared to think what they might say if they were called to give evidence. So off they went, leaving us behind. I tugged at Mum's pinafore and whispered, 'Mum, do they know?' She just looked at me. I knew what she was thinking.

'No. They're only busybodies an' want ter 'ear everythink so they can 'ave a good old gossip. An' don't yer forget what yer promised to say if anybody asks yer.'

When we arrived at the courts, Granny and Mum were out of breath. We struggled up the steps and entered a spacious hall. I was surprised to see so many people and all with such sad faces. Some were sitting on a long bench and others were gathered together in groups. It all seemed very strange. I'd never been inside this place before and I was afraid. I looked around and noticed four glass doors leading into different courtrooms. Mum was already peeping through the first one when a policeman crept up behind her and tapped her on the shoulder. She turned round and told him who we were and whose case we were concerned about. He asked us to follow him and he ushered us into courtroom two. We trailed in, in single file, with Granny bringing up the rear. When the policeman saw Granny's uniform he spoke to her very politely.

'This way, madam.' And he took her arm and let her to a seat.

The seating was just like the pews in our Mission Hall. The trial was in progress, but I didn't listen to what the judge was saying because I was too busy looking at the people round me. On the left side was the farmer and his wife and the farmer's brother, the man who'd taken us to the hop fields in his hay cart. Next to him sat a middle-aged man, very smartly dressed, in top hat, black cape and silver-topped cane. Then I saw my brother, looking as charming as ever as he stood in the dock. My gaze settled on the judge who peered sternly over the top of his spectacles. He towered over us in an upright, high-backed chair. Below, sitting at a long, oblong table, were several sombre-looking men, writing down what everyone was saying. The voices seemed to echo in this dismal, dark, dusty room with its oak-panelled walls. Mrs Phipps, Mrs Jones and Mrs Buckley sat in the row behind us. I'd never seen them sit so quietly. After a while my eyes were drawn to the gentleman opposite. My curiosity got the better of me and I whispered my question to Frankie, but before he could answer Mum hissed, 'That's Jack's boss. Now 'ush!'

However, when Frankie saw Jack he jumped up, waved and called out, 'Hello, Jack.'

Everybody turned their heads just like they do when watching a tennis match. It went dead quiet for a couple of seconds. Then the judge broke the silence. His voice boomed out to the constable standing by the door.

'Remove that lad at once!'

Frankie didn't wait to be removed. He ran out, and Liza followed him. I would've liked to have gone too, but I couldn't move. Once more there was silence, but just as the judge began to speak again Granny decided she wanted to go to the lavatory. She moved towards the door quickly and asked the constable where it was and I saw him smile as he whispered loudly that she'd find it in the hall. It was clear that the judge was not amused. He sat bolt upright in his chair and frowned at us over his glasses. I followed Granny out. The hall was nearly empty now, apart from the old policeman darting about from one room to another. Frankie was sitting on a bench reading a comic. We couldn't see the lavatory anywhere. Then Granny spotted another door tucked away in a dark corner.

'What's it say on theea?'

'Private Chambers,' I answered.

'Well goo an ask 'em if I can borrow one of 'em or I'll burst in a minute,' she complained, holding herself.

I was just as ignorant as she was. I thought they were chambers like the one we had under our bed. I was just about to ask a policeman, when a young lady came out of the courtroom. She could see Granny crossing and uncrossing her legs and said, 'It's over there in the corner. Mind the steps.'

Granny dived down the half-dozen steps for dear life, but when she tried the door it was locked from the inside and smoke was coming over the top of the door. Granny banged on the door and yelled out, ' 'Ow long yer gooin' ter be?' She was hopping from one foot to the other, but there was no reply. 'If yer don't 'urry up I'll do it on the floowa.'

I was scared stiff in case she did and I knew Granny might. Then the door opened and Granny rushed past the previous occupant, nearly knocking her over, flopped down on the seat and kicked the door shut. I couldn't look at the woman, I was so ashamed. When she started to ascend the steps I looked at her and saw the back half of the prettiest drawers I'd ever seen.

I was fascinated by this but felt too shy to tell her. Yet if I
didn't she'd be out of the door and it would too late. When
she reached the top step I ran up after her and cried out, 'Lady,
you've tucked your frock into the back of your drawers.'

Like a flash, she pulled the remainder of the dress out and
when she turned to thank me I could see it was Mr Skinny-
Legs's wife, I hadn't recognised her at first, she looked so
pretty in her blue dress with matching gloves and a pretty blue
picture hat with lace trimmings. She thanked me kindly and
asked how Jack's case was going. I said I didn't know and then,
struck with curiosity, asked why she was here too.

'I came to see Jack, but I'm afraid I'm too late. Anyhow, I'll
wait outside until we know the result.'

I was just going to ask how she knew about our troubles
when Granny emerged from the cubicle.

'Don't yer let me see yer talking to that brazen 'uzzy,' she
said, dragging me out of the door.

I had to obey and we returned to the courtroom, Granny to
be escorted by the policeman to her seat, and me making my
way as best I could to my place on the bench. Mrs Jones was in
the witness-box giving evidence. There seemed to be something different about her, but I couldn't put my finger on it. It
wasn't her clothes because I'd seen her dressed in these same
clothes as far back as I could remember. She looked pale
against the orange boa.

'No, sir,' I heard her saying to the judge.

'But you said you saw the prisoner that night with the van.'

She didn't answer, but began to fidget. Then she burst out,
'Phew! It's 'ot in 'ere!'

She pushed her boater back on her head and I could see why
she looked so strange. She was wearing a big red wig and as she
pushed the boater back the wig went with it. People in the
court began to titter. Even the judge smiled, but he was
obviously losing his patience and drummed the desk with his
fingertips.

'Silence!' he boomed out again.

Everyone obeyed, but they continued to grin broadly. The

judge turned once more to Mrs Jones and told her to listen to him.

'Now, did you see the prisoner at any time with the pig?'

'No, sir. After I 'ad the whisky I fell asleep. Yer see I was worn out an' tired. I'd bin . . .'

'That will be enough,' the judge interrupted, still drumming his fingers. 'We're getting nowhere. You may stand down.'

'Thank you, sir,' she said, getting down from the box. 'I wish I could tell yer mower but the truth is I don't know mower.'

He waved her away and called out sharply to the constable at the door.

It was Mrs Phipps's turn. All eyes followed her as she made her way noisily towards the witness-box. She climbed the steps and stood waiting. She looked very frightened, and held the rail to steady herself. I'd seen her and Mrs Buckley having a nip or two of gin from a medicine bottle before they went in. They needed Dutch courage, no doubt. The officer handed her a Bible and asked her to read the words that were written on a card. Everyone was so quiet now you could have heard a pin drop as he waited for her to begin.

'I carn't read,' she said in a hoarse whisper.

'Very well. Repeat after me.'

She repeated what he said word for word. Then she kissed the Bible and handed it back and looked across at the judge.

'You are Amelia Emily Phipps?'

'Yes, sir.' She nodded vigorously.

'Now, did you, on the night in question, see the prisoner with – '

'Can I sit down, sir?' she interrupted. 'Me legs are killin' me. Yer see I've got varcus veins an' if I stand too much they'll bust. I'll show yer if yer don't believe me!' she babbled, hitching up her frock at the same time.

The judge looked across at her and cleared his throat noisily. Everyone started to laugh at the sight of Mrs Phipps holding up her dress, showing all the holes and tears in her black woollen stockings.

'Sit down and answer the questions.'

He was red in the face and as he frowned his shaggy eyebrows pushed his glasses to the tip of his nose. He looked over the top of them at us lot in the court.

'Silence!' he almost shouted. 'Or I'll clear the court.'

Silence descended once again and he began slowly and deliberately:

'Now, Mrs Amelia Emily Phipps, I want you to tell me in your own words, and truthfully, what you saw on the night in question. Did you see the prisoner with the pig?'

'No, no. I dain't. I only told 'im I thought Jack 'ad took it.'

'You're a liar,' the farmer shouted across to her.

Suddenly there was a sharp crack as the judge brought down his gavel on to the desk in front of him. He banged it down several times before he got any kind of order.

'Now,' he said, addressing Mrs Phipps. 'I want you to tell me in your own words, and truthfully, what you saw on this particular night. Did you see the prisoner or anybody else with the pig?'

'No, sir! No, sir!' she repeated, and shook her head so fiercely that the cap seemed about to fly off.

'Did you tell the farmer that you knew who had stolen the pig?'

'No! No! I dain't. I only told 'im I *thought* Jack 'ad took it.'

Again the farmer called her a liar. Again the judge struggled to re-establish order.

'Now,' he said to the farmer, 'if I don't get some kind of order I shall dismiss the case at once.'

There was dead silence once more, not a whisper from any one. Then glaring at her, with the gavel still clutched in his hand, he waved Mrs Phipps from the witness-box.

'Step down! I'll question you again later.'

He blew his nose hard, making a noise like a trumpet. Then he called the farmer to the witness-stand but, before he moved, Jack's boss asked the judge for permission to speak. He said he could but to make it brief. Jack's boss said he had found my brother honest and trustworthy all the time he had been in his employ. He added that Jack was truthful and that he didn't believe that Jack had stolen the pig.

'I'll be the best judge of that,' the stipendiary replied.

I looked at him again – in fact I very seldom took my eyes away from that hard-looking old man while we sat in court. I was so afraid. I hoped and prayed that he'd dismiss the case so that we could all go home. The farmer mounted the witness-stand. Again the judge blew his nose and cleared his throat.

'Are you Mr Henry William Onions?'

'Yes, sir,' he answered.

'Now do you recognise the prisoner?'

'No, sir,' he answered at once.

'No? You mean to say that you don't know him?'

'I've never seen him before.'

The judge started drumming his fingers hard, with obvious impatience.

'If you say you have never seen this man before, how is it that he is charged with stealing the pig?'

The farmer jumped up and pointing across at Mrs Phipps shouted, 'She told me. She said she saw him put it in the van.'

All eyes turned in her direction as Mrs Phipps jumped up and denied his accusation. Once more the gavel banged down with enough force it seemed to split the desk.

'Put that woman outside!' he instructed the constable at the door.

She was led out and Mrs Buckley and Mrs Jones walked out in sympathy. Mum, Granny and I sat very still, too scared to move. I was trembling and so afraid that I might be called next to answer their questions. How could I lie to such a flint-faced man? His eyes penetrated you when he looked at you. I was fascinated by his face. He returned to question Jack. He asked several questions and told him to explain how he came to be at the farm. Then he sat back in his high chair and fixed my brother with his cold stare.

'Now, begin at the beginning.'

Jack looked handsome as he stood up to his full height and began. 'My father received a letter from my sister Kathleen to say would he fetch them all home as they were sleeping all together on bags of straw and they were all hungry. This is the letter, sir,' Jack said, and handed it to the constable to give to the judge. He read it and placed it on the desk and then spoke slowly.

'You were saying?'

'They were very short of money and food and – '

'That's a lie!' the farmer shouted. 'The missus gave – '

Down came the gavel again.

'Silence!' the court resounded. 'If I have any more interruptions I shall close the case.'

The farmer sat down, looking furious. Then the judge told Jack to continue. He sounded to me as if he'd rehearsed the answer over and over again. He spoke easily, without hesitation.

'My father asked me to fetch them home. I asked my boss if he would kindly lend me the works van, which he did. So that same night I drove to the farm, but when I knocked at the farmhouse door there was no answer. Then I drove up to the barn and found my mother and her friends. I told my mother I had come to take them back home.'

'Go on,' the judge said, looking Jack squarely in the eye.

'I drove the van along to the Pig and Whistle to have a drink of cider, and to see if I could find out where the farmer was, but when I inquired no one knew. The first time I saw him was when I was arrested, sir.'

'What happened after you left the public house?'

'I drove back. Everyone was asleep bar my mother. I asked her to wake my granny and my two sisters and brother. Then we all got into the van. That's the God's truth, sir.'

I waited for him to explain how the pig came to be in the van but he didn't mention it.

'Why didn't you wait to see the farmer and explain why you were taking these people away?' the judge asked.

'I hung about until after midnight, sir, but we had to go. I had to be in work by six o'clock the next morning and I'd promised to take the van back.'

The men in black who sat round the table were writing down what he said, word for word. Then the judge stopped drumming his fingers and stroked his chin. He looked first at Jack, then at the farmer and then round the room at the rest of us. I knew, and so did my mum, that Jack had lied and that if he were ever found out we would all go to prison. If only my dad was with me I would have felt safer. I knew I wouldn't be able to face that man's steel-grey eyes without speaking the truth. So I made up my mind to dash out, but just as I started to get up off the bench Mum caught hold of my plaits and pulled me down again. I prayed to myself and began to cry.

The judge was speaking again. 'Do yo wish to question the . . .'

The farmer was angry now, and he interrupted the judge again. 'If he ain't had my pig, well, who has? Tell me that!'

Once more I put my hands to my ears as the gavel banged loudly. The judge had finally snapped and he was furious.

'Case dismissed. Clear the court!'

My prayer had been answered and I didn't have to give evidence. I didn't stay to see the people leave. I flew out of there as fast as I could. I saw Frankie in the hall talking to the woman with the pretty frilly drawers and when she saw me she asked how my brother had got on. I told her the case had been dismissed. She smiled at me and sat down beside Frankie who was more interested in his comic than in Jack's fate. Then I saw Jack, Mum and Granny, beaming big smiles, coming towards us. Jack had eyes for no one but his fancy piece, as Granny called her. Almost at once I felt that I never wanted to see him again and couldn't stop myself tugging at his coat tail and upbraiding him.

'You lied, Jack. I won't ever believe you again.'

But he only grinned at me and put his hand in his trouser pocket and drew out a handful of change and selected a silver sixpence for me. He pushed it into my hand and it occurred to me that this was the second sixpence he'd given me. The other one was still under the floorboards beside my bed. This second gift made me even madder. To think he couldn't trust me to keep his secret without bribing me. I looked down at the sixpence in my hand and wondered what I could do with it. Then I heard Jack say, 'Come on, Lil. Let's go across the road and have a drink.'

Then I decided. I threw the sixpence down and called after Jack, 'I don't want yer sixpence, and you can have the other one back when I find it!'

I watched it roll across the floor and before Mum could stoop to retrieve it, Frankie had beaten her to it. He put it quickly in his pocket and ran off. Granny, who hadn't noticed what had happened, said she was going after Jack to have a gin to warm her up. However, Mum wasn't interested. She dragged me by the hand down the street. Passers-by could hear every word she uttered in her harsh, loud voice.

'What yer do that for? Come on! You bin 'iding money away from me, ain't yer?'

'No. I ain't yer,' I mimicked.

By now people were stopping and staring at Mum who was shaking me violently. But I didn't care any more what she said or did because I'd found the courage to answer her back. Suddenly I broke away from her and shouted that the sixpence was under the floorboards and then I took to my heels and tore down the street. Mum didn't follow me, but turned and marched off into the pub.

It was late in the afternoon by this time and I was hungry. I regretted throwing the sixpence away. Still, I think I'd have tossed a sovereign back at him, if Jack had given me one. Anyway, it was idle speculation to think about the tanner because Frankie had probably spent it by now. Then I had a thought, I would stand outside Mrs Gingold's window and if she saw me she might give me a twist of batter scratchings. I hurried along and turning the corner, I came face to face with Frankie eating fish and chips which he'd bought with the sixpence. My eyes fixed on them and my mouth began to water.

'Here, have a chip.' I grabbed a few before he changed his

mind, and stuffed them in my mouth. He was annoyed.

'Here, have 'em all,' he said handing me the remains. 'I'll go back and get some more.'

I sat down and finished them off and It didn't take long either. I was so hungry I even licked the vinegar off the paper. Then Frankie came back and let me help him with the second lot. What a lot of fish and chips you could buy then for tuppence!

Frankie still had tuppence left and that he shared with me too. I felt better when my belly had stopped rumbling. We strolled along together and Frankie didn't say a word. I was glad, really. I thought that at any moment he would ask me about the pig, but my brother was no fool, he knew when it was best to say nothing. Just as I was thinking what to say if he should ask, Jonesy ran up and they went off together, leaving me standing alone. There was nothing left to do except return home to face Mum. If there had been any other place to go I would have gone willingly. But I knew that wherever I went in our district people would ask me all sorts of questions, and I had no idea how I would answer them. I'd always tried to tell the truth and grown-ups had a way of getting round a child. So reluctantly I returned home. When I got indoors there was nobody there, so I sat down to wait for Mum. I'd only been there a few moments when I heard a noise like boards creaking and I dashed upstairs.

'Is that you, Mum?'

'Yes,' she called back. 'Come up 'ere. I want yer!'

When I reached the attic door I wasn't surprised to see that she'd lifted the boards.

'Where did yer say it was?'

'There.'

I pointed to the one beside the bed where there was a large crack. I knew she wanted the sixpence badly. She went on her hands and knees as best she could. The loose board came away in her hand when she tugged at it, for it was rotten and half eaten away. She felt around in the open gap but didn't find the tanner until she'd placed several piles of fluff and dust beside the bed first. I went back downstairs, wondering if all mothers were like mine. I knew we were living through very hard times, but we were a little better off than some. My dad was working, after all, but you only had to mention money and Mum was all ears. She counted every penny on the fingers of her left hand. When it came to farthings I always did the reckoning, but the Lord help me if she discovered I'd made a mistake. She followed me downstairs and when I looked at her I could see she was pleased with herself.

'Get the bag and fetch some stewin' meat and vegetables. We'll 'ave a nice pot o' stew fer yer dad when 'e comes 'ome.'

She never bothered about us kids all day but it was always the same, 'yer dad must 'ave this', and 'yer brother must 'ave the other', until I was sick and tired of the sound of her voice.

Then I saw her self-satisfied grin and I said defiantly. 'No! I'm not going! That sixpence belongs to me.'

Like a shot she raised her hand to strike me, but before it came down I backed away.

'If you dare hit me again, I'll tell Dad, Mary and everybody else about that night in the barn and about the pig!'

She turned pale and her hand droppped to her side. Flopping down in the chair, she demanded, 'Come 'ere!'

'No!' I gripped the door knob, ready to run out.

'Come 'ere,' she said, 'I'm not gooin' ter 'it yer any more.'

I wasn't sure what she was going to do, so I left the door ajar, ready if I needed to make quick getaway and slowly I edged towards her. She changed her tone of voice and smiled at me.

'Get me yer dad's cap off the door, an' the bag. I'll goo meself.'

I couldn't believe my ears. I had actually defied her and she'd done nothing to me. Quickly I reached down the cap and handed her the shopping bag and, keeping my distance in case she changed her mind, I watched her push the cap on the back of her head and march out without another word. I was sure she was going to punish me when she returned but I determined to disappear until Dad came home. Frankie and Liza always did that and got away with it. Then I thought, if I don't have my punishment she'll never forget. She always said, 'There, that's what I owe yer,' when you were least expecting it. That was one reason why I was always nervous. I was sure she didn't love me, and at times I think I hated her, although at others I was sorry for her. After all, I was lucky to have a mum of any kind, some kids round our way had no mother at all. They were welcome to mine at times, though. I tried too hard to make her love me and I always did the wrong thing, the result was that I was afraid.

After she'd left for the shop, I tried to think what I could do to please her. Then it dawned on me that I needn't bother. I had the secret of why she had a black eye and I knew all about the pig. It was this secret that stopped her from hitting me, and she was afraid I would break my promise and tell Dad. I realised that I had a weapon to defend myself with and I made up my mind to use it whenever I needed to.

I jumped up from the chair but I sat down again quickly. I could hardly see. There were little flashes of light in front of my eyes. I was afraid. This had never happened to me before. I felt sick and there was a nasty taste in my throat. I rushed for the bowl but it had dirty clothes in it. I couldn't use the sink either, it had the crocks in it, so I rushed outside with my hand to my mouth. I didn't want to retch in the yard in full public view, so I ran down toward the lavatory. But Frankie and his friends were kicking a can about and I felt too weak to brazen my way past them. I leant against the wall and Annie Buckley approached me.

'What's the matter with yower Katie, Frankie?'

'Yow ain't 'alf white!' I heard someone say.

I felt dreadful and didn't want them around me.

'Go way! Go way! All of yer!'

Then the gang round me parted and Maggie Bumpham pushed her way towards me.

'My God!' she said, but her voice sounded far away. 'Yer look as if yer dyin' an' yer white as a ghost! What's the matter with yer?'

'I think I am dying, Mrs Bumpham, and I can't see either!' I

184

cried out in what must have been a pitiful voice, and my eyes filled with tears.

She put her hand on my forehead and roughly pulled my eyelids apart and peered into my eyes. She propped me against the wall and fetched out a backless chair for me to sit on. The flashes subsided and I became aware of my surroundings. Maggie pushed my head back and tried to pour salt water down my throat. The kids crowded round to watch the performance. I lurched out of the chair and tried to spit it out but I'd already swallowed most of it. I tried to run away, but before I could, she grabbed me and told Jonesy and Frankie to hold me down. Then, while I struggled, she pushed her grimy fingers down my throat as far as she could. I thought I would choke. I heaved twice. The the only meal I'd had that day slid down the drain. I felt better when my stomach had emptied and the flashes subsided. I dashed for a drink of water.

I looked to Frankie for sympathy but got no support.

'You shouldn't 'ave bin so greedy with the chips,' was all he said.

They continued playing their game and I walked indoors. I looked in the bit of cracked mirror on the wall. I was still very pale but I felt better when I sat back in Dad's chair. Soon after Mum walked in. She looked tired and harassed and she didn't look my way. She knew I was there but she didn't speak, and had her back to me. She tipped the food on to the scrubbed table top. I watched her sorting things out. She looked pathetic, and I felt sorry I'd made her go to the shop.

'Mum,' I said. But she didn't answer.

'Mum,' I repeated. 'I'm sorry. I won't tell anyone or say a word to Dad. Really I won't, Mum.'

Then she turned and faced me.

'What yer bin dooin'?' She saw how pale I was. 'Are yer sickenin' fer summat?'

'I've been sick, Mum,' I said.

But I said nothing else, only that I was feeling better.

'Very well. You can 'elp me get yer dad's tea ready.'

I wrung the clothes out and emptied the bowl, then I took it

185

down the yard to fill it with clean water. The yard was deserted. The kids had gone off to play in another – they always fled when they saw our mum. When I returned, Mum had aready got the pot on the fire in readiness for the stew. I placed the bowl on the table.

'Can I peel the potatoes, Mum?' I asked, eager to make it up with her.

'No! I want 'em cut thin. Yer can scrape the carrots while I skin this rabbit.'

I watched her hang the rabbit by its two back legs from a convenient nail and with two deft tugs she had it skinned. I began scraping the carrots at one end of the table while she chopped up the rabbit into small portions at the other. I didn't look at her, but I could feel her eyes on me all the time. When she'd completely dismembered the rabbit and it was in the pot she sat down and called me over to her. 'Now I'm for it,' I thought.

'But I haven't finished the carrots yet.'

'Never mind about them. I want ter talk ter yer.'

I slowly edged round the table towards her.

'Now,' she began looking me straight in the eye. 'Yer remember what yer said this afternoon? About 'ow yer was gooin' ter tell yer dad?'

I was too afraid to answer, so I nodded several times and all the time she fixed me with her stare.

'An' do yer remember yer made me a promise not ter tell yer dad?'

I nodded again.

'Well,' she continued. 'I'm gooin' ter promise yow this. If yer'll keep yer promise not to say a word to 'im or anybody else about the pig or anythink what's 'appened, I'll never 'it yer again.'

I threw my arms round her and said all in a rush, 'I'll never tell a soul, cross my heart, Mum, and hope to die!'

'All right! All right! she answered and impatiently pulled my arms from round her neck and waved me away.

So, I thought, while she keeps her promise I'll keep mine.

After that day she never did hit me again – with the cane or her heavy hand. But there were times when I would rather have felt either than the lashings she gave me with her tongue.

I finished scraping the carrots while Mum put them in the pot with the rabbit. I wiped down the table and spread a sheet of newspaper over it. It was not many minutes before Dad came in, closely followed by Frankie, Liza and Granny. Dad washed his hands as usual, picked up his newspaper, took the spectacles I handed him, and proceeded to settle in his chair without a word. I could see he wanted to be left alone but Mum was very fidgety and kept glancing across at him. Then she could contain herself no longer and she burst out with the news.

'He got off, yer know!'

Dad carried on reading.

'Sam!' she persisted, 'Our Jack got off, yer know. I told yer 'e never kept that pig. 'E took it back ter the farm.'

Dad slowly looked up over the top of his glasses and stared coldly at Mum.

'I don't want to hear another word about Jack or the pig.'

Then, pushing his glasses back on to the bridge of his nose, he recommenced reading his paper. But Mum couldn't leave well alone. She thought Dad should hear about the court hearing. When Mum was excited about anything she kept on and on until she got every little detail off her chest.

'But, Sam,' she began, but got no further. Dad slapped the paper down, pushed his chair back, and went across to her.

'Now look here, Polly. I don't want to hear any more. I've already heard enough from outsiders. Now get my supper ready, I'm clammed.'

I watched him take down the lavatory key and go out into the yard to find a refuge. Just after he'd gone out Granny came in and started questioning Mum.

'What's all this fuss about? I knew Jack wouldn't pinch a pig. That farmer's took 'im for somebody else. Still, I'd like to know who did take it, wouldn't you, Polly?' She rambled on and on.

'No I wouldn't!' snapped Mum. 'An' don't yow start!'
Then Granny's temper really exploded.

'Nobody tells me anythink that goos on in this 'ouse. I'll be glad when I can goo back to me own place. An' yer keep yer supper. I'm goooin' ter bed!'

'You're not going anywhere, Mother!' Dad said as he entered. 'You'll sit down with the rest of us and eat. Now, let's not hear another word. And you, Katie, call Liza and Frankie in. It's about time they were here.'

Then we all sat down round the table and while Mum dished out the food, Granny sat with a self-satisfied smirk on her face. Not another word was spoken and later, when Jack came in, Dad didn't even look at him. In fact he didn't speak to him for days, and each time he returned Dad would deliberately walk out and go to the local for a drink.

16
How Things Turned Out

Our neighbourhood soon settled down again to the dismal daily struggle for a crust. Although we didn't know it then, the world was about to be shattered by the Great War but looking back I doubt if it made much immediate difference to many of us – except the young lads who enlisted for the Front. Our brother Jack was one of these, and I well remember taking my first job cleaning the school corridors for money to buy khaki wool to knit him a pair of socks.

The circumstances in which I started work were typical of my sort of people. Mum wanted to make me useful so she asked Mrs Morton, the caretaker's wife, and it was agreed I should get half a crown for Friday night and Saturday and of this Mum would be given one and sixpence. I didn't relish the thought of this job much because I was terrified of Mr Morton. He was a weedy little man who had an unsavoury reputation in our neighbourhood. I suppose today 'Weary Willie' would be regarded as a pervert, but then his peculiar antics were accepted as ordinary enough.

On my first evening, Mrs Morton left me to get on with my cleaning while she carried on with other jobs. I took off my clogs and knelt down to start scrubbing. I hadn't been long working when I was startled by the sensation of heavy breathing down the back of my neck. I sprang to my feet and found Weary Willie grinning at me and leering through his pebble-thick glasses. I was scared stiff wondering what he wanted. Then I felt his hot, smelly breath on my face and he squeaked in his peculiar high-pitched voice, 'The missus ses yer carn't clane the flowa without this.'

With that he slapped a big gob of soft brown soap into my hand. It felt and looked repulsive and I let out a scream. At that sound Mrs Morton appeared and inquired if he was bothering me. I could only nod dumbly. She just pushed a paraffin rag into my hand and told me to rub down the benches. Meanwhile Weary Willie had vanished. I was still frightened though, and I decided to turn the gaslights up to brighten the corridor more. As I was standing on the bench, stretching to reach the brass tap, I felt a cold, clammy hand on my bare thigh. In my shock and fright I fell off the bench on top of him and we both landed on the floor in a heap. His head hit the bucket and the soapy water gushed all over him. I found my strength and pushed the rag I was still clutching into his face and as he lay there spluttering I escaped down the corridor. I ran home as fast as my legs would carry me and fell through the door into our kitchen sobbing, 'Mr Morton . . . Mr Morton . . . !'

Mum knew at once what was wrong. I can see that now. She probably knew what to expect from him. 'What's 'e done to yer?' she demanded, shaking me.

I couldn't explain clearly, partly because I wasn't sure myself exactly what had happened, but what I did say was enough for Mum. She grabbed my wrist and dragged me back up the hill. When we entered the school corridor Weary Willie was having his hair dried by his wife. When Mum saw him her jaw set and she strode towards him in her familiar determined manner. Mrs Morton could only look on helplessly as Mum grabbed him by the shoulders and shook him violently.

'Yer dirty little ram!' she shrieked. 'If I ever catch yer pesterin' my child agen, or anybody else's kids, I'll swing fer yer! An', yow!' she added, rounding on his wife.

' 'E dain't mean any 'arm, it's the only little comfort 'e gets, teasin' little girls,' she whined.

'Comfort!' Mum was furious. 'Comfort? 'E betta watch out or next time I'll cut 'is bit a comfort off!'

With that Mum strode out, hauling me with her. When we got home I was sent to bed and Mum threatened to tell Dad what had happened, but I knew she wouldn't. He had said I was not to help the caretaker and that it was a job she could do herself. However, I never earned those few coppers and Jack didn't get his khaki socks, but fortunately he survived without them.

This incident happened when I was eleven, just after the outbreak of war. I didn't earn any more until I left school at fourteen, except by begging or running little errands. It was 1917 that I finally started work, and lots of girls and young women were earning good wages. My first job paid twelve shillings and sixpence for a 48½ hour week. I pressed and drilled brass army trouser buttons. It was an easy job to learn, but after deductions for cleaning, tea and overalls I received only ten shillings. Later, I went into piecework and could earn fifteen shillings, but when piecework rates were reduced I moved on.

I lived on the edge of the Jewellery Quarter and it was in one of the many jewellery trades that I worked next. This area was, and still is, one of Georgian and Victorian residential houses centred on St Paul's Square which today is Birmingham's only remaining eighteenth-century square. The individual rooms of the houses are still rented off to craftsmen and small manufacturers who ply their various trades. In my young days many houses were still occupied by families but, as they left, the landlords would encourage jewellers to come in, so that eventually there was a different trade thriving in each room. They were mostly outworkers making jewellery of every description – gold watches and chains, diamond rings, wedding rings and gold bracelets.

My first job was in a room which had obviously been somebody's kitchen. On the gas stove were pots of bubbling glue and I was shown how to make jewel boxes from plywood, cardboard and velvet. Although it was not hard work and I received fifteen shillings a week in wages, I left after a month because I was expected to carry packages containing what I discovered were illicit diamonds. When I realised this I left in a hurry. I stayed in the Jewellery Quarter though, and eventually settled down to work as an enameller, enamelling small brooches which were very popular then, and later badges and motor plates. I wasn't able to become skilled immediately because, in common with most employers then, my first boss would teach me one process only and that was how to 'lay on' enamel. In order to learn all the other processes I had to move from firm to firm, and pick up the trade bit by bit.

My skill as an enameller was very valuable to me after my husband died and I had to bring my children up alone. We'd married in 1921 and were very happy together, but married life was very different form being single. I had to give up work whenever I was pregnant, and being pregnant made it hard to keep accommodation because we could only afford to lodge in rooms, and landladies weren't keen on children. We had four at that time, two boys and two girls and all the while they were young we had a struggle to make ends meet. My husband, Charlie, was out of work most of the time and made a paltry living buying sawdust from the sawmills and selling it to pubs and butchers. This brought in two shillings or half a crown a day, but it was miserably insufficient and he became depressed and gradually took to drink. My father's health declined and he died in 1927, broken by a life of hard work and poverty. I managed to work intermittently as an enameller between pregnancies and I worked up to two days before my fourth confinement. In general, though, I couldn't keep a job because I had to look after the children and found time-keeping difficult.

Bad luck seemed to haunt us then. My father died, as I've said, soon after the birth of Jean, my second daughter. Then, not long after that, my eldest son, Charles, was knocked down and killed by a meat van on his way home from school. After that my husband's health seemed to deteriorate but he managed to do odd jobs and seemed to be drinking less. For a short period after this things went well. I managed to find a job with a Mr Brain who allowed me to bring my baby to work so I could feed her during working hours and while John, my other son, was at school my mum looked after Katie. However this good fortune didn't last. Mr Brain closed down because he had so little work and I was out of a job.

I had to look for work, it was either that or parish relief, and rather than this I took in washing and mending, but the earnings from this were nothing like sufficient. In common with most women then I knew nothing about birth control and I became pregnant again at about this time. This meant I was less capable of the heavy work involved in washing and mangling but I had to struggle on. The illness which Charlie suffered from became much worse as well. He was doubled up with stomach pains for which the doctor gave him injections and tablets and I nursed him, but his condition steadily deteriorated. The doctor returned and when he saw how Charlie was he ordered an ambulance to take him to hospital. That same night I went into labour and I gave birth to a baby girl, my third. Poor Charlie did not live to see his daughter though, he died three days later on 26 April 1931.

I was shattered. I had no real home, no job and no money. I was turned down when I applied for a widow's pension because Charlie didn't have enough insurance stamps on his card. How could he, when he'd been unemployed most of our married life? I had to turn to the parish and I'll never forget the humiliating and degrading way that the stern-faced inquisitors treated me. I determined that if the Lord gave me strength again I would do something better with my life than sitting there helplessly begging for a crust.

I was given food and coal vouchers eventually, but not before I had pawned everything except the clothes we stood up in. Still, what was given was not enough for us and I had to moonlight as an enameller in order to survive. Even then I couldn't cope. Life was unbearable with Mum, and I was at my wits' end. Finally, I had to let my children go into a Dr Barnardo's home. I was heartbroken, but what could I do? We were starving and helpless; there was only Mum and me and so I decided to let them go where they would at least be clothed and fed. The home turned out to be better than I had expected. It was in Moseley which was still quite rural then, and the matron was a kindly soul. I still wept bitterly when I had to leave them there, but they were laughing and chatting with the other kids soon enough, and I knew I'd done the right thing. That was not what my Mum and the neighbours thought. I was the worst woman in the district!

I went back to work full-time and moved to a furnished room. I visited my children regularly, but it took years for me to fulfil my promise to myself and to them to have them home and they were growing up and away from me. It was not until the Second World War broke out that my chance came. My boss offered to supply me with outwork if I could find suitable premises. This I did eventually. It was a top-floor room and rat-infested, but that didn't deter me, Mr Butler kept his word, and I began enamelling red and green Castrol badges at seven shillings and sixpence a gross.

After a while work began to pour in. Other firms called to see if I could help them complete their orders, and I had to take on young girls to help me. I soon had a thriving business.

All my spare energies and money went into providing the home that my children had never had. I rented a three-bed-roomed house with a large garden and was in seventh heaven furnishing it. Then I applied to have my children back. By this time they had been evacuated and I had to wait, but they eventually returned – the girls that is, because John was a naval cadet on HMS *Ganges*.

Later I bought a house and a small car and we went to see him. We moved just in time because our rented house was bombed soon after we left. My mother and my sister Mary were not so lucky. They were killed in an air raid which completely destroyed our house in Camden Drive and those of the old neighbours from my childhood who still remained there. My son was luckier, though. He survived the war on HMS *King George V*.

Today, although they are widely scattered, I've a large family of whom I am very, very proud indeed.